SCREEN LEGENDS

BRUCE YACCATO

McArthur & Company
Toronto

First published in Canada in 2006 by
McArthur & Company
322 King St. West, Suite 402
Toronto, ON M5V 1J2
www.mcarthur-co.com

This paperback edition published in 2007 by
McArthur & Company

Copyright © 2006 Bruce Yaccato

All rights reserved.

The use of any part of this publication reproduced, transmitted in any form or by any means, electronic, mechanical, photocopying, recording or otherwise stored in a retrieval system, without the expressed written consent of the publisher, is an infringement of the copyright law.

Every attempt has been made to secure permission for all material used, and if there are errors or omissions, these are wholly unintentional and the Publisher would be grateful to learn of them.

Library and Archives Canada Cataloguing in Publication

Yaccato, Bruce   **Screen legends / Bruce Yaccato.**

Includes bibliographical references. _ISBN 1-55278-615-3 (bound).
ISBN 978-1-55278-668-0 (pbk.)

1. Motion picture actors and actresses--Canada--Biography.
2. Motion picture producers and directors--Canada--Biography. I. Title.

PN1998.2.Y33 2006   791.4302'8092271   C2006-903856-2

Design by *Mad Dog Design Connection*
Printed in Canada by *Transcontinental*

The publisher would like to acknowledge the financial support of the Government of Canada through the Book Publishing Industry Development Program (BPIDP) and the Canada Council for our publishing activities. The publisher further wishes to acknowledge the financial support of the Ontario Arts Council for our publishing program.

10 9 8 7 6 5 4 3 2 1

To Amy and Ben

Table of Contents

Marie Dressler

B. LEILA MARIE KOERBER, COBOURG, ONTARIO, 9 NOVEMBER 1869
D. SANTA BARBARA, CALIFORNIA, 28 JULY 1934

NO ONE COULD EVER ACCUSE MARIE DRESSLER of getting by on her good looks. She titled her 1924 autobiography *The Life of an Ugly Duckling*. To call her "plain" would be a compliment. But she was one of Hollywood's all-time great comediennes. And that plain appearance and salt-of-the-earth manner made fans and critics alike idolize her.

Reviewers would single her out for her "extraordinarily sympathetic personality" that always brought a "genuinely human touch to her roles," usually as a gruff old gal with a loyal-to-a-fault heart of gold.

She began life just two years after Canada's Confederation as Leila Marie Koerber in the bucolic Ontario hamlet of Cobourg, near Toronto. She recalled hamming it up for her family from the age of 5. Against her father's wishes (and what are fathers for?) by her mid-teens she was performing on stage in Michigan. She had two gifts: the ability to make people laugh, and a singing voice good enough to perform in an opera company for three years.

She climbed surely if not quickly from stock to vaudeville and, by 1892 at age 23, to Broadway. Stardom came after she was cast as the lead in the smash 1896 musical comedy *Lady Slavey*. Her greatest hit, and eventual entree into the film business, came in 1910 when *Tillie's Nightmare* made her rich and famous beyond anything she'd dreamt. For an idea of her image, Marie played a "homely, boardinghouse drudge" named Tillie Blobb.

As Tillie, she caught the attention of fellow Canadian Mack Sennett, Hollywood's first comic genius and inventor of the hugely successful Keystone Kops. Years earlier, back in 1902, Sennett had been a labourer with pretensions to show biz. By 1914, Sennett himself was a big-time producer and director, easing the very actress who'd once been kind to him into the new medium of film.

Tillie's Punctured Romance (1914), a historically important film, was the first full-length feature comedy. Until then, even some *films noirs* considered classics were "one-reelers," shot on a single spool of film. It featured Marie opposite a fast-rising comic star named Charlie Chaplin. She recalled little of the encounter later, except for being slightly appalled that Chaplin would show up every day with the same food stain on his suit jacket.

Watching the film today, Chaplin's emerging greatness is apparent, and some of Marie's ham-handed, over-the-top vaudevillian antics seem embarrassing. But it was a hit, and several sequels were made.

During World War I Marie worked full-time on the war effort, campaigning for War Bonds and performing for troops. Strangely, it appeared her career was over by the war's end.

In 1917, Marie supported Broadway chorus girls in their strike against Broadway theatre owners and producers. They won and went on to form the Actor's Equity Union, but Marie was, in the eyes of producers and owners, a dangerous, traitorous radical despite her wartime efforts. She became a pariah, blacklisted both on Broadway and in Hollywood. With her career apparently over, it seemed time to write her memoirs, the aforementioned *Ugly Duckling*. She turned 55 with a bleak future.

Her exile lasted until 1927, when a fellow Canadian, director Allan Dwan, offered her a bit part in his next movie, *The Joy Girl*. The painful wilderness years were over but there was no sign that the next five years would bring superstar status, an Academy Award and tributes from her biggest fans, Franklin and Eleanor Roosevelt!

More than a few silent stars failed to make the transition to the advent of sound, but Dressler's projection and elocution, born of years on stage, not only helped her make the cut, they propelled her to diva status when she was nearly 60 years of age.

A couple of well-received silent comedies followed *The Joy Girl* and Marie went from blacklist to A-list. She signed with MGM and landed a part in Garbo's first talking picture, *Anna Christie*. "Garbo Talks!" was the buzz, but the critics welcomed her back.

The *New York Times* noted:

Marie Dressler, who plays Marthe, may overact occasionally, but most of her performance is exceptionally clever. She, with all Marthe's bibulous

Tillie's Punctured Romance *1914. With Charlie Chaplin. Keystone Film Company*

nature, elicits sympathy for the dissolute woman and often she relieves the sordid atmosphere with effective comedy. Miss Dressler has done good work in audible screen offerings, but her speech, expressions, and her general gesticulations make this far and away her outstanding film characterization.

Dressler's next comedy, *Min and Bill*, had tragic overtones. She played Min Divot, the owner of a squalid waterfront hotel whose love interest is Bill, a hard-drinking fisherman, played by Wallace Beery, making them two of the era's most popular and least glamorous leading actors. In one scene, Min pretty much beats the stuffing out of Bill for his wandering eye. All the while, she tries to protect her adopted daughter from their sordid life. It struck a chord with audiences and the Academy, who awarded her the Oscar for Best Actress in 1931.

MGM began promoting her as the greatest actress alive. In *Emma*, in 1932 she gave what is widely regarded as her greatest performance, "one of the finest character studies that has come to the screen" by the actress "whose film work has earned the highest praise in the English-speaking world." *Emma* is the story of a housekeeper who marries her employer and is rejected by his children. It brought another Academy Award nomination as Best Actress, but she lost out to a lesser-known upstart named Katherine Hepburn.

Her role as the long-suffering Annie Brennan in 1933's *Tugboat Annie* garnered more rave reviews. It was the real-life story of a heroic woman trying to save the family business, the Pacific Coast Tugboat Narcissus, from a well-meaning but alcoholic husband, played by Wallace Beery.

Then she was cast as the lead in what the studio called "The Supreme Screen Triumph of MGM. The Most Glamorous Production of all Time." And *Dinner at Eight* was nothing if not lavish. MGM's slogan was "More Stars Than There Are in Heaven" and the studio trotted out a boatload of them. The film was written by George S. Kaufman and Edna Ferber, and directed by George Cukor. Marie had top billing over John and Lionel Barrymore as well as Jean Harlow and Wallace Beery, all megastars in their own right.

Here she was no downtrodden angel. She played Carlotta, a former star well past her prime who becomes part of an ill-fated dinner party that the viewer never gets to see. From her first entrance, she is larger than life, a compelling presence with impeccable timing, easily outshining the cast's other big time stars. *Dinner at Eight* is a true tour-de-force and well worth an evening's rental.

In the last year of her life, she made her last movie, *Christopher Bean*, which her fickle patron at the *Times* described as "a joy to behold . . . Miss Dressler affords heaps of mirth."

She died the following summer of 1934.

There is a museum and an annual film festival in her honour in her home town of Cobourg, Ontario. She may not be a household name now, but she held her own

Tugboat Annie *1933 with Wallace Beery. AMPAS*

with greatest legends Hollywood ever had to offer. The woman who came to fame as Tillie Blobb went on to deliver some of cinema's greatest performances with strength, compassion and a down-to-earth dignity that touched the hearts of millions of fans.

Raymond Burr

B. NEW WESTMINSTER, BRITISH COLUMBIA, 21 MAY 1917
D. SONOMA, CALIFORNIA, 12 SEPTEMBER 1993

THE NEXT TIME YOU'RE WATCHING AN EPISODE OF *Boston Legal* or one of the many franchises of *Law and Order*, try to remember that Raymond Burr's stellar portrayal of the lead character in *Perry Mason* was the first courtroom-based weekly drama to be required prime-time network viewing.

Perry Mason was one of the icons of that era known as the Golden Age of Television. For 271 episodes from "The Case of the Raging Redhead" on September 21, 1957, (could it really be fifty years ago?) to "The Case of the Final Fadeout" in 1966, *Perry Mason* and its cast were perennial Emmy Award winners and money in the bank for what was then a lucrative, hard-fought struggle for ratings supremacy on Saturday nights for CBS. As surely as Ralph and Alice would patch things up on *The Honeymooners* or *Dr. Kildare* would save the patient, or for that matter, the sun would rise in the East and set in the West, Perry Mason would win the case and solve the murder. Aficionados recall that Perry lost only three cases but overturned two convictions by the end of the show and only lost a civil case (and who counts those?) because the judge was running for re-election and playing politics. It does make one wonder how his rival attorney, Hamilton Burger, played by William Talman, kept his job, what with going 0 for 271 and all.

It was something of a nice, ironic career twist for Burr. His first, last and undying love was for the stage. In movies he was almost always cast as a thug, gangster, drug-runner, killer and/or heavy (in more ways than one — lifelong weight problems would have him eventually tip the scales at 300-plus pounds). No one would have guessed his biggest triumph would later come as a model of invincible lawyerly probity and integrity on the small screen.

The Burr clan had deep roots in Canada, having fled Ireland's County Carlow for the New World in the 19th century, stopping in Victoria before settling in New Westminster. His father was a hardware salesman. This was the home, even then, of one of Canada's great sports dynasties, the lacrosse powerhouse, fetchingly named the Salmonbellies, who, by the time of Raymond's birth, were on their third consecutive national championship and who remain a force in the sport to this day. With his precocious physique, he perhaps could have joined them to the screen's great loss. But in 1922, when Raymond was 5, his mother left with kids in tow for California. Raymond grew up in what was called at the time "a broken home."

His first recorded stage performance came in junior high with a singing part in *Naughty Marietta*, which earned him a job as a radio host on *The Slumber Hour*. He enrolled in the prestigious acting school at the Pasadena Playhouse, but apparently couldn't afford to stay very long. To help his family survive the Great Depression of the 1930s, he worked at everything from ranch hand to forest ranger.

The story line becomes little murky here, but at some point he went to visit his father in New Westminster and by some unexplained chance, this apparently led to his joining a touring theatre group in 1936, which took him to Toronto and a seminal meeting with film director (and Burr mentor) Anatole Litvak. Without much formal training the handsome, imposing young Burr could act well enough to persuade Litvak to enlist him in another troupe heading overseas to Australia, India and England, including playing Macbeth in the Bard's very hometown of Stratford-on-Avon in Warwickshire.

He met and married an English actress, Annette Sutherland, and they had a son, Michael Evan. With World War II erupting on the Continent, Burr headed for home, with wife and son to follow at the end of her acting contract.

There are fair-sized portions of Burr's life that recall the confusion legendary scribe and fellow BC native Allan Fotheringham would place under the heading of "Department of Fuzzification." For one, his biographies claim he studied for a while at the University of Chungking (now Chongqing) in southwest China. One source claims his father took the family there. Not very likely. Another says he managed a piece of land there, without a clue as to when.

But back to Mrs. Burr. Whatever reason Burr had for going on ahead to the US without his new wife and son, it had truly terrible consequences. Leaving their son behind with her parents in London, Annette set off to join her husband in 1943, but the commercial airliner she was on was shot down by the Luftwaffe off the coast of Portugal, killing all on board. Sadly, it would not be the last tragic chapter in Burr's life.

Then there's his World War II record. Everyone says he joined the US Navy after the death of his wife. Some put him in the fighting on Okinawa. Slightly fewer go so far as to say he was shot in the stomach, wounded so severely that he had to endure a series of operations through the years. A very few have him awarded a Purple Heart. The US Navy, when contacted about this distinguished service, politely and diplomatically say there is no record at all of a Raymond Burr.

It *can* be confirmed that his first recorded screen role came in *San Quentin* (1946) as bad guy Jeff Torrance. Over the subsequent eleven years, until *Perry Mason*, he made about seventy appearances, almost all of them critically unacclaimed except for two very different kinds of classics.

In 1954, there was the great Hitchcock film *Rear Window* with Jimmy Stewart as a photographer in a cast and wheelchair who, with too much time on his hands, watches his neighbours for something to do and finds there's something bad going on. Or according to the trailer:

> Through his rear window and the eye of his powerful camera he
> watched a great city tell on itself, expose its cheating ways . . . and
> Murder!

Thelma Ritter, as his nurse, and his girlfriend, played by Grace Kelly (who never looked more beautiful), investigate the evil-looking Lars Thorwald (Raymond Burr). You have to watch to see how it plays out. Ruining the ending of a Hitchcock film should be a serious criminal offense if it isn't already.

Burr followed his fine performance in that great film with a portrayal of a Muslim insurgent, Captain Ahmed Shir, in *Khyber Patrol*, directed by Seymour Freidman. He also played reporter Steve Martin in the schlock cult classic, the seminal Japanese-monster-who-ate-Tokyo piece of cinematic history *Godzilla: King of the Monsters!* (1956). (It was actually made in 1954 as *Gohira* and repackaged for US theatrical release in 1956.)

> SEE! A monstrous sea-beast . . . surging up from the ocean! . . . A city of
> six-million wiped out by its death ray blast ! . . . Giant ships swamped!
> Jet planes swept from the skies! Trains ripped from the rails! MORE!
> MORE! MORE! SEE EVERY SCREEN-SHATTERING THRILL.

*With Frank Sinatra in **Meet Danny Wilson** 1952. Corbis*

Yes, *Godzilla* really was made by director Ishiro Honda, a protégé of no less than Akira Kurosawa, one of the most influential directors of all time. Burr's character, Steve Martin, is a reporter who, on a stopover in Tokyo, witnesses a centuries-old dinosaur re-awakened by nuclear testing destroying everything in his path. There were countless sequels that led bad-movie fans around the globe to equate Godzilla with the term "cheesy." Burr reprised his Steve Martin role in 1985, this time as a Godzilla specialist. The *New York Times* was highly amused.

Though special-effects experts in Japan and around the world have vastly improved their craft in the last 30 years, you wouldn't know it from this film. Godzilla, who is supposed to be about 240 feet tall, still looks like a wind-up toy, one that moves like an arthritic toddler with a fondness for walking through teeny-tiny skyscrapers instead of mud puddles. The point seems to be that Godzilla, being a "living nuclear bomb," something that cannot be destroyed, must rise up from time to time to remind us of the precariousness of our existence. One can learn the same lesson almost any day on almost any New York street corner.

For the rest, he played the occasional beefy police detective. Once he was Grand Vizier Boreg al Buzzar in *The Magic Carpet* (1951) with Lucille Ball. Another time he played Alexander Dumas fils in *Black Magic* (1949) with Orson Welles and Akim Tamiroff. Why we'll never know. But, it being an Italian co-production, he at least had the personal thrill of meeting Pope Pius Xll. He was big on Popes, though it would be hard to say he was just a good Irish Catholic boy.

But mostly Burr was typecast as the Bad Guy. In fact, The Really, Really Bad Guy. He developed an expertise in dying violently at the end of movies, to much applause in the theatres. Frank Sinatra offed him in *Meet Danny Wilson* (1952). Errol Flynn killed him in *The Adventures of Don Juan* (1948). Even women enjoyed killing him, like Lizabeth Scott in *Pitfall* (1948).

In his biography, he's quoted as saying, "Early in my career when I played all those villains and brutal gangster parts, I think my Canadian relatives were ashamed of me. As the years and parts changed, I hope they enjoyed my work." And in fact he seems to have been one of those too-rare people who became more generous-spirited in the face of personal adversity. In 1953, his 10-year-old son died of leukemia. In 1954, he remarried, only to lose his new bride to cancer. His response was to adopt a small army of foster children and treat casts and crews in the kindest of ways they would recall fondly. He worked for the B'nai Brith, CARE and the March of Dimes and founded his own philanthropic organization, the Raymond Burr Foundation. He made dozens of trips, visiting American troops in Korea and Vietnam.

And then came Perry. Perry Mason, the invincible trial lawyer, had a little-known quarter-century of history before it became a TV classic. The original mysteries were written by Erle Stanley Gardner in the 1930s. Some of them were made into truly terrible films in the same decade by Warner Brothers, including one featuring Richard Cortez as a kind of Latino version of the title character.

A successful radio version ran in the 1940s. Then Gardner set up his own production company, Paisano Productions, to adapt his greatest character for the new medium of television. He chose Burr personally, legend holding he did so over the vociferous objections of his colleagues and wife. But even though there are whole books written on the series (especially *The Perry Mason TV Show Book*), once again the Department of Fuzzification intrudes.

It would appear the dreaded gangster actor got the audition based on his role as District Attorney R. Frank Marlowe in the 1951 drama *A Place in the Sun*, with Elizabeth Taylor and Montgomery Clift. Uncannily like another legendary TV series starring a Canadian, namely *Bonanza* with Lorne Greene, the initial reviews were harsh. *TV Guide* was underwhelmed with Burr's initial efforts comparing his dramatic presence to a corporation executive on his way to, and slightly late for, the 4:12 club car from Grand Central.

Perry Mason was all pure formula, but Burr's two Emmys show how masterly his performance was. His serene gravitas would make you, without hesitation, place your life in his hands, as did 271 satisfied customers wrongly accused of murder.

He did need a little help from some friends in 1963 when he underwent surgery to remove cancerous polyps. Under his "direction," lawyer "friends" of his argued his cases in court while Perry was allegedly away in Europe. The pinch-hitters were impressive, including Bette Davis and fellow Canuck Walter Pidgeon. Mason, though, never batted an eye or broke a sweat. When he lifted his considerable bulk from behind his desk, to calmly but forcefully, state, "I object, Your Honor," one couldn't imagine him being overruled. Always by mid-episode his case would look doomed to failure. His hapless opponent Hamilton Burger would finish some cross-examination apparently terminally damaging to Perry's client, smirking that "I've-got-you-now" smirk, as if, duh, he never learned that Perry always had an ace up his sleeve. The camera would zoom slowly to Mason in medium close-up, staring impassively into the distance, with dramatic, ominous music all fading into commercial.

Somewhat ironically, for years *Perry Mason* fought toe-to-toe in the Saturday night ratings war with *Perry Como*. It is ironic in the sense that the only two shows beginning with "Perry" ever produced (not counting British, Australian or Norwegian television) should run at the same time. Mason prevailed in that one, but would eventually succumb to new competition from *Bonanza*. Burr was glad to see the show end, tired of the schedule, the hours, the repetition (although he did get an honorary law degree). He had also been the highest paid actor on TV and had banked enough to buy an island in Fiji.

Raymond Burr went on to star in another long-running hit series. *Ironside*, featuring Burr as a wheelchair-bound detective, debuted in 1967, the same year he returned to New Westminster as the Grand Marshal of the Canadian Centennial Year Parade. *Ironside's* run lasted until 1975.

He took a break in 1973 long enough to make what had been his dream project, playing Archbishop Angelo Roncalli (the late Pope John XXlll) and his efforts in World War II to save Italian Jews from Nazi death camps.

You would have to be a trivia monster to recall his third and least successful series, *Kingston Confidential*, which lasted just four months in 1977. There followed some film work in the aforementioned *Godzilla* reprise and a funny cameo turn as the judge presiding over the case of the hapless failed pilot Ted Striker in *Airplane 2*.

From 1985 to 1993, Burr made some two dozen episodes of *The Return of Perry Mason*. Such was the series' lasting renown, and the actor's celebrity, the debut episode knocked the unbeatable Bill Cosby off the top of the ratings chart. Burr had truly become an iconic figure in North American culture. He spent more and more time being the "farmer I always wanted to be." His favourite thing was growing and breeding orchids, including one for his Perry Mason colleague Barbara Hale (Della Street).

Robert Benevides was an old actor friend of Burr's who became executive producer of *Ironside*. He had a farm in the Dry Creek Valley, and planted grapes in 1986 that produced a good vintage in 1992, a year after Burr's doctors found the tumor that would kill him in 1993. The Raymond Burr Vineyard website explains the connection.

> By some coincidence, and not a little skill, the 1992 Raymond Burr
> Cabernet Sauvignon is very like the man; big, full of gusto, complex
> and jubilantly alive. Raymond Burr didn't want the vineyards named
> for him. But Robert Benevides, his partner, colleague and companion of
> 35 years, after much struggle and thought, decided that, in this case,
> the parallels of man and wine could not be separated; it is not so much
> a memorial to Raymond Burr as it is his living, breathing presence.

The biography on the website for New Westminster's wonderfully restored Raymond Burr Centre for Performing Arts tells the rest:

> After his death, his ashes were interred alongside his parents and grand-
> parents in the Fraser Cemetery in New Westminster. Raymond's loyalty
> to his Canadian roots was evident in his words and deeds. Throughout
> his life he proudly maintained dual citizenship as an American and a
> Canadian: "I get a joy out of claiming I'm Canadian. I have the fortu-
> nate situation in that I'm a citizen of both countries."

Yvonne De Carlo

B. MARGARET YVONNE MIDDLETON, VANCOUVER, BC, 1 SEPTEMBER 1922

YVONNE DE CARLO'S AUTOBIOGRAPHY IS DEDICATED TO: All the Kings, Princes, Lords, Millionaires and Truck Drivers I have known. It's an interesting read about an interesting life in a time and place that no longer exists. She is refreshingly candid about her path to success and the artistic merit of many of her films. *Time* magazine called her "The Queen of the B's"… as in B-grade movies. But still, her career spanned five decades on screen, stage and television.

Her story provides a glimpse into the grittier side of "making it" in Hollywood. One online biography describes her perfectly:

> A vibrant, full-bodied performer with a rich voice and a lushly sensu-
> ous if somewhat odd beauty, Yvonne De Carlo achieved stardom in the
> 1940s in some of the more bizarre escapism of that era. During her
> heyday and later in character roles, she acted in remarkably few films
> that could be called first-class.

She was much better at being a bombshell than an actor, but then so were Lana Turner and Ava Gardner. The sexy dances in skimpy outfits in long-forgotten movies may seem easy to dismiss now. But it's also easy to imagine the promise of a De Carlo premiere on the local screen making hearts skip a beat and hands scrambling to find the nickel or dime it would cost to see.

She came up the hard way, back in the day when dames were dames and men were pigs, enduring boorish talent agents who insisted she hike up her skirt to show her legs, who would ask if she would mind an inspection of her "upper assets" by the boss. She would rehearse until her feet bled just to advance to the front row of the chorus girls in a supper club, in the hopes of offering a better view for the movie mogul who would whisk her off to stardom. And ironically for all that, she would be best remembered for a cult classic that dressed her in green makeup, black fingernails and distinctive white-streaked jet-black hair.

She was born Margaret Yvonne Middleton to a mother obsessed with making her a star and a father whose permanent address was One Step Ahead of the Law. He disappeared when "Peggy" was just 3. Mother Marie and daughter would live a hand-to-mouth existence for over a decade. Sometimes they lived with better-off relatives on Comox Street or in Kerrisdale, sometimes living "on relief" (The Great Depression's version of welfare) in threadbare flats. Somehow, though, there were always dance lessons. Lord only knows what made Marie think that if she could only get herself and Peggy to California, Something Good would happen. If a word described Marie to a "T," that word would be "moxie." She was a super salesperson when it came to her precociously beautiful, talented daughter. Peggy was not blessed with an angel's voice like Deanna Durbin, although she would make several successful recordings. Nor was she as fortunate as Fay Wray to have a theatre stage at Hollywood High to be seen on.

Peggy's big break came at a swimsuit competition in Venice Beach, between Hollywood and Santa Monica in 1940. She finished second, winning the small fortune of $25 and the attention of a guy who knew someone who could get her an audition to dance at a ritzy supper club. It was there she declined to have her "assets" verified and was rejected. She did catch on at the Florentine Club, which was somewhat less ritzy, yet still frequented by enough stars that she was soon being hit on by some of Tinseltown's elite. Sterling Hayden, Jimmy Stewart, Franchot Tone, Burgess Meredith (whom she called Buzz), Orson Welles and big band leader Artie Shaw were all captivated by her. She artfully recalled the backstage atmosphere: "A kaleidoscope of false eyelashes, makeup and mesh stockings. There was the tinny clatter of shoe taps against the boards as the girls hurried to their places."

Peggy had adopted her middle name, Yvonne, and Marie's maiden name, De Carlo, as her stage name. It was from her mother's Sicilian bloodline that she got those exotic looks. Artie Shaw told her to take singing lessons and to get an agent. She did both, and was rewarded with a small part in her first feature in 1941, *Harvard Here I Come*. It was a dreadful B-movie, she wrote, but "I didn't know it was dreadful." Her agent was earning his keep, getting her an interview with the head of Paramount Pictures. The result was another bit part, as one of Dorothy Lamour's handmaidens in the Bob Hope/Bing Crosby hit *The Road to Morocco*. She was just one of many, part of the scenery really, and hard to find in the actual movie. But there is a publicity photo shot on set that captures her at 20 years of age, sublimely beautiful, with an air of vulnerability and innocence that could melt your heart. That she'd already travelled many hard miles seems impossible to imagine.

It all led to a six-month contract at Paramount for more money than she'd ever seen. Her next two efforts, she recalled in a self-deprecating way, included one in which "only my left shoulder survived the editing" and the next, another "dreadful bomb." Many more bit roles followed so that until 1945, the only onscreen credit she got was in *The Deerslayer* as Princess Wah-Tah. The movie starred Bruce Kellogg and Jean Parker. Even in the unlikely event you could find it, don't go there.

Despite every sign to the contrary, she was on the verge of some of her best work. On the way, she recalled another dreadful audition, in too little tiger skin, with a script so bad, "even I knew it." It was something of a coming of age for her, though, as she relates in a passage from her autobiography that will make you laugh if you've had anything remotely to do with the wonderful world of film: "I always assumed a script wouldn't be all bad if a group of businessmen were willing to spend a fortune to make a movie out of it. But I was learning."

It had been five years since the Victory at Venice Beach and the roles remained microscopic and must have been deeply unsatisfying. Sure she got to play in a movie with Alan Ladd and Veronica Lake. But "Cigarettes, sir?" was all she had to say and she was done before lunch. A lot of aspiring young actresses would have (and did) give up and go home in defeat, but not Yvonne. By about page 60, her book becomes one part *bio*graphy, one part *film*ography and one part *man*ography. Her roles *off* screen became juicier than those *on* screen.

When she was in Vancouver on some shore leave after receiving a hero's welcome, she met Howard Hughes who had flown his DC-3 into town just to meet her away from the studio publicity police. He watched her movies over and over, intrigued. Though as De Carlo herself noted, "Howard was on a different frequency than the rest of us." They flew back, touching down, as it were, in Vegas and Pebble Beach and remained "close" for several years.

There was the torrid romance with Prince Aly Khan, son of the Aga Kahn and another with the son of the Shah of Iran. When, as a 28-year-old she told reporters, "I collect jewelry, furniture and men. It's so hard to find a husband earning more money than I do. The world is suffering from a shortage of serious bachelors," it sounded less true confessions than shrewd marketing in the femme fatale biz.

Her admirable persistence paid off in 1945 in *Salome, Where She Danced*, at long last her big role, and a commercial success for Universal. She was billed as "The Most Beautiful Woman in the World!" In it she plays a beautiful Viennese dancer who falls in love with an American journalist during the Franco-Prussian War, where they meet Robert E. Lee and flee the clutches of Bismarck to Arizona and…well, you've probably heard enough. Oh, to have been a fly on the wall of *those* rewrite sessions. She did earn some nice reviews for *Salome*:

From *Variety* . . . "a looker with lots of talent who should go far."

From the not insignificant *LA Examiner*: "a grand honey who casts the most torrid shadow in Technicolor of any person in years . . . completely equal to inspire wolf whistles."

The *New York Times* wondered if her dancing might attract the attention of government censors, launched by Mr. Hays: "Miss De Carlo has an agreeable mezzo-soprano singing voice, all the 'looks' one girl could ask for, and, moreover, she dances with a sensuousness which must have caused the Hays office some anguish. The script, however, does not give her much chance to prove her acting talents."

Meanwhile, *Time* magazine said: "Miss de Carlo, a newcomer to the screen, is not exactly persuasive as the great artist, but as a woman, especially in her Salome number, she brings the house down."

Her next starring role came in 1947's *Song of Scheherezade*, again as an exotically beautiful dancer, tempting, torturing and inspiring the great real-life Russian composer Nicolai Rimsky-Korsakoff to write his signature masterpiece, "Scheherezade," based on the tale from *The Arabian Nights*.

She never professed to be making high art or, frankly, to the need to make it. She seemed to be having a fine time in a life most people on the planet would trade theirs for in a heartbeat. She did, deservedly, take pride in four acclaimed performances. She called singing in an LA production of the Johann Strauss Jr. classic opera *Die Fledermaus*, "the aesthetic high point of my life." She was outstanding as Sephora, the wife of Moses (Charlton Heston) in Cecil B. DeMille's 1956 epic *The Ten Commandments*. Even the always critical *Times* paid its respects: "Yvonne DeCarlo as the Midianite shepherdess to whom Moses is wed is notably good in a severe role." And in a 1953 charmer *The Captain's Paradise*, with Sir Alec Guinness as a ferry steamer captain with two ports, two lives and two wives in Gibraltar and Morocco, *Time* magazine said:

As wife No. 2, Yvonne de Carlo does the job of her life. For the first time a director (Anthony Kimmins) has understood that her exuberant wiggles, suggestive ogles and painted sneer of sexual overconfidence

With Dorothy Lamour, Bob Hope and Bing Crosby in **The Road to Morocco**. *(1942) Universal*

need only the least exaggeration to change a glamour girl into a raucously earthy figure of fun.

In 1955 she retired to marry and have a family. The lucky guy was Bob Morgan, a handsome man-mountain and a Hollywood stuntman. They soon had their first son, Bruce. Then a horrible on-set accident cost Morgan his leg and De Carlo her retirement. She had to re-emerge to make a living in a business not known for its sympathetic treatment of middle-aged women. John Wayne jumped in with an offer to appear in his next movie, *McClintock!* (1963). She did some regular work on television staples *Bonanza*, *Playhouse 90* and *Death Valley Days*.

Then she was offered the role for which she will probably be best known forever — Lily, mother to the lovable family of vampires and living dead called *The Munsters* (1964). For some reason, sitcoms sending up horror films were in vogue in the early

Sixties. *The Addams Family* on ABC and *The Munsters* on CBS debuted within a week of each other. *The Munsters* had impeccable comedy bloodlines. It was developed by two writers who'd written both the radio classic *The Amos 'n Andy Show* and the TV classic *Leave it to Beaver.*

They were surprisingly clever. Lily opened a beauty salon in an early Munster episode called "The Most Beautiful Ghoul in the World," a nice play on De Carlo's early billing for *Salome.* Most of the family has been dead for at least 150 years, which leads to great one-liners like "I've never been so insulted since the day I died." Sort of an undead version of *The Honeymooners. The Munsters,* though popular, was cancelled inexplicably after only two seasons. But fan clubs still abound.

Another substantive artistic achievement would come in the 1970s in a Tony-award winning Broadway play by Stephen Sondheim called *Follies.* And calculate these odds. Vancouver native De Carlo appeared with a fellow British Columbian, Penticton-native Alexis Smith in the cast. Smith won a Best Actress award, but De Carlo's rendition of the touchingly apt "I'm Still Here" was a memorable showstopper.

Nothing was a better place to come from than what she had early in life. Yvonne De Carlo was a signature product of the Golden Age of the Hollywood talent factory, a deeply flawed, totally exploitive but undoubtedly romantic and long-gone era. She had battled her way into a world where men had all the power, and learned to take everything they could throw at her and use them for great fun and much profit.

It's tempting to end as she does in her book with the classic Sondheim lyric, "I'm Still Here" (which can make you really sad you weren't there to see her sing it):

Plush velvet sometimes,
Sometimes just pretzels and beer.
But I'm here.
I've run the gamut
From A to Z
And three cheers, dammit,
C'est la vie.
I got through all of last year
And I'm still here.
Lord knows at least I was there.
And I'm here . . . Look who's here.
I'M . . . STILL . . . HE-E-E-RE!

And close curtain. Dim lights. Fade applause. Tip your cap. Good on you, Peg.

Claude Jutra

B. MONTREAL, QUEBEC, 11 MARCH 1930

D. MONTREAL, QUEBEC, NOVEMBER 1986

TO LOOK AT THE LIFE AND WORK OF CLAUDE JUTRA is to ponder the price of genius.

This country has produced no director more talented than he. For years his 1971 masterpiece *Mon oncle Antoine* was considered the best Canadian movie ever made. He counted the giants of film making around the world as his fans and friends. By all accounts he was a lovely man, generous of spirit. But the tortured soul and fragile psyche seem a terrible price to pay for inspiration. Van Gogh painted up a perfect storm, but would you really trade places with him?

Jutra was a prodigy, winning his first film award in his teens. But he deferred to his parents' wishes, graduating from medical school, becoming a doctor and artist just like his father. The Jutras family (Claude dropped the "s" later because he said there was only one like him) must have been the most documented family in Quebec, as the young artist endlessly played with his camera.

Much has been written about his relationship with his demanding, possessive mother who seems straight out of a Tennessee Williams play. It profoundly affected his work, making the theme of the troubled boy struggling to find his way in a grown-up world a constant in his films. Jutra called himself a "perpetual child." The other recurring theme, an eerie foreshadowing of later events, had to do with his characters tending to jump off piers and bridges into water. This was a strange obsession from some deep-seated emotional dungeon.

Jutra and his friend and colleague, the brilliant cinematographer Michel Brault, idolized cutting-edge, international directors. In Paule Baillargeon's moving documentary on Jutra's life, *Claude Jutra: portrait sur film (2002)*, Brault recalls the "completely crazy" prank they once pulled, bluffing their way into the New York hotel suite of the great Italian director Federico Fellini to interview him. Afterward, they noticed his breakfast was unfinished, so they stole a sacred piece of toast that "belonged" to their hero.

He called *Mouvement perpetuel* (1949) his first real film. He did some TV work, and even hosted a show about movies. At the National Film Board, he collaborated with the legendary Norman McLaren on the short film *Il était une chaise* (English title: *A Chairy Tale*). An experiment in stop-motion animation, it is twelve minutes of whimsical charm. Jutra is the actor denied a seat by a difficult and agile chair. After chasing, wrestling and pleading, he finally discovers the secret to making the chair stay still. It was nominated for an Oscar in 1958.

He made his first feature, *Les mains nettes*, in 1958, and with it washed his hands of Montreal, moving to Paris at the invitation of one of France's most eminent film makers, Francois Truffaut. Jutra was in heaven. In the midst of the cresting of the New Wave of French cinema, he found himself directing a film based on a story by Cocteau, with Truffaut producing. His ever-troubled mother bombarded him with letters pleading for his return. He responded by leaping off to Africa with another legend, Jean Loach, to make a documentary, *Niger: The Young Republic*.

When he did finally head home, he chose wrestling as the subject of his next film, *La lutte*. The *zeitgeist* of Montreal in the 1960s was a potent combination of the Age of Aquarius and political upheaval as Quebec belatedly entered the 20th century. The Quiet Revolution inspired intense nationalism. The intellectual ferment of the 1960s, the emancipation of the French-Canadian people from exploitation by English bosses and the heady experience at the centre of avant garde movie making propelled Jutra to another level. It was he who launched the wave of talented, angry, sovereignist directors who dominated Quebec's film scene for the next two decades.

Jutra's breakthrough film was *À tout prendre* (*Take It All*) in 1964. The international community noticed. The *New York Times* wrote:

> This dizzily eccentric picture, made by a young Canadian, Claude
> Jutra, who wrote it, directed it and plays the leading role, is a totally
> subjective statement of his own egotistical concerns during the course
> of an actual or imagined (he never tells us which) love affair. He han-
> dles the camera and direction with such inventiveness and flexibility.

À tout prendre 1964. *Bruno Massenet*

This is a film that will totally frustrate and confuse an average moviegoer. But it was a watershed in Quebec film and it made the pros sit up and take notice. Two of the greats, John Cassavetes and Jean Renoir, raved about it. It won the Canadian Film Award for Best Picture.

Oddly, with his new "heavyweight" status, he followed his breakthrough with the imaginative but slight *Cineboom* and a short documentary about the then-new phenomenon of skateboarding, *Roli-roulant* or *The Devil's Toy*. They came after a year teaching at the prestigious film school at the University of California at Los Angeles, where it was said he hung out and ingested many substances with a young film student named Jim Morrison, the lead singer of The Doors, one of the great bands of all time, before Morrison crashed and burned at an early age.

Back home in Montreal, Jutra's whole life was altered in a split second. Out of money, as usual, he was driving his Vespa across the Jacques Cartier bridge and crashed. His friends said he was never the same after that. Brault said life became much more tragic for him.

After his avant garde period and mind-altering West Coast experience, he, again oddly, chose to make a historical film from the bad old days of Francophone sub-servience. But *Mon oncle Antoine* (1971) would lead to international renown. Set in the asbestos mining town of Thetford Mines, it depicted a boy growing up as he watches the town's men die horrible, premature deaths mining the poisonous stuff that makes the English boss rich. Jutra had been at the famous strike there in 1949, where mineworkers protested conditions, along with the province's senior labour leaders and a rich Montreal dilettante named Pierre Elliott Trudeau. The film was his touching homage to the brave, downtrodden people of Thetford. The *Times* called it an extraordinary film. The venerable Pauline Kael, in of the *New Yorker Magazine*, called it a masterpiece and put Jutra up there next to his hero Renoir.

But as quickly as *Mon oncle Antoine* made his superstar status, *Kamouraska* (1973) compromised it. Though he and his star, Geneviève Bujold agreed to reject their Orders of Canada, they agreed on little else. He even fought with his old pal Michel Brault. The result was an exercise in tedium. The *Times* trashed it as "second-rate gothic fiction." There was the suggestion that the historic epic was out of touch with the province in its post-October Crisis ferment, and Jutra's *nationaliste* credentials were called into question.

If *Kamouraska* had been a disappointment, *Pour le meilleur et pour le pire* (*For Better or Worse*) (1975) was a complete disaster. He was now broke, discredited and unwanted.

He had only one job offer. In an almost cruel irony, he spent one night celebrating the election of the Parti Quebecois in 1976. Then the one-time Golden Boy of Quebec film left for the centre of Canada's Anglo corporate universe, Toronto. He was just there for work. There were no calls from his home province to come back. No job offers. He was an exile, mockingly called English Canada's favourite French director.

In Toronto, he made the film adaptation of Margaret Atwood's *Surfacing*. It was memorable in a bad kind of way, not what a struggling film maker needed. While no one was calling with work, the city of Montreal was calling him intently. He returned to no great acclaim, back to le Carré St. Louis, just off St. Denis Street, the absolute centre of Quebec's left-wing, separatist artistic community. He did what he could to get by with commercials and some theatre. His roommates recalled bizarre moments like arriving home to find Bertolucci over for a visit with his old friend.

The memory lapses that had begun in Toronto now became more acute. Paule Baillargeon says in her documentary that while shooting *La dame aux couleurs* in 1984, Jutra had no idea what he'd shot an hour before. In his last role, incredibly, he played a doctor who tells a patient his diagnosis of Alzheimer's.

In *Le dément de lac Jean-jeunes* in 1948, a demented man ends it all by jumping in and drowning.

In *À tout prendre* it was the character played by Jutra himself who took the fatal plunge.

In 1986, suffering greatly in body and soul, "with the angels of death flying around me," he left a few goodbye notes, instructions on feeding his cats, stuffed a note under his belt that read "I am Claude Jutra" and headed down to the dark, mysterious waters of the mighty St. Lawrence. He was only 56.

The Quebec film community that once seemed to turn its back on him embraced him in death. Since 1999, the awards given for excellence in film are called the Jutras.

Norma Shearer

B. MONTREAL, QUEBEC, 11 AUGUST 1902

D. MONTREAL, QUEBEC, 12 JUNE 1983

IF YOU'D BEEN THERE IN 1920 and told the great showbiz producer Flo Ziegfeld that the young woman in his office, yes, that short, chunky teenager with a cast in one eye would become *the* quintessential Hollywood leading lady, he'd have choked on his cigar.

Norma Shearer wanted to join the famous Ziegfeld Follies but the great impresario told her point blank she didn't have the legs or figure to be a Ziegfeld Girl. Around the same time, another showbiz legend, the great film director D. W. Griffith, told her she didn't have the face to be a film star either. That might have been the end of Norma's dream if not for yet a third legend who saw her in the long-lost silent film *Stealers*, in which Norma had her first noticeable role as Julia, the virtuous, organ-playing daughter of a crooked travelling preacher.

Irving Thalberg was a junior executive at Universal in New York, but he would become a powerful second-in-command to Louis B Mayer at MGM. Maybe it was the lighting and the camera angles, or maybe D.W. and Flo just missed the boat. But Thalberg found the young actress captivating and set out to find her. In 1921, Shearer was retreating in utter defeat back home to Montreal. By 1925, she would be voted MGM's biggest star.

Edith Norma Shearer was born into the lap of luxury in one of those lovely mansions halfway up Mount Royal in Montreal's blueblood enclave of Westmount. Father Andrew had a successful construction business. Norma went to Westmount

High, learned to ride, play piano and do all those things debutantes need to know. She recalled her youth as a "pleasant dream," but it all came crashing down in the Depression that followed the end of World War I. Mr. Shearer lost the business. The family lost the mansion and Norma had to find work. Her first job was playing piano in the window of a music store. She then graduated to playing in a silent movie theatre.

One day her mother Edith had had enough of poverty and her husband and set out to leave both far behind. She sold the family piano and bulldog (for 30 bucks). Impulsively, with just the slightest encouragement from friends and relatives with tenuous connections to the business, armed with letters of introduction to Ziegfeld and one of film's First Families, the Selznicks, she took Norma and sister Athole off to New York City.

Fame and fortune were not waiting with open arms at the 42nd Street bus depot. There was much pavement pounding, door knocking and involuntary dieting. Like just about every Canadian trying to make it in the movies at that time, Norma ended up working for (if underwhelming with her looks) D.W. Griffith at Biograph. But despite her boundless ambition and optimism, two events saved her first New York excursion from total disaster.

First, there was the role in *Stealers*, which would lead to Thalberg, And her mother had taken a few of their precious remaining dollars and sent her daughter to a controversial eye doctor named Norman Horatio Bates. Bates would achieve fame when the great English author Aldous Huxley was cured by the "Bates Method" in the 1940s and wrote about it in *The Art of Seeing*. After a Napoleonic retreat in 1921, with the Montreal winter and the family fortunes even bleaker, the eye doctoring paid off with modeling work — for fur coats no less.

What happened next remains a tad murky. Universal sent word that they had a part for her. Mother and daughter rushed to New York, where the deal fell apart over the studio's refusal to pay Mother's train fare to Los Angeles, a ticket the Shearers couldn't dream of affording themselves. But the people she'd modelled for in Montreal offered contacts, helping Norma into her highest profile role to date — as Miss Lotta Miles on the Kelly-Springfield Tire Company's billboard on Columbus Circle.

There followed a short flurry of roles, small but well-received. And finally an offer from the Mayer Corporation: six months at $250 a week, a small fortune for anyone in that era, let alone a family fallen on hard times. Throw in train fare for Mother and they were off to LA.

At the Mayer Studios, they were greeted by a small, young-looking man whom the Shearers mistook for an office boy. He was in fact the boy-wonder, 23-year-old vice-president of the studio, Irving Grant Thalberg, the young executive who'd been attracted by Norma's performance in *Stealers*. Under the tutelage of the brilliant man who would become an Oscar machine (*Grand Hotel, Broadway Melody, Mutiny on the Bounty*), Shearer would become known as the First Lady of MGM.

The wagging tongues amongst the chattering classes of Hollywood (which come to think about it is pretty much everybody) held that Thalberg was in love with the beautiful actress (though the extent of her beauty was still being debated) and was her Svengali, molding her into a star, advancing her cause with his considerable power at court. She was nothing without him, her rivals said — or at least hoped.

It is true that under his influence, she reached the pinnacle of her career, including Oscar gold. And there is some merit to the theory that her Oscar was as much, if not more of an homage to her boss for his creation than a tribute to her actual performance. On the other hand, Svengali had come within inches of firing her after what Shearer called a "hideous" screen test in 1923. Mayer insisted she was a write-off, but Thalberg let her have one more chance. After all, Garbo's first test was terrible too. Shearer knew she was one step away from oblivion and proceeded to run the table with a baker's dozen decent, profitable movies, only one of which Thalberg had anything to with.

The Most Popular Actress at MGM award (from a poll of theatre owners) was won by her efforts alone.

Still, the Shearer/Thalberg relationship and the circumstances that led to her sexy superstar status are all fascinating and mysterious. This was during the era of the Hays Code, named for the man who was sent to clean up Hollywood after a decade of lurid scandals, sexual assaults, vehicular homicides and hard drug use. It laid down the laws of acceptable content and by extension, behaviour:

General Principles

1. No picture shall be produced that will lower the moral standards of those who see it. Hence the sympathy of the audience should never be thrown to the side of crime, wrongdoing, evil or sin.

2. Correct standards of life, subject only to the requirements of drama and entertainment, shall be presented.

3. Law, natural or human, shall not be ridiculed, nor shall sympathy be created for its violation.

Consider it a crude precursor to the rating system of today. Established in 1930, it wasn't enforced until 1934, the interval being an important era in cinema history known as the Pre-Code Years when women were permitted to engage in relatively normal human behaviour that the Code would put beyond the pale for thirty years or so.

Best Actress 1930 for **The Divorcee**. *Corbis*

Much of Shearer's cachet came from playing what were then edgy, risqué roles, playing women with a sexuality usually denied them. In a perceptive online essay at *BrightLights*, Gary Morris offers clues to the aura Shearer had then:

> Shearer mesmerized Depression-era audiences who longed for both the escapist fantasy of sexual freedom (and equality) and the reassuring return to dreary conventional roles.

It explains why some of her films were so popular at the time and seem so trite now, since the envelope of sexual explicitness has gone where Mr. Hays couldn't have imagined.

Imagine what it must have been like in 1930 watching *The Divorcee*. How bold it must have seemed when she goes home with Another Man, the camera focused on the upstairs window as the curtains close and the light goes out. When she tells her unfaithful husband, "I have balanced our accounts on that note," it's quite stunning for anyone from the generation who grew up with sitcoms in which our favourite married couples, Lucy and Ricky, Ozzie and Harriet, June and Ward had to sleep in separate beds. Yet here was Norma's character, Jerry (a man's name), admitting onscreen to an extramarital affair without apologizing, begging for mercy, having a scarlet letter burnt onto her or dying a horrible harlot's death.

It must have been bracing, brazen stuff at the time. Sure there's Norma in her Deco silk/chiffon/fur outfits (curiously covering all from throat to ankle) from her wardrobe which, sold at auction, would surely erase all third world debt. One supposes this is to make the star look like a Classy Dame, but her world is full of spoiled, pompous, drunken brats who spend far too much time wearing white tie, drinking highballs and calling each other "DAH-ling." You can search high and low for evidence of Oscar-winning activity, but it is very difficult to find. The gorgeous publicity stills, though, of her reclining impeccably coiffed and gowned do show a woman to die for. The great *New Yorker* film critic Pauline Kael wrote: "Shearer's specialty was always sexual suffering in satin gowns . . ." If you're really into this, watch Shearer in *The Divorcee*.

Equally mystifying is her marriage to Thalberg. They were married in 1928 by E. F. Magnin (Rabbi to the Stars), without having spent much time together, except professionally. She was underwhelmed from the start by his appearance. He thought of firing her at least once. Moreover everyone knew he'd been born with an inoperable heart defect and from birth the prognosis was that he'd be lucky to live much past 30. He'd just suffered his first heart attack three years before Norma decided that becoming Mrs. Thalberg was a good idea. Her biographer Gavin Lambert tells of Shearer making a balance sheet that ended up with way more reasons to marry him than not. For his part he *was* obsessed, romantically and professionally, but not with Norma. His unrequited love was for the sister of one MGM's biggest stars, Norma Talmadge. He finally gave up on her. At work he doted on Garbo, Mayer's great discovery. He finally settled on Shearer. Lambert called it not so much a marriage as "a merger." And he reports the fur was soon flying, especially from Shearer arch-rival and *Mommy Dearest*, Joan Crawford, who feared that her career was doomed. "What can I do?" she's supposed to have said. "Norma's sleeping with the boss."

Crawford decried the merger as a calculated career move made by Shearer, "knowing that Irving was going to die on her." Just to add to the "What *were* they thinking" aspect, Thalberg wanted to deny her the lead role in *The Divorcee* on the grounds she wasn't sexy enough! God's teeth, man, if Hollywood's sexual icon doesn't do it for you, if the whole point is to be Henry Higgins to her Liza Doolittle and she's not sexy enough, why on earth marry the woman? And turning down your own wife for a role she covets? Why not just say, "I'm looking forward to sleeping on the couch for the rest of my born days"?

Mrs. Thalberg had a string of hugely successful commercial hits, with mixed critical reaction. In *A Free Soul* (1931), Shearer sets her sights on Clark Gable's gangster character. Again, for *The Barretts of Wimpole Street*, box office was no problem and she got good reviews for her portrayal of invalid poet Elizabeth Barrett Browning. "Miss Shearer's Elizabeth is a brave and touching piece of acting," said the *Times*, who also applauded her Juliet in the movie adaptation of the Shakespearean play, though many had warned her she was much too old to play the part. Thalberg was too tired to attend the premiere and died soon after at age 37. He'd been talking of living on borrowed time.

The day of his funeral, at the Wilshire Boulevard Temple, 7,000 people showed up. All the other studios observed five minutes of silence. Rabbi Magnin called the couple's love greater than Romeo and Juliet's, an unfortunate mix of hyperbole and cross-promotion.

It wouldn't be unkind to think of her husband's long-expected death as something of an emotional release for her. What it did for certain was put her at war with "The Chief," Louis B. Mayer. One of Mayer's first moves after the funeral was to move in with his partner and claim Thalberg's share of company profits. Shearer took them both on while negotiating a lucrative new contract with them. Clearly this was not someone who needed the protection of an influential husband. She won, too. Mayer, the most feared man in Hollywood, backed down and the royalties due to the estate of the creative genius behind the throne rolled in.

Professionally, she made some seriously bad calls. She turned down offers to play Scarlett O'Hara in *Gone with the Wind* (1939) and the lead role in *Mrs. Miniver*, for which Greer Garson would win Best Actress. She obsessed about playing Marie Antoinette to the point of frequenting the Austrian State Archives in Vienna for research. With a huge budget, it remained her favourite film, though most critics dismissed it as a turgid, overstuffed costume drama. Her last two films are long forgotten.

All of this was fodder for the "She's nothing without Irving" school of thought. Yet she did make another classic in 1939. In the cat-eat-cat world of *The Women*, she again plays the rich, stylish wronged woman. But this time she had the esteemed George Cukor directing, with a strong script from Anita Loos and crackling energy from a bevy of formidable actresses in enthusiastic support in a kind of tame template for *Sex and the City*. Rosalind Russell is deliciously catty. Joan Crawford (of Shearer's real-life mutual hatred society) is the epitome of extramarital evil. It is Shearer at her best:

> The tonic effect of Metro-Goldwyn-Mayer's film of Clare Boothe's
> *The Women* is so marvelous we believe every studio in Hollywood
> should make at least one thoroughly nasty picture a year. And even
> Miss Shearer's Mary sharpens her talons finally and joins the birds of
> prey. It is, parenthetically, one of the best performances she has given.

After all, maybe it was Crawford's character, Crystal Allen, who got in the last scratch: "There's a name for you ladies, but it isn't used in high society . . . outside of a kennel."

The *All Movie Guide* writes that, "No one will ever know what made Shearer choose the tired old farce *Her Cardboard Lover* as her last film." But, in 1942, she literally finished her scenes, walked off the set and announced her retirement. Soon she announced her second marriage, at age 40, to a 28-year-old ski instructor and pretty much disappeared. She lived into her eighties, but was very unwell in old age.

Norma Shearer's riches-to-rags-to-riches story is unusual and touching. Her relationships and success are more difficult to fathom. She should be, by right, a feminist icon for her groundbreaking roles of "modern" women. But she's not, perhaps because she overdressed for the part and offered no public avowals of the principles behind those roles. Not all of her films have aged well, though *The Women* will always remain worth seeing.

One has to admire the iron will of a woman who could overcome the early dismissal of two showbiz greats, physical flaws and death to accomplish what she did. You don't get nominated for six Oscars and take on the likes of Louis B. Mayer in real-life poker without formidable talent. Her iconic persona, like Madonna's, was her real work of art. Yet long after she had disappeared from the screen, no less than the renowned Alfred Hitchcock was heard to lament, "Where are the Norma Shearers of the world?"

Raymond Massey

B. TORONTO, ONTARIO, 30 AUGUST 1896
D. LOS ANGELES, CALIFORNIA, 29 JULY 1983

TO READ RAYMOND MASSEY'S AUTOBIOGRAPHIES (*When I was Young* and *A Hundred Different Lives*) is to meet a prince among men whose serenely cerebral, yet charmingly self-deprecating contentment with life leaps off of every well-written page. Someone who is, as the French say, *très confortable dans sa peau*, very comfortable in his skin. In the foreword to the second volume of Massey's memoirs, the also-legendary Christopher Plummer described him as follows:

> Offstage there is nothing "actorish" about him. No frills, no posturing.
> He is gregarious, generous, jovial, gentle, an admirer of Trollope and
> racy limericks, and a hell of a lot of fun.

Massey would be among our greatest artistic exports for his stage career alone. That some of the greatest performances ever seen on film were his only adds to his legendary status.

The Masseys may be Canada's most overachieving family of all time. Raymond was the distinguished thespian, brother Vincent was the first Canadian-born Governor General, and the family, who could trace their New World roots back to Puritans fleeing England in 1630, ran the immense farm machinery company Massey-Harris since 1847. (Of course, the Sutter family of Alberta, who did put six sons in the NHL comes close.)

Massey is one of a very few to have two stars on the Hollywood Walk of Fame, one as a movie star on Vine Street and the other on Hollywood Boulevard for his famous role as the fatherly Dr. Gillespie in the classic TV series *Dr. Kildare*. He is also quite likely the only actor in the English-speaking world to have his professional stage career begin in Siberia.

Raymond was wounded in World War I and recovered. In 1918 he enlisted in a Canadian brigade that went to fight in support of the "White" Russians against the "Red" Bolsheviks, who were in the process of taking power during the aftermath of the Russian Revolution.

To say there wasn't much action is an understatement. Massey recalls it as "rotting for months." He did a little skit at the officers' mess and was summoned by the commanding officer to mount a full-fledged show to boost morale and give the men something to do, and it was a great success.

With his mother's encouragement, he had become enthralled by the theatre at an early age. Though it didn't sit well with the males of the family, captains of industry and all, Raymond never really had any other ambition. After his Russian sojourn, he dutifully tried to follow in the hallowed industrial footsteps of his forebears. He reported for work at the company's main plant in Toronto to begin working his way to the top. His starting salary was $25, which was almost immediately cut to $22.50. He knew he wasn't cut out for the job, and the theatre "kept beckoning." He quit, took a boat to England and got his first stage gig in 1922, in Eugene O'Neill's *In the Zone*.

By decade's end, he was a critically acclaimed star on the London stage. In 1928, he took a small film role in a bizarre "futuristic" science fiction movie called *High Treason*, set in the distant future year of 1950 on the brink of war between the US and a united Europe.

Massey wrote matter-of-factly:

It was inevitable that I would go into movies sooner or later. Yet the experience of those years in the movies counts for very little to me as a stage actor. The actor who works on stage and screen must accept the sad truth he is following two different professions . . . I am not a theatre snob who looks on movie work as a form of slumming. I detest such snobs.

In 1931, he played Sherlock Holmes in *The Speckled Band*, which, as the *New York Times* review noted, opened in New York when he was playing Broadway for the first time:

Raymond Massey, who is now appearing in Hamlet at the Broadhurst, portrays Holmes. He is not quite the prototype one was accustomed to see in the drawings in the Strand Magazine stories, but his diction, expressions and gestures are so satisfactory that there is no doubt he makes a far better Holmes than Clive Brook did in Basil Dean's picture, *The Adventures of Sherlock Holmes*, which was released two years ago . . . Mr. Massey's performance is pleasing, intelligent and restrained.

He hired an agent, from one of filmdom's powerhouse families, the Selznicks, and headed west. He recalled not exactly taking the town by storm:

After three days and four nights in a Pullman compartment I crawled off the Santa Fe Chief at Pasadena feeling like death. Nobody turned out to meet me. I took a taxi to the hotel in Hollywood and had a bath.

Bucked up by a stay at San Simeon with newspaper magnate William Randolph Hearst, he returned to Universal studios to make his movie *The Old Dark House*. He glumly noted he was told it was good though he never saw it: "The long and colourless juvenile part I was given did not permit much acting." What he leaves out is the fact that, however dreary the part, he made his Hollywood debut in a classic. Though little seen and hard to find today, *Dark House* is one of the best of the Universal horror flicks of the early 1930s, starring British great Charles Laughton and the emerging Boris Karloff. The *All Movie Guide* accords it "Grail-like status" among horror fans. It was directed by the undisputed master of the genre, John Whale, still a cult hero, who would go on to make *Frankenstein* (1931), *The Invisible Man* (twice in 1933 and 1966) and *The Bride of Frankenstein* (1935), with that memorable performance by Elsa Lanchester.

Massey expected something to follow, but nothing developed except a reduction in his golf handicap. He fled the West Coast for New York and when no play materialized, he kept going, all the way back to London.

Later in 1933, Massey travelled home to Toronto with a pre-Broadway tour of a play called *The Shining Hour*. The performance, he thought, went well. The crowd, including their Excellencies the Governor-General and Countess of Bessborough, applauded enthusiastically. The Canadian reviews, however were terrible, predicting doom on Broadway — where in fact it was soon to be a huge hit.

In 1934 came the movie that Massey said was the most fun of all to make. *The Scarlet Pimpernel* was based on the classic novel about Sir Percy Blakeney, the fey-looking Englishman who is secretly part Zorro and part Robin Hood, rescuing innocent French nobles from the revolution's Reign of Terror. The arch enemy of "that damned elusive Pimpernel" is the Darth Vader of 18th-century Paris, Citizen Chauvelin, played with evil élan by Massey. Pauline Kael deemed it one of the most durable of all swashbucklers with Leslie Howard as the hero, Merle Oberon "looking unhumanly beautiful" and applauding Massey's "snarling villain." It was produced by the great Alexander Korda,

the Hungarian ex-pat who was almost single-handedly dragging the British film industry into a position to compete with Hollywood.

In 1937, he was Cardinal Richelieu in *Under the Red Robe*, set in 17th-century France during the persecution of the Hugenots. Massey played the good Cardinal with such intensity that he scared the wits out of a 10-year-old schoolboy named Christopher Plummer:

> For it was a face not just molded for horror — it was wise and devout .
> . . carved from oak; drenched in Melancholy; it had seen ghosts and
> war, sorrow and death. To a boy of ten, it could terrify!

It's one of those minor historical ironies that the two most renowned renderings of the American legend Abraham Lincoln came from Canadians. In 1930 Walter Huston played the doomed president under the direction of the silent movie master D. W. Griffiths. But Griffiths never came to terms with the use of dialogue, and only a truly heroic performance by Huston makes the film and its long, wordy set-pieces remotely watchable.

Massey came to Abe through the Pulitzer Prize–winning play written by Robert Sherwood called *Abe Lincoln in Illinois* and went on to star in the film adaptation. It's a fascinating piece in a lot of ways. It's bold structure, beginning with Abe as a very young man and ending with his first election to the Oval Office. If you're one of those addicted to Lincoln and Civil War lore, Massey's performance is uncanny. It seems as if the Great Man himself has come alive, rising off all those many pages written about him. The iron will behind the self-effacing wit, the deeply felt humility and calm demeanour, the sudden debilitating flashes of despair and depression. While Mary Todd, his wife, played by Ruth Gordon frets, huffs and puffs, Massey plays Abe as supremely unconcerned. As the returns trickle in with the very State of the Union hanging in the balance, he reads incoming wire copy from the key battleground of New York: "Seems there's a paper in New York that says I have the soul of Uriah Heep in the body of an orangutan."

The *New York Times* was effusive.

> He looks the part, he is the man, he speaks the lines as Lincoln must
> have spoken them, or should have spoken them. We recognize that it is
> unfair to take performance for granted, but that will be Mr. Massey's
> fate: you will simply think of him as Lincoln.

David Herbert Donald, whose brilliant 1985 biography of Lincoln also won a Pulitzer concurred:

My favorite film portrayal of Abraham Lincoln will always be that by
Raymond Massey. I remember seeing the film as a small boy, and I have
looked at it several times since. Massey seemed to have just the right
figure for the part, the slightly shuffling walk, the keen eyes. I found
him utterly believable — something I can't say of some other actors
who have tried to play the part.

Lincoln is considered by many to be his cinematic masterpiece (his only nomination for
Best Actor, but he lost to Jimmy Stewart for *The Philadelphia Story*), but there would
be many more intriguing and always challenging roles.

49th Parallel in 1941, about German sailors landing in Canada's far north, was
nominated for Best Picture and actually won the Oscar for Best Writing, Original Story.
In that one Massey plays Andy North, who makes a very late but crucial appearance
right near the film's end. *All Movie Guide* heartily approves of the product and director Michael Powell's use of, "Riveting suspense, superb writing, good cinematography,
and some of the finest actors of the day."

In 1943, Massey volunteered for the US Marines at the age of 47. When it hit
the papers, he was summoned by Prime Minister Mackenzie King's Minister of Defense
Colonel J.L. Ralston, who insisted that Massey join the Canadian forces instead or the
King government would look bad. Massey was introduced to his new CO, a General
Stuart. They immediately repaired to the Rideau Club for an "excellent luncheon."
After a desultory year pushing paper, Major Massey went back to real work.

It may be the kind of statement that begins arguments, but Frank Capra's 1944
nutbar black comedy *Arsenic and Old Lace* is one those classics that has aged extremely
well and still makes for a nice evening's entertainment. The sweet little old Brewster
sisters have taken up a hobby: inviting drifters in for a glass of their elderberry wine
spiked with poison, and then burying the victims in the basement. One might well wonder how many gallons of elderberry wine were needed to come up with this premise.

Cary Grant plays a theatre critic who discovers what his aunts are doing for fun.
He has two brothers. One believes he's Teddy Roosevelt, demands to be addressed as
"Mr. President" and runs up the stairs like San Juan Hill with drawn sword, yelling
"Chaaaarge!" Mr. Grant's other brother, Jonathon, played by Massey is about as hyster-
ically funny as a psychotic murderer just out of prison can be. He is scarred and made
up to look like Boris Karloff playing Frankenstein. And he is upset with the old sisters.
They've killed about as many people as he has, and he is apparently very competitive.
The *Times* was so-so on the movie, but glad about Massey's return:

Abe Lincoln in Illinois *1940. Photofest*

The picture serves to welcome back Raymond Massey after an extended leave. While it is a little breath-taking to hear "Honest Abe" shambling around sounding like Lincoln but looking like Boris Karloff, that's the condition that prevails.

Television would soon beckon but before then came some serious roles in adaptations of classic novels and plays. In 1947 he appeared in the film adaptation of Eugene O'Neill's harrowing stage epic *Mourning Becomes Electra*. If you know anything about the play, you would have thought it unfilmable and you might have been right.

Massey then played a newspaper publisher in Ayn Rand's own adaptation of her novel *The Fountainhead* (1949), with Gary Cooper and Patricia Neal. Pauline Kael called it one of those unintentionally funny films. And to properly give credit where its due, here is the *Times'* redoubtable Bosley Crowther with one of the most scathing critical putdowns of all time: "*The Fountainhead* is a picture which you don't have to see to disbelieve."

Massey played James Dean's father in a production of John Steinbeck's *East of Eden* (1955) that won an Oscar for Best Supporting Actress and was nominated for three more, including Best Director for Elia Kazan. And he was a general in Norman Mailer's war epic *The Naked and the Dead* (1958).

But the role that the Yuppie Generation remembers him best for is the avuncular Dr. Leonard Gillespie on the hit TV series *Dr. Kildare* (1961–1966). The extremely successful series was based on films from the 1940s about a young daring handsome doctor (played by Lew Ayres) and his kind, wise mentor, played by no less than Lionel Barrymore. On television, Kildare was played by Richard Chamberlain and the series ran for five solid seasons.

Massey, at age 80, was with Chamberlain again one last time in his final hurrah on stage in Tennessee Williams' *Night of the Iguana*. He called *Night of the Iguana* his "little finishing canter," quoting Oliver Wendell Holmes:

> The riders in a race do not stop when they reach the goal. There is a
> little finishing canter before coming to a standstill. There is time to
> hear the kind voices of friends and say to one's self, "The work is done."

Mack Sennett

B. MICHAEL SINNOTT, DANVILLE, QUEBEC, 17 JANUARY 1880
D. WOODLAND HILLS, CALIFORNIA, 6 NOVEMBER 1960

MACK SENNETT'S IS ONE OF THE MORE PLEASANTLY ASTONISHING success stories. It begins with absolutely no clue or reason to suspect that he would become a giant in a medium that had yet to be invented when he was born.

Long odds are a prerequisite for even entering the road to icon status, but where others who made the climb were handsome, beautiful, childhood prodigies or blessed with stage work at Hollywood High, Sennett was just a farm boy from Quebec's Eastern Townships with a decent education and an equally decent bass voice.

From that beginning, he somehow became "The King of Comedy" in the silent movie era. His comic innovations resonate to this day.

Sennett came to have an unsurpassed eye for talent, all the more impressive in the early chaotic days of a fledgling film industry. Charlie Chaplin, Gloria Swanson, W. C. Fields, Bing Crosby, Mabel Normand, Stan Laurel, Marie Dressler, Wallace Beery — all became stars eventually, but Sennett was the first to recognize their potential.

It would be difficult to exaggerate his stature in that time before sound. But pay close attention to the adoration in this passage from Frank Capra, who would become one of Hollywood's most esteemed film makers (*It Happened One Night, Mr. Deeds Goes to Town, It's a Wonderful Life*). In 1924, at the apogee of Sennett's career, Capra sought work in the Master's studio:

I looked and gaped for the first time at King Mack's towers . . . more
famous in comedy circles than the towers of London or Babel.

Sennett's autobiography, *King of Comedy*, and some biographies about him are
great reads, but tend to be more works of fiction than history. It seems as if the King of
Comedy had to rewrite his life to add more gags, to make it funnier. Sadly it's easier to
document his way down than his way up. But even when a few details are iffy, the life
story of an absolute genius is always worth telling.

We do know he was born Michael Sinnott in 1880 in the village of Danville,
between Drummondville and Sherbrooke. His Irish Catholic family had come from
County Wexford to farm. He referred to his singing as mooing on the lonely roads of
Quebec. His mother encouraged the unlikely dream that he would sing professionally.

Mack and his two brothers were shipped off in their teens to an exclusive school
in Montreal, indicating that the family had done well. The parents headed hundreds of
miles east to open a hotel in Lac Megantic, one of Canada's least known and most beautiful regions. The Anglo country rubes were soon singled out as the "S'nott" brothers and
they literally had to fight for their existence. At the age of 17, Sennett left with the rest
of the family for Connecticut and eventually Northampton, Massachusetts where his
showbiz life began.

Some voice lessons had upgraded the vague notions of mooing to an ambition
to sing with the Metropolitan Opera in New York. By 1902 he was in the Big Apple,
but how he got there is anyone's guess. He may have just got tired of slogging at the
pulp mill with his father, packed up to seek stage fame and fortune, changed the name
just enough to end the "S'nott' jokes and left.

Mack's version also involves the renowned stage actress (and Cobourg, Ontario
native) Marie Dressler. Sennett schemed to get an interview with the star. Somehow he
knew a prominent local lawyer named Calvin Coolidge (the future 30th president),
who was persuaded to write a letter of introduction. Upon receipt of said letter and said
pulp mill worker/opera singer, Ms. Dressler graciously offered the services of her own
producer, the legendary New York impresario David Belasco.

In reality, he disappeared into the seedy world of burlesque halls, where performers kept one eye on dodging missiles launched by unruly audiences and the other
on the exit, just in case there was another police raid. Biographer Simon Louvish turned
up one actual credited performance for Sennett on Broadway in 1907 in *The Boys of
Company B*.

The next year would prove to be a seminal one. Every hungry actor in New York
heard the word that the Biograph film company was hiring. Sennett made his way there
and was hired at about the same time as a young man from Kentucky named D. W.

Griffith. Sennett began acting in Griffith's films in the summer of 1908, and quickly became a leading man.

Let's clarify what the term "film" meant in those days. They were referred to by the number of reels they ran. A one-reeler was about ten minutes, a two-reeler, which quickly became the industry standard, ran up to twenty. They were shot in a day. In today's computer-generated effects world, they seem primitive, with grotesquely over-the-top hamming for the camera. But think back to your first video game experience. How primitive was that, and how many quarters did you happily sacrifice, marveling at the novelty?

Griffith was film's great innovator and Sennett, while overacting for the camera, watched him direct and took it all in. Griffith later called him "indispensable" on shoots and was impressed enough to allow Sennett to pinch-hit for other absent directors. He was put in charge of Biograph's comedy films. In 1912, at the age of 32, he set out on his own, finding the financing to form Keystone Studios.

The *Encarta Dictionary* describes both the qualities and derivation of "slapstick:"

Boisterous comedy: comedy with the emphasis on fast physical actions, farcical situations, and obvious jokes that do not depend on language.

Early 20th century: Slapstick: a device made of two flat linked pieces of wood, formerly used in comic performances to simulate the sound of a blow.

The Quebec farm boy mastered a steep learning curve and become a movie mogul unto himself. In the hands of masters, even slapstick could be an art form and Sennett, with his astutely chosen stable of actors, *was* a master.

Some of the most enduring symbols of early silent comedy were Sennett concoctions. The hysterically hopeless Keystone Kops careened into situations they only made even more hopelessly chaotic. The depiction of bumbling authority left audiences howling with laughter. The age-old scene of the virtuous maiden tied to a train track by a mustachioed bad guy comes directly from a Keystone film, *Barney Oldfield's Race for a Life* in 1913, featuring Ford Sterling and Mabel Normand respectively as the villain and maiden. Normand was a Sennett discovery who would become a major star and with whom Sennett would have a longstanding, acrimonious and indeterminate relationship. He never did marry or have children.

In the realm of film innovation, Sennett may not have invented the pie in the face as a comic device, but his studio refined it to technical perfection, as described by Sennett protégée Del Lord:

You don't throw it like a shortstop rifling to first base. You push the pie
towards the face, leaning into your follow-through. Six to eight feet is
the limit for an artistic performance.

The Sennett Bathing Beauties were another staple of his productions, scantily clad
women being for good or ill a perennial attraction.

Sennett also continually broke new ground. In 1914 he made the world's first
feature-length comedy. *Tillie's Punctured Romance* ran seventy-three minutes in a star-
studded production that was the first feature for future superstars Charlie Chaplin and
Marie Dressler. Chaplin left Keystone the following year and was succeeded as Sennett's
Clown Prince by the somewhat-forgotten (though legendary in comedy circles) Ben
Turpin. Turpin was married to a Canadian comic actress from Quebec City named Carrie
Lemieux, though that wasn't what made him famous. He was the son of a French-born
candy store owner in New Orleans, where he'd wandered around vaudeville until some
undiagnosed condition caused his eyes to become permanently crossed. He made his
first film at the age of 38 and those eyes and thick moustache were his trademarks. His
best work came whenever he was cast as a parody of a handsome leading man, especially aping silent heartthrob Rudolph Valentino, in 1924's *The Shriek of Araby*.

Always looking for publicity, Sennett took out a $25,000 insurance policy with
Lloyd's should Ben's googly eyes for some reason straighten out.

Keystone had merged into Triangle Films in 1915, which reunited Sennett and
his old mentor D. W. Griffith. The slapstick king branched out a bit, directing less, producing and managing the business side more, which not coincidentally was where the
occasional financial crises that would one day prove terminal began.

He began making a few romantic comedies, mostly in honour of another of his
discoveries, a stunning teenager named Gloria Swanson, who in time would be one of
Hollywood's most distinguished actors, best remembered now for being "ready for her
close-up" in *Sunset Boulevard* (1950). With a dignified presence even in youth, she
quickly (and to her, mercifully) graduated from being one of the pie-in-the-face girls to
a star in her own right. She provides an interesting, if not flattering description of her
place of work:

> It was a world of falling planks and banana peels and wet paint and
> sticky wads of gum; of funny looking fat men with painted moustaches
> blowing the foam off beer at each other, of stern battle-axes wielding
> rolling-pins and cute little giggling hoydens being teased, tickled and
> chased.

Mack Sennett's Keystone Kops. Photofest

Newcomers were initiated to the "Sennett Commandments" uncovered by biographer Louvish:

> Thou shalt punch the time clock at 9,12,1 and 6.
> Thou shalt not speak to directors without permission of the name on the gate.
> Thou shalt not feed Pepper the cat.
> Thou shalt not be seen carrying a book.
> Thou shalt not gurgle the grape on these holy premises.

He continued to amass his great fortune and was treated as Hollywood royalty. *Photoplay* dispatched no less than renowned American novelist Theodore Dreiser to interview Sennett about his philosophy of comedy. He answered:

> People want to laugh at something. Mostly other people's troubles, if
> they're not too rough.

Still, the 1920s was a vexing decade for him. He bought a mansion with liveried butlers, and brought his mother down to live. He bought a large piece of land and to promote its value, erected a huge sign of white letters lit by bulbs spelling "HOLLY-WOODLAND."

It soon fell down, but was put back up, minus the last syllable, and remains an unforgettable sight on the Hollywood skyline.

His on and off relationship with Mabel Normand became ever stormier, and scandal became a regular visitor.

In 1921, former Keystone Kop and Sennett favourite Fatty Arbuckle was at the centre of the shocking death of a young actress, the alleged victim of a lurid sexual assault. This lifted the lid on the seamier side of Hollywood, of drugs, booze and sexual excess. Sennett issued a statement in support of his one-time star, who would eventually be acquitted, but whose career and life were ruined. Arbuckle died in his sleep at the age of 46.

Mabel Normand was involved in two fatal shootings, one of which included Sennett as a suspect. One was never solved, and in the other her chauffeur was found guilty. It all brought a crisis of reputation to the movie world, and the threat of government censorship if the moguls couldn't control their own.

Sennett would never recover from two more crushing blows in the late 1920s. The first was the advent of sound. Sennett was not the only one to fail to make the transition from the silents. The attrition rate was especially high among comics, including the great Chaplin himself. Only W. C. Fields and Laurel and Hardy graduated successfully. Sennett just couldn't figure out how to marry dialogue with a pie in the face. Though he made a few well-received short films in the 1930s with Fields and Bing Crosby, he was done.

Worse still, the stock market crash of 1929 wiped him out. He officially declared bankruptcy in 1933, listing liabilities of $925,681 and assets of $1,600.

Not until 1938 did the Academy of Motion Picture Arts and Sciences award him an honorary Oscar, and the tribute was eloquent and moving:

For his lasting contribution to the comedy technique of the screen, the
Academy presents this special award to that master of fun, discoverer
of stars, the sympathetic, kindly, understanding genius, Mack Sennett.

The presenters were two of his greatest protégés: W. C. Fields and Academy President
Frank Capra. Tears streamed down his face and all he could manage was "Thank you."
It was Charlie Chaplin who best summed up Sennett's rise and fall:

Mack Sennett had a feeling for comedy that has never been equaled.
Unhappily, his inability to sense the subtle changes that were taking
place in public tastes led to his downfall. If we could have had only
silent movies forever he would still be the World's King of Comedy.

He and his legacy faded into obscurity, though there was a Broadway musical in the
1970s called *Mack and Mabel* in which Robert Preston played Mack. In the 1992
bioflick *Chaplin*, Sennett was portrayed by fellow Canadian Dan Aykroyd.
His headstone in Culver City, California's Holy Cross Cemetery reads:

MACK SENNETT

1880–1960

BELOVED KING OF COMEDY

The greatest of the S'nott brothers of Danville, Quebec.

Colleen Dewhurst

B. MONTREAL, QUEBEC, 3 JUNE 1924
D. SOUTH SALEM, NEW YORK, 22 AUGUST 1991

COLLEEN DEWHURST HAD A WONDERFUL LIFE. It wasn't a charmed life by any stretch, but it was a full one. She was fortunate to be brilliant at her profession, which she loved so much she would have worked (and sometimes did) for nothing. "Once an actress," she said, "always a waitress." But on and off her beloved stage, as an actor, friend, lover, mother, it was a full life, full of passion, pain, applause, achievement and what must have been a level of satisfaction most of us dream of. Full of great art, many cigarettes and many bottles of white wine it was never, it seemed, for one moment dull or complacent. Though she died too early, she sure didn't get cheated out of anything, except perhaps wealth, which she had little regard for anyway.

One of the most complimentary things you can say about a hockey player is that he (and she these days) held nothing in reserve, instead "leaving it all out there on the ice." That was Colleen Dewhurst's approach to life. She became known as THE definitive interpreter of the harrowing and demanding dramas of Eugene O'Neill, a label that came to vex her. She lamented that her obituary would read "O'Neill interpreter died somewhere yesterday."

It's kind of funny, actually, reading the American-based websites about her life. Her father was a professional athlete and given the Canadian specific, they all presume he must have been a hockey player. In fact he played for the Canadian Football League's

Ottawa Rough Riders. One of the most significant contributions he made to his tomboy daughter's young life was teaching her how to throw a punch to avenge the abuse inflicted by the Mean Girls in high school. One Mean Girls' broken nose later, she was left alone. She was, and would remain, a feisty lass. It was once written that she had a face that belonged on Mt. Rushmore, omitting that she also had a temper like Mt. Etna.

As playing in the CFL in those days was not a way to make your family rich, Dewhurst (and this is no small achievement) had to work at odd jobs to pay her own way into and through the prestigious American Academy of Dramatic Arts. There was no doubt about what she wanted to be.

She made her debut on Broadway in 1946, while still in school, in *The Royal Family*. Dewhurst had a remarkable presence as a stunningly handsome rather than delicately beautiful woman. One of her early and favourite stories was about actually turning down the great Joseph Papp, who was essentially God to aspiring Broadway actors back in those days. He had invited her, sight unseen, to audition for a production of *Romeo and Juliet* he was mounting. Her autobiography records the conversation like this:

Dewhurst: Have you ever seen me Mr. Papp?
Papp: No
Dewhurst: Well I couldn't play Juliet even when I was thirteen.

The impression she left was positive enough for Papp to cast her in the somewhat less romantic *Titus Andronicus* as Tamora, Queen of the Goths.

In 1958, she signed on to an off-Broadway production of *Children of Darkness*. This was less notable professionally than personally, as this was where she met her soulmate, George C. Scott. They were both married at the time, though not to each other, and after a pair of messy divorces, moved in together and eventually married. Then divorced. Then re-married. Was it George Bernard Shaw who observed that second marriages represent "the triumph of hope over experience?" What would he have quipped about second marriages to the same person?

Scott was a brilliant, multi-award winning actor, a formidable man. Their connection was obviously profound. As a husband, he seemed to be a hundred miles of bad road. Still, Dewhurst adored him always, and refused to speak ill of him when she was dying.

There is just not enough time or space to share all the superlative reviews Dewhurst received over time, so, let's hit the heights.

Her greatest personal triumph was her unequaled portrayal of Josie Hogan, the Irish-American farmer's daughter, alongside Jason Robards in Eugene O'Neill's *Moon for the Misbegotten*. Her first performance of this defining role was in Spoleto, Italy in 1957, with the accomplished stage director Jose Quintero. It was December 1973 before it would open on Broadway, to much acclaim. Lavish would be an understatement. Dewhurst, with more than a little pride, notes in her book the review written by the great theatre critic of the *New York Times*, Clive Barnes:

> There are some performances in the theatre, just a few that urge along as if they were holding the whole world on a tidal wave. I felt that surge, that excitement, that special revealed truth . . . This is a landmark production that people will talk about for many years. It seemed to me an ideal cast . . . in one of the great plays of the twentieth century. *(December 31, 1973)*

She wrote that "it was the most wonderful Christmas and New Year's I had ever celebrated and the best time of my life."

She explained her own theory as to why she had such a touch with O'Neill's women:

> They feel, they need and they act. Their greatest mistakes, which often create great tragedies, always have as their basis, love.

Co-star Jason Robards offered a touching recollection of the experience:

> I will never forget listening to Colleen screaming "Father, Father, I love you." It just broke my heart hearing it every night. What the hell are you going to do? Play this every night for a year and go home and tear your heart out? No, the play does it for you. And the rest of the time, you might as well have a good time out there.

They made their epic stage performance into a TV movie, one of her seven Emmy nominations. Dewhurst's Emmy award win, though seemingly a long way from O'Neill (and Albee et al) to a sitcom on the small screen, was something she managed to pull off. Her memoirs record that the final choice for playing the mother of ace reporter Murphy Brown, in one of the best television series ever, came down to Colleen Dewhurst and Lauren Bacall. Both would have been superb, and Dewhurst won the role and an Emmy. Ms. Brown, wonderfully played by Candice Bergen, was a formidable TV journalist, fondly nicknamed by the show's anchorman as "Slugger" for her hard-hitting reportage. Of course, Mom, (Dewhurst), who raised such a forceful young woman, made her daughter seem like a walk in the park, by comparison.

For all her fabulous performances and the great dramatic lines she got to deliver, few are likely better remembered by more people than this, one of TV's all-time classic great lines:

Big Valley *with Barbara Stanwyck. Corbis*

Murphy: "It was bad enough you making the waiter take the steak back, but did you have to follow him back and make the chef eat it?"

Avery: "If you keep letting people get away with shoddy work, then you end up with President Quayle."

(And on the off-chance you don't remember Dan Quayle, rest assured it is an absolutely devastating line.)

Much like Kate Reid, most of Dewhurst's screen success came on television. *Murphy Brown* was one, but she was welcome on the best series there were to be had: *Dr. Kildare, Alfred Hitchcock Presents, The Big Valley, Moonlighting* and, slightly below the bar, *Love Boat.*

But for Canadians she is best remembered as Marilla in two movies about that venerable Canadian institution, *Anne of Green Gables. Anne* had a long tradition of film adaptations dating back to the silent movie era in 1919. There were also versions made in the 1930s and 1940s. It took a good Canadian boy named Kevin Sullivan and an unbelievably precocious young actor named Megan Follows to capture it, along with Dewhurst, in 1985, for television audiences around the world.

Her reputation and talent earned her roles in some great films. But they weren't really her priority. She had grand supporting roles with Sean Connery in *A Fine Madness,* and was Diane Keaton's mother in the Oscar-winning Woody Allen movie *Annie Hall.* Perhaps she most enjoyed playing opposite her talented son Campbell, in the Julia Roberts movie, *Dying Young:*

> Mr. Scott, who cuts a dashing figure and enables the coy, bashful
> flirtation between Victor and Hilary to be drawn out more slowly and
> teasingly than would otherwise have seemed possible. Also in the film,
> and providing a kind of grace note, is Colleen Dewhurst, Mr. Scott's
> mother (George C. Scott is his father), who plays a knowing
> Mendocino resident with a colorful past, a garden maze and an
> unfortunate gift for foretelling the future. Mr. Scott's exceptional
> assurance and his mother's in these scenes are very much in tune."

Her memoirs close with a speech she gave to the graduating class of Sarah Lawrence College.

> Listen, my darlings, It's terrific out there. What it's about is joy. It's
> about joy and agony and pain and believe me you can't go around it or
> under it. You've got to go through it.

Ruby Keeler

B. DARTMOUTH, NOVA SCOTIA, 25 AUGUST 1909
D. RANCHO MIRAGE, CALIFORNIA, 28 FEBRUARY 1993

THE BUCOLIC HAMLET OF COLE HARBOR, NOVA SCOTIA quite rightly takes great pride in its home-grown hockey superstar Sidney Crosby. A gifted talent, the gods have blessed him with a combination of skill, grace and tenacity. Down the road a piece, the city of Dartmouth lays claim to its own home-grown superstar, the legendary dancer and actor Ruby Keeler.

It is true that, at times, she may have looked as if she was taught to dance by Clydesdales. But she did star in three of the greatest musicals of all time in one year. She captured hearts and filled seats. Before the stylish grace of Rogers, Astaire and Charisse, Ruby Keeler was the First Lady of Hollywood dance. In *A Biographical Dictionary of Film*, David Thompson allows that in just a few films she made herself "widely remembered as the pert, dancing sweetheart of Warners' musicals of the 1930s." Amazingly she earned legend status after making just eleven films.

Ethel Keeler was one of six children born to an impoverished Irish-Catholic family in Dartmouth, Nova Scotia who hoped that a move to New York City would bring better times. For a time, life in the Land of Opportunity proved no better than it was back on the shore of the Bedford Basin. There was barely enough to keep everyone clothed and fed. But good fortune eventually paid a call in a way that none of the Keelers ever dreamed of.

One of the nuns at St. Catherine of Siena's Catholic School thought Ruby showed some promise in her dance class and suggested formal training. Mrs. Keeler somehow scraped together enough money to enrol her promising daughter in the School of Rhythm and Tap of the musical impresario Jack Blue. Mr. Blue, too, saw promise. Enough to take her along to see the musical giant, George M. Cohan. (*Give My Regards to Broadway, Yankee Doodle Dandy, Over There*). She auditioned, the boss liked what he saw and there she was, a chorus girl in a Cohan production of *The Rise of Rosie O'Reilly*. At $45 a week she was earning more than her father and became the family's salvation. The only minor complication was that she was under-age, 14 at most, on a big Broadway stage! A little embellishment in her paperwork took care of that. From there, the charmingly naive nun's protégée and alumnus of St. Catherine of Siena's personal and professional life took some rather piquant twists and turns.

As *Rosie O'Reilly* was closing, she was noticed very favourably, not by the Bolshoi Ballet, but rather by the owner of a fairly notorious New York nightclub, a "speakeasy," one of those illicit and illegal establishments that thrived in the era of Prohibition when the public sale of alcohol was illegal. Easily one of the worst pieces of legislation ever passed by a democratically elected government, Prohibition measures encouraged an entire generation of Americans to become comfortable with flouting an ill-advised law of the land. Anyway the speakeasy owner was just one of many men captivated by the sensual innocence of the sweetest kid you'd ever meet, and he hired her to perform at his esteemed establishment. It was there that she became generally known as the "girlfriend" of Johnny Costello, aka Johnny Irish, apparently a genuine New York gangster — somewhat like Tony Soprano without the therapy. Not to reflect on Miss Keeler's virtue during those teenage years, but it's difficult to imagine keeping a mob boss happy by eating cotton candy at Coney Island and repeating, "Gosh, Johnny, you're really a swell guy." Few people would dare flout the law as Mr. Costello was known to.

Keeler was a collector of men's hearts, and by the age of 17, her collection included that of "The World's Greatest Entertainer," Al Jolson. The son of a cantor from Srednik, Lithuania, he was the first person in history to appear actually singing on film. *The Jazz Singer* (1927) was the first commercially released talking film, and it made him a superstar.

They married in 1928. Ruby was 18 and Jolson was 42 (or 44 or 46 depending on the account). He was the most famous man in the world. What else was a young girl from Oak Street to do? It must have seemed like a good idea at the time. Some feared Johnny Costello might get annoyed and deposit Mr. Jolson in several pieces deep in the

East River. Either Jolson was too big a name to knock off, or Johnny was a romantic cold-blooded killer at heart and just wanted his girl to be happy, the big lug.

She was not only piling up conquests often and seemingly with little effort. Her rise to stardom seemed to be remarkably free of struggle and adversity. She went from school to Cohan to the "speak" and then, after starring in *Show Girl* (1929) for the great stage producer Flo Ziegfeld, on to Hollywood with her famous husband to Warner Brothers.

Of course the marriage would become its own private hell. Ruby's career was about to explode, and by the 1930s, Jolson's was clearly on the back nine. He became well-known for attending Ruby's stage performances and jumping up to sing along with her numbers. She later called the marriage a long mistake (she filed for divorce in 1939) and remained sufficiently bitter to deny permission to use her name in the movie *The Al Jolson Story*. It's said their relationship was the plot for the oft-made classic, *A Star is Born*.

In the early 1930s Warner Brothers reveled in its gangster dramas and stable of stars with "edge" — Bogart, Cagney, Jean Harlow, Bette Davis. With the advent of sound, so many musicals were made so badly, it was completely discredited as an art form. But in 1933, Warner Brothers reinvented the musical with the help of the brilliant choreographer, Busby Berkeley. He took big stars (William Powell, James Cagney, Una Merkel, Ginger Rogers), great scores, lavish sets, budgets that would have been the envy of third world dictators, packaged them together and topped them off with the sweet little thing Depression-era audiences would fall in love with: our girl Ruby.

And except for getting an unexpected check in the mail or a really good white chocolate cheesecake, what really could be nicer than hunkering down and watching those three wonderful 1933 musicals — *The Gold Diggers of 1933*, *Footlight Parade* and especially *42nd Street*. The *New York Times* deemed the latter "invariably entertaining":

> . . . it is for the most part a merry affair and in it Ruby Keeler (Mrs. Al Jolson) makes her motion picture début. Her ingratiating personality, coupled with her dances and songs adds to the zest of this offering. It is a film which reveals the forward strides made in this particular medium since the first screen musical features came to Broadway."

Keeler plays the adorable, unassuming Peggy Sawyer, who shyly ducks through the chorus girl audition crowd, making her entrance. No one could seem less cut out for fame. She even faints during a grueling rehearsal. Wonderful musical numbers like, "Shuffle Off to Buffalo" on board a train and "You're Beginning to Be a Habit With Me" will stick in your mind for weeks. Just give in. Resistance is futile.

An uncharacteristic but delightfully hard-boiled Ginger Rogers is very funny as "Anytime Annie." And wouldn't you know it, the star breaks her ankle just before opening night. They turn to Annie, who defers to Peggy/Ruby. You can take a wild guess about how it all turns out. And yes, the Director (Warner Baxter) utters the immortal line:

> Sawyer, you're going out there a youngster, but you've got to come
> back a star!

After the Big Three, the studio seemed to try and make the same movie over and over. In 1935, she actually co-starred with husband Jolson in *Go into Your Dance*, a reasonably well-received film the *Times* called above average:

> If the reactions of the Capitol's patrons are to be believed, the
> husband-wife combination should prove a popular one. At the risk of
> causing a family squabble, this corner must set itself down as of the
> opinion that Mr. Jolson is the better half.
>   It is his enthusiastic presence that pulls the picture into the
> safety zone of musical entertainment. When he is absent from the
> screen one's attention is likely to stray, even in the face of Miss Keeler's
> nimble dancing. *(May 4, 1935.)*

Keeler went on to make just five more films, including the forgettable *Sweetheart of the Campus* in 1941. Having already dumped the husband, she then dumped the movie business too. She met a handsome wealthy real-estate agent on a blind date, married, and finally had the family she'd been longing for.

She pretty much lived happily ever after, except for her husband's death in 1969. It was only then that she considered one of the many comeback offers that had been rolling in for nearly thirty years. She agreed to dance in the remake of a decades old play called *No No Nanette* (from whence "Tea for Two" comes). She was by then past 60, and Broadway can be a very unforgiving place.

Thankfully it was a triumphant return. She never looked more comfy or lighter on her feet. She was the picture of grace, and there wasn't a grumpy nit-picking reviewer in sight. The redoubtable Clive Barnes of the *Times* no less said:

> One of the show's many charms is the amount of dancing—not
> unexpected, when it is remembered that the production has been
> supervised by the great Busby Berkeley, who once made Hollywood a
> world fit for tap dancers, and stars Ruby Keeler, who, way back when,
> was sent on that stage by Warner Baxter, an unknown, and came back

*As Bea Thorne in **Footlight Parade** 1933 with James Cagney. Warner Brothers*

a star. Ruby still is a star. Admittedly Miss Keeler is making acting into one of the arts of conversation, but she dances like a trouper and wears indomitability shyly like a badge of service. She is just enormously likable." *(January 20, 1971.)*

She was called The Queen of Nostalgia. It's a warm feeling you get looking at her star on the Walk of Fame at 6370 Hollywood Boulevard. Critical disdain, the public adulation, chucking it all for love and family, the wonderful last hurrah. She was a good Irish-Catholic Bluenose girl and she deserved that star.

Deanna Durbin

B. EDNA MAE DURBIN, WINNIPEG, MANITOBA, 4 DECEMBER 1921

SHE MUST HAVE BEEN A REMARKABLE YOUNG WOMAN. How many people could have the strength of will to walk away from the addictive allure of Hollywood superstardom before turning 30?

Deanna began life as Edna Mae Durbin, the daughter of recently arrived immigrants from Lancashire, England. The gods blessed her with the vocal chords of an opera diva. And though she went to California with her family at a very early age, the blessing did take place at the Grace Hospital in downtown Winnipeg in December of 1921. She studied voice and dreamed of a career in opera. The thought of making movies never crossed her mind until she was discovered by a Hollywood talent agent at a school recital at the age of 14.

That voice made her a star at 16: at US$400,000 per film, she was the world's highest-paid actress by 21, then suddenly retired at 27. She was credited with single-handedly saving Universal Studios from bankruptcy during the Great Depression. One critic said she could have made movies from seed catalogues and still have filled theatres. Her perky, plucky persona was so loved by fans around the world that her picture had a special place on the wall over the bed of a young, desperate Jewish girl in Amsterdam named Anne Frank.

These days Deanna Durbin movies rarely show up on TV. They're hard to find in even the most serious classic video stores. Her contemporary youthful stars, Judy Garland, Mickey Rooney and Shirley Temple are still famous. Deanna, in her day, was bigger than all of them, yet now, outside of a devoted cult following, she is virtually forgotten. In fact, her very first screen appearance was along with Garland, in *Every Sunday*, a short feature made for MGM in 1935. The studio signed Judy to a long-term contract but let Edna get away to rescue Universal, and the rest is history.

Three Smart Girls (1937) was the first of her eight straight blockbuster hits. Watching it for the first time can still cause goosebumps, hearing that gorgeous, soprano voice coming from that little chicken-wing of a girl. It's a lighter than air confection that features Deanna's singing and scheming to reunite her estranged parents. This involves, among much else, charming the entire NYPD by singing an aria from Puccini. High art it is not, but as a vehicle for a fresh new face, it's brilliant. It is totally predictable and formulaic, but it's as charming today as it was when first released. The exuberant, determined young woman manipulates all the unsuspecting adults around her to the happiest of endings.

After *100 Men and a Girl* (featuring legendary classical conductor Leopold Stokowski), *Mad About Music* and *That Certain Age*, her salary per film leapt to a quarter of a million dollars. She was just 18 and, more importantly, she was awarded a special Oscar (along with Mickey Rooney) in 1939 for "their significant contribution in bringing to the screen the spirit and personification of youth, and as juvenile [sic] players, setting high standards of ability and achievement."

She had become the most popular performer of the Great Depression. Her irrepressible spirit, perfect manners and charming onscreen disposition made her the daughter that parents wished for, the role model for young women seeking to rise above the gloomy times. Universal nurtured her profile with a regular spot on the great Eddie Cantor's CBS radio show. She began a serious recording career. But Deanna and all the studio's men couldn't avoid the most career-limiting move that could befall her. She grew up to be a glamorous, talented woman with ambitions to serious acting credentials.

She wasn't even allowed to be kissed until her sixth movie, *First Love* (1939). The lucky guy was future star Robert Stack, and it was so controversial that not a single studio photograph was ever made. The Kiss stunned the movie-going world from Hollywood to London, England. Who could foresee that it was the beginning of the end?

Durbin was active in the war effort. Combat pilots painted her name and likeness on the nose of their planes. But there was no question that her box-office magic was waning.

In 1944, at the advanced age of 23, she played a down-and-out singer in the film noir *Christmas Holiday*. Her character married a doomed killer on the run played by future dancing star Gene Kelly. Tragic endings of Deanna Durbin films were not what her audience was used to. She followed that with *Lady on a Train*, a sort of mystery/comedy. It remains a bit of a train wreck to watch, but it firmly established two things.

As Penny Craig in **Three Smart Girls** *1936. Universal*

First, she COULD act and act well. Less happily, it also confirmed that her devoted fans much preferred her as their fondly remembered teenage heroine.

Durbin endured the remainder of her contract and after *For the Love of Mary* in 1948, now all of 27 years old, she retired and never looked back. A fellow Canadian, perhaps filmdom's greatest superstar, Mary Pickford, won fame, fortune and renown by playing young women well into her own adulthood. But Deanna would not make that compromise. She left the glamorous Hollywood life so many dream about apparently without a second thought, taking her considerable fortune to a reportedly happy life in Paris, dismissing all attempts to bring her back to stage or screen.

Writing about her life isn't easy. Her career lasted a dozen years. Her life as a total recluse spans five decades. She married her third husband, director Charles David,

*Deanna Durbin with Gene Kelly in **Christmas Holiday** 1944. Universal*

in 1950 on the condition he protect her from "spiders, mosquitoes and reporters." Tall mythical tales have grown through the interstices of real-life fact.

One website claimed that she was a favourite of Winston Churchill, that he would screen all her films personally before their release in Britain and that he would often celebrate Allied victories by watching her 1937 film *100 Men and a Girl*. I had the privilege of asking Churchill's renowned biographer, Sir Martin Gilbert, about these rituals. He replied, "Who's Deanna Durbin?"

It's not surprising that myths abound about a great star who last spoke to the media in 1949. But it's hard not to admire a woman who rose from the obscurity of Gallagher Avenue in Winnipeg to the pinnacle of stardom and obscurity, all on her own terms.

Alexis Smith

B. GLADYS SMITH, PENTICTON, BRITISH COLUMBIA, 8 JUNE 1921
D. LOS ANGELES, CALIFORNIA, 9 JUNE 1993

WHAT ARE THE ODDS? Two young, talented Canadian actors move to Hollywood to seek fame and fortune. Both are saddled with the decidedly unglamorous name of Gladys Smith. The first changes her name to Mary Pickford and becomes the Silent Era's biggest star. The second, about forty years later, chooses the more exotic first name Alexis, keeps the Smith, and is nicknamed Hollywood's "Dynamite Girl."

The name change was all she needed. She could dance, act and stop traffic on a dime. The story of Alexis Smith is a tad bittersweet, one of much promise and frustration but with a happy ending. There are three images of Smith that tell her story and linger in the mind.

First the smiling young ingénue, achingly pretty and wholesome. A Homecoming Queen whom even the Captain of the school football team might struggle to ask to the Prom.

Then, the sultry siren, smoldering in silk, reclining on a love seat (said to be Garbo's) with that impossible glamour and beauty that exists only in the world of film and just takes your breath away. It shows an accomplished, confident professional.

And finally, at 50, still a great beauty, dancing her way to awards and acclaim and onto the cover of *Time* magazine, sweet payback to all the studio moguls who squandered her talent and creativity in films and roles beneath her true merit.

Most Canadian actors in Hollywood have a story about why they ended up there. Stage stars recruited by studios; ailing parents seeking a nice climate and so on. Why the Smiths left Penticton for Tinseltown is unknown. But it was clear that young Gladys had loads of talent and an appetite for hard work. She was something of a dance prodigy. Only 13 years old, she made her stage debut at the Hollywood Bowl, no less, in a production of the ballet, *Carmen*.

Life was kind. She went to Hollywood High (and who wouldn't wish they'd done that?), and won a state acting contest. She wasn't discovered by chance at a drugstore soda fountain. She worked hard, studied theatre at LA City College, and hoped that the studios would come calling. Warner Brothers offered her a screen test and signed her up with big plans. She was 20 years old.

The studio didn't exactly blast out of the gate. Though she played in eleven movies in her rookie year, 1941, most were uncredited. She paid her dues and her early filmography contains roles such as "Phone Gossip # 4" in *You Couldn't Say No*. Not to mention the "Girl who says 'I Wish I Were Dead'" in *Flight from Destiny*.

But film No. 9 marked her real debut, *Dive Bomber*. Directed by Michael Curtiz of future *Casablanca* fame, the film features significant star power with Errol Flynn, Ralph Bellamy and Fred MacMurray racing to find a cure for the altitude sickness that was killing dive bomber pilots. Smith plays an already-married woman who fancies both Flynn and MacMurray.

"The Other Woman" role was one in which she was often cast. Some of her best reviews came from her portrayal of Cecily Latham, the love interest of neighbour Humphrey Bogart whose hobby was poisoning his wives. *The Two Mrs. Carrols* was dismissed as a "soap noir," but it was noted that Miss Smith "is delightfully selfish in a fine part." As Bogart refuses to leave his marriage, the "fresh-faced ingénue" delivers a look of icy contempt harsh enough to drop a large predator at 50 meters.

She even played The Other Woman with another woman in the trashy adaptation of Jacqueline Susann's *Once Is Not Enough*. Smith co-stars with Kirk Douglas as his nasty wife, a still-in-the-closet lesbian who takes a shining to Melina Mercouri. It may have been the very first onscreen same-sex kiss.

There's a little irony here, in that she also starred with Cary Grant in 1946's *Night and Day* as the wife of the brilliant songwriter Cole Porter. Porter's then-notorious homosexuality was completely sanitized, as Hollywood still considered the subject the love that dare not speak its name. The *New York Times* praised the leads for "providing enough character and star power to make the audience forget the silliness of the script."

Alexis Smith often played the same part of the saintly, long-suffering significant other of brilliant, troubled men. Linda (i.e. Mrs. Cole) Porter, Olivia Clemens opposite

Alexis Smith. Hollywood's "Dynamite Girl."

Frederic March's epic effort in *The Adventures of Mark Twain* (1944); the love interest of Errol Flynn again in *Gentleman Jim* (1942) as the famous boxer Gentleman Jim Corbett.

Critics loved the "zany side" she revealed in her foray into musical comedy in Frank Capra's *Here Comes the Groom* (1951) with Bing Crosby. It was written that "Crosby, Franchot Tone and Jane Wyman all turn in fine performances, but Alexis Smith does considerably much more than that."

The making of *The Young Philadelphians* in 1959 was pivotal in Smith's career and life. The film features a striking performance by Paul Newman as a brilliant, unscrupulous yet somehow honourable lawyer who manipulates everyone, but saves the life of his old pal Robert Vaughn (who was nominated for an Academy award for his role). Smith was then pushing 40, a dangerous age for Hollywood actresses, yet she was still being cast as women of great beauty and sensuality.

Her unorthodox "entrance" in the film consists of a medium-wide shot of her on a ladder, waist-down from the rear in stocking feet, flaunting those dancer's legs for all to see. That this woman who stopped the young Newman dead in his tracks could be married to an aging lawyer who spends his days writing a book about the Sherman Anti-Trust Act strains credibility. She falls for Newman (who wouldn't?) and plays the breakup scene, lovelorn and dignified in a black negligee. In an unusual Hollywood plot twist, Newman wins the Big Case *and* Gets The Girl.

It showed she had been blessed with timeless beauty. But it also showed that even after holding her own with almost all of the great leading men of the time—Newman, Grant, March, Flynn, Crosby, Charles Boyer, even Jack Benny (of course as a beautiful angel in the camp classic *The Horn Blows at Midnight*)—the juicy leading ladies' roles she had coveted were now passing her by.

By 1960 she was out of Hollywood. Her husband, Craig Stevens, to whom she would be happily married for forty-nine years, was doing well in television. Later that decade, the two began touring in stage shows together.

In 1971, she won a role in *Follies*, a Stephen Sondheim musical about the reunion of ex-showgirls at a soon-to-be-demolished Broadway theatre. She won a Tony Award as Best Actress and with it the acclaim she'd spent decades searching for on Hollywood sound stages.

Over the next two years, she was invited onto the *Johnny Carson Show* a half-dozen times. She was on the cover of *Time* magazine, which rapturously wrote:

Alexis Smith is the living, dancing refutation of F. Scott Fitzgerald's axiom that there are no second acts in American lives. At 49 she is in

*As Phyllis in Stephen Sondheim's **Follies** 1971. Martha Swope*

the best second act of her life. Her blue-green eyes catch the light and the audience's rapt attention; her body seems beyond the aspiration of girls half her age. *(May 3, 1971.)*

The attention spurred a return to screens big and small after a 16-year break. A regular gig on *Dallas*; a role as Jodie Foster's aunt in *The Little Girl who Lives Down the Lane*; with Burt Lancaster and Kirk Douglas in *Tough Guys*, with the *Times* noting she was "looking mighty good, thanks."

She was gracious about her missing a home run in the movies, admitting the frustration but refusing to blame anyone but herself:

People frequently said it was a shame Warner Brothers typecast me, and I don't believe that. I believe I typecast myself . . . I was not that creative.

Her last film appearance came in Martin Scorsese's *The Age of Innocence* in 1993. He was one last addition to the long list of Hollywood's great directors who were entranced by the radiance and talent of Gladys, that hard-working girl from Penticton, BC.

Beatrice Lillie

B. TORONTO, ONTARIO, 29 MAY 1894

D. HENLEY-ON-THAMES, ENGLAND, 20 JANUARY 1989

HONESTLY WITH MOVIE PEOPLE YOU JUST NEVER KNOW. Beatrice Lillie was crowned "The World's Funniest Woman." All the more impressive that she was awarded that crown by Noel Coward, one of the wittiest men of all time.

In 1952, she opened her Tony-award-winning show *An Evening with Beatrice Lillie*. The reviews were unbelievable: "She is still the funniest, most delightful, most enchanting woman in the world." President and Mrs Truman reverentially attended. It ran for 275 performances then went on tour, even to Canada.

So picture this meeting of movie moguls in Hollywood in 1958: One starts by noting the reviews and box office and says: "This *Evening with Lillie* thing is huge. Don't you agree we should make it a movie or at least a TV special? She's a legend, we should at least have her on tape. We could cash in, big-time." Another one says, "No. I have a better idea. Let's bring her all the way to California, put her in really crappy movies, with lousy scripts, no plot and really weak supporting casts. And if she says anything funny, we can just leave it on the cutting room floor." A third says, "Of course we'll have to pay her a lot of money." The previous one exclaims, "Of course we will. And if we do this right and make them as bad as we can, we won't get any of that money back." The chairman ends the meeting declaring, "I like this plan. Good work, Ipkiss. Now, don't just sit there Smedley, get out there and find the worst scripts money can buy."

OK, so maybe it didn't happen *quite* like that. But how else to account for the

American and British film industry squandering such a great talent and immense celebrity, not to mention a substantial international revenue stream? The *World's Funniest Woman*, the female Charlie Chaplin who had the world howling with laughter you would think would have movie moguls salivating to sounds of "Ka-ching, Ka-ching!" Such was her acclaim in Britain during World War II that Prince Philip, the Duke of Edinburgh, later said "We wouldn't have won the war without her." Granted the movie people only had, oh, forty or so years to figure it out. The tragedy is that almost nothing remains for us to see what all the fuss was about. This from an industry that can finance a sequel to *Legally Blonde*.

Actually it was partly her own fault. She was on the stage for forty years and was much more comfortable playing to an audience than a camera. But in her autobiography, she wrote that she felt so badly treated by the studios (she sued one of them, too) that

> For reasons we hold to be self-evident, I chose playing in vaudeville any
> day, week or year to working in Hollywood.

Despite the rather mixed blessing of not having a film career, Lillie had enough praise from her stage and radio career to last several lifetimes. No one else in this entire volume can hold a candle to the glow of her reviews, superlatives over the years and across the Atlantic.

For instance, for *This Year of Grace* in 1928:

> It is more devastating to see one corner of her mouth twitch than to
> see some comedians fall down stairs.

Her friend, collaborator and ardent admirer, Noel Coward wrote of "the piercing lethal beam of her dreadful irreverence and her implacable humor."

The most sophisticated of seniors laugh just recalling her, and relate that her comedy came more from timing than content. She was a true giant in her time, but in an archaic mode of comedy, from back in the time the Toronto Maple Leafs won an occasional Stanley Cup.

Beatrice Gladys Lillie was born in Toronto's west end or as she puts it in her memoirs, *Every Other Inch a Lady*:

> I was born at a very tender age because Mother needed a fourth at
> meals.

Her parents were appalled to discover Bea and younger sister Muriel playing house under freight cars in the railyard near their house. She called it "Canadian roulette."

Her first ambition was to work in a booth at the Canadian National Exhibition.

She went to the same school as Mary Pickford had. But Beatrice, with her mother and sister, developed musical entertainment talents and formed the Lillie Trio. They played for everyone from social clubs to mining camps. Muriel's marriage and move to London broke them up. Beatrice was sent to school in Belleville for a time, then her mother summoned her for the two of them to sail for London just in time for World War I. But she often returned on tour to her hometown, and seemed to genuinely recall it with great fondness.

> A little bit of heaven had fallen down from the sky onto the shores of
> Lake Ontario. So they sprinkled it with stardust and called it Irish
> Toronto.

She wrote this on being feted by Mayor McBride ("with a brogue as thick as Irish coffee"):

> He said "Your singable beauty has endangered you to thousands."
> I thanked him from the bottom of my galoshes.

Bea went straight for the dance halls and got spots as an "extra-turn," someone to occupy the audience during intermissions of regularly scheduled shows. Her break-through act was "Upon the Death of his Beloved Wife" in which she impersonated a husband sobbing his way through Irving Berlin's "When I Lost You." She was bloody good, as she would have said, and the sobbing act cracked up Andre Charlot, who was a big deal in theatrical production in London back in the day. He hired her on the spot and the very next day World War I broke out.

One night at supper at Simpson's-in-the-Strand, she was introduced to the handsome and dashing Bobby Peel, a scion of the once distinguished but then much diminished baronetcy. The first Sir Robert Peel built a great fortune. The second had been a great prime minister. The rest seemed to have devoted their considerable time and energy frittering away the family's status and wealth. When Bea's "Bobby" ascended to the title, he continued that tradition with an apparent fondness for gambling. He and Bea married in 1920. Five years later they became Lord and Lady Peel, a title she enjoyed for the rest of her life.

She took Broadway by storm as part of a traveling version of *Charlot's Revue of 1924* (or as she liked to call them, Charlot's Harlots). Decades of raves began that January night. The *New York Times* said:

> No amount of advance description can take the edge off the enjoyment
> that is to be had seeing and hearing Miss Lillie sing "March with Me."
> There is no one in New York comparable to Miss Lillie.

As Maria Wislack in **On Approval** *1944.*

Her biographer, Bruce Laffey, describes that scene like this:

> "March With Me" with Bea, dressed as Britannia, and leading a battalion of similarly dressed Girl Scouts, crashing into her followers while attempting to retain her sword, shield and dignity.

The audience, he reports, was "hysterical." The US tour ended in Los Angeles where Lillie met Valentino, Chaplin, Fairbanks and Hearst, and also made a movie called *Exit*

Smiling, coincidentally co-starring with fellow Canadian Jack Pickford, brother of Mary. Lillie remembers it this way:

> Most of the time I couldn't make out what the movie was all about. Neither could anyone else. I was used to working for months to perfect a gesture. Here we were due to finish in five weeks. I doubt whether "Da Lawd" himself could have made much sense of the goings on on set.

For quite some time she refused to see it. An awful feeling, she said, watching yourself and knowing there's nothing you can do about it. Some critics called it first-rate clowning. Bea thought it was "a piece of cheese" and so did the movie-going public.

So a pattern of sorts developed. Every few years a mediocre movie, then back to the stage for more lavish praise. In 1926 after the *Exit Smiling* debacle, she starred in *Oh, Please!* Various reviews are quoted in her biography:

> Miss Lillie is as astonishing as ever. Her comic gift is the best in the world.

> She proves to be a whole show needing just a backdrop and her eyebrows.

The show ended in New York and Lillie met and became close with the likes of Fanny Brice, Harpo Marx and the legendary Algonquin Round Table with Dorothy Parker and Robert Benchley. Her lightning-quick wit was perfect. Overhearing a chorus girl gushing about taking a house on Leicester Square, she replied "That's very nice, dear, but you must put it right back."

On Bea in *She's My Baby* (1928), Alexander Woolcott wrote that the play

> . . . leans so heavily on the comic from Canada that she will be black and blue by the end of the week.

She spent more and more time in New York, bought a flat overlooking the East River and in 1930 made her first feature film, *Are You There?* And the *New York Times*, as per usual, trashed the film, but loved her:

> There is very little reason for seeing "Are You There?" except for Miss Lillie . . .

She had a hit radio show for a while. "Hello, hello and so on from the sweetheart of show biz." Her sponsor was a dairy ("Let's pour a can of milk over junior and see if he evaporates, too").

In 1934, the fifth baronet Sir Robert Peel, her husband, died suddenly from complications after an attack of appendicitis. She didn't miss a performance. She never remarried. Some said it was because she wanted to keep the title she would have to forfeit if she did. She did however meet a handsome Marine 28 years her junior named John Huck, who became her constant companion and died a day after she did.

Her next film effort came in 1938. She seemed to enjoy the experience, staying with her friend Fanny Brice, then in La La land.

With the outbreak of war, her son enlisted in the Royal Navy. Bea set out to perform for the military from the Navy's northern base at Scapa Flow to Tripoli for the heroic Eighth Army of Field Marshall "Monty" Montgomery and for Eisenhower's troops in Algeria.

> *I'm madly keen to entertain the troops.*
> *I don't mind if it's singly or in groups.*
> *I'll entertain in barracks*
> *Or even a large marquee.*
> *I'll give them swing,*
> *Or Wagner's Ring,*
> *Or selections from Rose Marie.*

She was in Manchester in 1942 when word came that her son was missing in action. She was devastated. Laffey cites a friend's observation that that was the day that Bea began her own death. She obsessed about her late son and the circumstances of his death to the point of visiting the harbour in Ceylon (Sri Lanka) where his ship was sunk by Japanese bombers.

Her next foray into film was 1948's *On Approval*. The headline in the *New York Times* read "Not Enough Lillie!"

> And when, on those rarer occasions, Miss Lillie is permitted to be herself, the film reaches its intended goal of humorous irreverence. On the whole, however, this comedy of errors, which might have been delightfully gay, is disappointingly dull. *(January 29, 1945.)*

Her crowning professional achievement opened at the Booth Theater in New York on October 2, 1952. Noel Coward remarked that *"An Evening with Bea Lillie* is one of the most enchanting things that could ever happen to anyone." "The Greatest Comedienne of All Time," they said. You know the drill, reviews too good to be true. But they *were* true. It ran for 275 nights, won a Tony, then toured for years. Laffey writes the Booth rocked with laughter every night. It must have had everything to do with the eyebrows.

It sounded all rather grand, with Noel and Fannie and Harpo, and the Royal Family. Lillie was summoned to Buckingham Palace once for a Royal Command Performance in honour of Queen Juliana of the Netherlands. She asked the Master of

Beatrice Lillie, Lady Peel. The World's Funniest Woman.

the Household what to do. He answered, "Oh about ten minutes I should think." She began by saying, "I shall sing a song by Noel Coward, who shall remain nameless."

Her final appearance on the big screen came in 1967. *Thoroughly Modern Millie* was a musical comedy with Julie Andrews and a Mary Tyler Moore, who looked like she may still have been in high school. Lillie played a conniving old sort who ran the women's hotel where the girls were staying. The *Times* said she was "jimdandy."

She ends *Every Other Inch a Lady* asking, "Is there anyone for Venice?" and with her favourite motto. "*En Avanti*. It's always better farther on."

Fay Wray

B. CARDSTON, ALBERTA, 15 SEPTEMBER 1907
D. NEW YORK, NEW YORK, 8 AUGUST 2004

THE YEAR WAS 1931, AND FILM ACTRESS FAY WRAY was in New York, playing in a Broadway clunker called *Nikki*. She adored the male lead, Archie Leach, who was tall, dark and impossibly handsome and gracious. He seemed to hang on her every word.

Archie would soon move to Hollywood and achieve much acclaim and fortune after changing his name to Cary Grant.

So some months later, when Wray was in the office of her friend and producer, Merion Cooper, and he told her she was about to work with the "tallest, darkest leading man in Hollywood," she was excited, expecting to see her ideal man Cary ushered into the room. She was crushed when Cooper pointed to a model of Kong, the darkest, tallest and (hairiest) leading man Hollywood would ever see.

You can't blame a girl for being disappointed at missing a chance to work with Cary Grant again. But Kong, though a good deal less handsome, gave young Wray a measure of immortality. *King Kong*, released in 1933, is still considered one of the great films of all time.

The prologue to her memoirs (entitled *On the Other Hand*, which is quite witty if you've seen the movie), is addressed to "Dear Mr. Kong." She almost wistfully writes,

> For more than half a century you have been the dominant figure in my public life.

So it was a real living legend that His Worship the Mayor of Cardston invited back for the town's 75th anniversary in 1962. Wray always wrote, often well. She recorded the day,

> As we approached the Canadian border the sky was swept with somber hues. The landscape to right and left was flat, seeming to go on to infinity . . . prairie land, wheat land.

She was certainly bigger news than the other big name invited, Prime Minister John Diefenbaker. She enjoyed the RCMP musical ride and the rodeo. She was made an honorary member of the Blackfoot First Nation as Kisk-sta-ki-aki, which she understood as "Beaver Woman." She was thrilled at seeing the Northern Lights. But a visit to the old family ranch at "Wrayland" about 40 kilometers from Cardston brought back a flood of memories. The log cabin her father built was long since gone. Mostly she remembered the withering winters, temperatures of minus 55 Fahrenheit, and six-foot snowdrifts that locked them in. The family's health problems had eventually taken them south to Utah, Arizona and finally California, from the Northern Lights to the bright lights of Hollywood.

She had begun acting at Hollywood High. A chance encounter led to a screen test with Fox and her very first film, a small role in *Gasoline Love* in 1923 at the age of 17. Her first big role came two years later in *The Coast Patrol*, alongside the unforgettably named Spottiswoode Aitken.

She soon signed on with Universal, whose specialty in the mid-1920s was the Western. Movie lengths were still measured in reels rather than minutes. Wray began doing "two-reelers," twenty-five minutes max. She soon graduated to feature-length "five-reelers" with one of the studios biggest stars, Hoot Gibson. Still, the genre was saddled then with the less-than-flattering generic nickname "Oaters."

But her work was highly enough regarded for her to be named as one of Hollywood's most promising starlets in 1926 by the Western Association of Motion Picture Advertisers. It may sound like several steps down from an Oscar, but at that time the Academy and its awards had yet to be invented. It was impressive company to be in. Along with Fay the Advertisers singled out Joan Crawford, Janet Gaynor (who would win the first Best Actress Oscar in 1929), Delores del Rio and Mary Astor, future stars all.

For Wray stardom came early in the 1928 silent classic *The Wedding March*. Renowned director Eric von Stroheim was entranced with young Fay's beauty. She was at once innocent and sensual, and elusive in the sense that she could look completely stunning in many different ways. She had so many different "looks" that it's sometime hard to identify her.

King Kong *1933. Corbis*

It was the time of her life. Sixty years later she would recall it with great affection, especially von Stroheim himself. "The word genius," she wrote "was suitably applied to him." She played Mitzi, an ill-fated young woman who falls in love with a Prince (von Stroheim), but is forced by her parents into an engagement with an oafish butcher she loathes. Lust, jealousy, murder and mayhem ensue. The film was over budget, too long, so behind schedule that it was released as a silent when "talkies" were taking over. But Fay loved everything about it, especially, in one way or the other, the brilliant, cantankerous director himself (von Stroheim, as he often did, doing double duty).

She married a rising young writer named John Monk Saunders and the two ran and played with Hollywood's elite. They partied with Cole Porter and Charlie Chaplin; beat legendary violinist Jascha Heifetz at ping pong; watched the 1932 Olympics from the private box of Hollywood's Royal Couple Mary Pickford and Douglas Fairbanks. (Canada finished 10th with 15 medals). Wray never would be overly impressed with her celebrity.

Back at work, she was paired with Gary Cooper as "Paramount's new glorious young lovers." The collaboration survived the transition to sound from *The Legion of the Condemned* and *The Kiss* to one of her best performances in *One Sunday Afternoon*. She was much in demand and amazingly prolific. From 1932 to 1933 she started a new film every fourth Friday and by the end of 1934, twenty-three of her films had made it to the screen. For reasons unknown, many of them were horror or science fiction films. Even before Kong, she was known as The Scream Queen for movies like *Doctor X* and *The Vampire Bat*. In *The Most Dangerous Game*, screams abound as she and Joel McCrea are pursued by a maniac whose idea of fun is hunting humans.

There may be people who don't know about *King Kong*, or its remake, but the critics raved.

Here is a summary from the *All-Movie Guide* that tells what happens when Carl Denham, a documentary film maker with an apparent death wish takes Fay (in a blond wig) as Ann Darrow to meet a tribe in the deepest jungles on the far-off uncharted Skull Island:

> The chief and witch doctor spot Denham and company and order
> them to leave. But upon seeing Ann, the chief offers to buy the "golden
> woman" to serve as the "bride of Kong." Denham refuses, and he and
> the others beat a hasty retreat to their ship. Late that night, a party of
> native warriors sneak on board the ship and kidnap Ann. They strap her
> to a huge sacrificial altar just outside the gate, then summon Kong, who
> winds up saving Ann instead of devouring her. Kong is eventually taken
> back to New York, where he breaks loose on the night of his Broadway
> premiere, thinking that his beloved Ann is being hurt by the reporters'
> flash bulbs. Now at large in New York, Kong searches high and low for
> Ann. After proving his devotion by wrecking an elevated train, Kong
> winds up at the top of the Empire State Building, facing off against a
> fleet of World War I fighter planes.

Mordaunt Hall in the *New York Times* called it "a fantastic film . . . worked out in a decidedly compelling fashion . . . Miss Wray goes through her ordeal with great

Fay Wray: "A beauty at once innocent and sensual."

courage." *(March 3, 1933.)* People were blown away by the special effects, cutting-edge for that era, it was the *Star Wars* of its time in a way — a touching, if loud, retelling of the *Beauty and the Beast*. The *All-Movie Guide* also asked "Has anyone ever screamed so eloquently?" Another critic remarked that Fay's character, Ann, was "a combination of sex appeal, vulnerability and lung capacity."

At the premiere, Wray was mortified with all the screaming. She had not only screamed on set, she had spent hours locked in a sound booth, being urged to recall terrible nightmares and to scream onto the tape until she could scream no more. She called them "My Agony Arias."

And she was no one-hit wonder. She followed Kong with *Shanghai Madness* with Spencer Tracy; *Viva Villa* with Wallace Beery, directed by the great Howard Hawks; *The Affairs of Cellini* with Frederic March; and *Bulldog Jack* with Ralph (later Sir Ralph) Richardson.

But there would and could be no sequel to Kong and in a way she never escaped his grasp. Despite the occasional foray into serious drama, it was mostly damsel in distress roles she was offered. She calmly notes in her memoir without a tinge of bitterness that she found herself making a lot of B-movies after *Kong*.

Personal adversity was ever-present for a time. Her ex-husband committed suicide. Her second husband had such chronic health problems that Way semi-retired to help take care of him. She had a mini-comeback in the 1950s, most notably in *Tammy and the Bachelor* with Debbie Reynolds, Walter Brennan and a then-obscure Canadian actor named Leslie Nielsen. There was a fair bit of TV work, but after *Gideon's Trumpet* in 1980 with Henry Fonda, she packed it in.

She lived a good, long life. She made a hundred films in a career that began in the silents of a young industry, and lasted well into the Age of Television. She wrote that she felt good "that I was a little, even a very little part of the Golden Age of Cinema." She made an annual pilgrimage to the Empire State Building. "A good friend died up there," she would say. There's a permanent exhibit in honour of her and Kong there now.

But what makes your eyes tear up is how, after she died in the summer of 2004, they dimmed the lights of the Empire State Building for fifteen minutes. A silent, moving tribute to a film legend, a rancher's daughter from Cardston, Alberta.

Florence Lawrence

B. FLORENCE ANNIE BRIDGWOOD, HAMILTON, ONTARIO, 2 JANUARY 1886
D. LOS ANGELES, CALIFORNIA, 28 DECEMBER 1928

CHANCES ARE THAT NOT A SINGLE ONE OF Hollywood's movie stars has any clue of the debt they owe to the daughter of a humble carriage-maker from Hamilton, Ontario. Florence Lawrence was the first actor to emerge from the blur of the primitive early days of silent film into stardom. Today's omnipresent, global, multi-media star system began with her in the early 20th century.

She was born Florence Annie Bridgwood on Jackson Street in 1886. Her mother, Lotta, was an ambitious stage actress of some renown. She had "The Amazing Baby Flo" on stage at the age of 3, a cute little dancer with an amazing ability to whistle popular songs. After her father's death in 1898, Florence and her mother wended their way south through Buffalo and eventually to unemployment in New York City.

The legendary bright lights of Hollywood and Beverly Hills in California were a long way off. The fledgling, struggling, dubious new industry of movie-making was based on the East Coast in very unglamorous places such as Flatbush in Brooklyn, in Fort Lee, New Jersey and in Cuddlebackville, NY. With little to lose, mother and daughter auditioned for the great inventor and film pioneer, Thomas Edison, whose company was mounting a production of the life of Daniel Boone. And they won their first roles as, logically enough, Boone's mother and daughter.

Little Floie, as her mother called her, saw herself on screen for the first time in 1907 and was appalled at how she looked. Fortunately, others disagreed and roles with the early giant studio Vitagraph Pictures kept coming. And coming. According to the Internet Movie Database, she made forty-six films in 1908 alone. They were great epics, no less: *Romeo and Juliet*, *Julius Caesar*, *Antony and Cleopatra*, *Macbeth* — all compressed by the early technology into one film reel, ten to fifteen minutes long, in a week of shooting.

The following year, in 1909, her new beau and future husband, Harry Solter, brought the 23-year-old Flo to the attention of a failed actor turned director named David Wark Griffith. D. W., as he came to be known, took a shine to her pleasant onscreen presence and stole her away for his Biograph Picture Company for the small fortune of $25 a week. She wouldn't even have to make her own costumes or paint the backdrops either.

It was the biggest break of her life. Griffith would soon be the towering genius of film, almost single-handedly in North America dragging the somewhat trashy amusement into a respectable art form. Florence now had the best director, considerable experience and plenty of confidence, but her lasting celebrity would have to wait for the invention of something hilariously mundane. Of all the wondrous things being developed and refined at the time — camera technology, shooting and editing techniques — the star system that she pioneered needed the arrival of a radically new concept that was to date totally unheard of: the movie critic.

In 1908, the publication *Moving Picture World* began reviewing films, rather than just re-printing the plot lines. Up to this point, there were was no long credit roll and no actor was identified by name. Churning out product week after week to pay the bills was all studios could manage. There was little time or thought for publicity.

In an unprecedented move in 1908, *MPW*'s reviewer singled out an actor in *The Taming of the Shrew*, writing "My first duty is to speak in unreserved praise of the lady who took the part of the Shrew." That was Flo.

The next year, she went on to make an astounding sixty-five films, including Griffith's groundbreaking adaptation of Tolstoy's *The Resurrection*. Fan mail poured in, begging for the name of the beguiling actress. She became known as "The Biograph Girl" until Biograph fired her in 1910 under murky circumstances. She signed on with IMP, and became "The IMP Girl." The Hollywood star machine dates from that year when Florence became the first actor named in a promotion campaign in *Moving Picture World*, pitching a movie "that gives Miss Lawrence the best opportunity she's had to work up some hilarious comedy." *Billboard* followed with the accolade of Florence as "the Queen of moving picture actresses."

In an eerie echo of what would come to pass, IMP launched a cheap publicity stunt, leaking rumours of her premature death, only to unveil their new superstar

Resurrection *1909. Library of Congress*

unannounced at a media event in St. Louis. Crowds that were usually reserved for presidents mobbed the train station.

The mysterious quality that made her so loved by fans worldwide was her presence, described as "graceful, expressive, emotional, talented to many degrees. A face that is fascinating rather than beautiful." But behind the facade there were worrisome signs. Even by 1910, she was writing her mother about back problems and nervous breakdowns.

Her 1912 effort *Flo's Discipline* bombed big time despite her renown, and she retired in a huff to her grand estate in New Jersey for good. Or at least until six months later when she learned that her new Canadian rival, Mary Pickford, was being paid

$2,000 a week. She returned to the screen, her devoted fan base intact. In 1914, while making *The Pawns of Destiny*, she collapsed, after repeating a scene in which she rescued a much larger actor from a "burning" building. The effort aggravated her back problems. She was an invalid for two years, deepening her depression.

She fought back with a comeback try in a six-reel feature, *Elusive Isabel*, in 1916. It was dismissed as a third-rate disaster. Another attempted comeback in 1921 met a similar fate. For fifteen years she would survive on bit parts, often uncredited, that were thrown her way by sympathetic old friends, especially at MGM. Her last notable role (though without dialogue or credit) came in *One Rainy Afternoon* in 1936.

Two years later, in dreadful pain from the back injury that had become a chronic bone disease, forgotten by even the messenger boys on the studio lot, she wrote a note saying "I am tired. Hope this works" and swallowed a deadly cocktail of cough syrup and ant poison. Fellow Canadian expatriate Mary Pickford, a film superstar yet to be surpassed, wrote,

> She was by far the best actress in the early days of Biograph. Many of us learned from her the craft that has given us so much over the years. That she should need to end her life in this way is sad. But there is only so much pain one can endure. The industry has lost a great talent.

Flo was otherwise barely remembered and was buried in an unmarked grave in the Hollywood Memorial Cemetery on Santa Monica Boulevard. In 1991, an anonymous fan bought her a simple bronze headstone, engraved:

FLORENCE LAWRENCE. THE BIOGRAPH GIRL. THE FIRST MOVIE STAR.

Glenn Ford

B. GWYLLYN SAMUEL NEWTON FORD, STE. CHRISTINE, QUEBEC, 1 MAY 1916

HE WAS HANDSOME AS ALL GET OUT, with just a little devilish hint in that smile. He was one of the most popular leading men of his generation, making Columbia Pictures vast sums of money. He gave tremendous performances in some of the great classic films of all time. Yet his awards list runs three lines. Oscar never smiled on Glenn Ford. He received two Golden Globe nominations — in 1957 for *The Teahouse of August Moon* and in 1958 for *Don't Go Near the Water* — and a Golden Globe Best Actor win for *Pocketful of Miracles* in 1961.

On the other hand, the list of his humanitarian and military awards runs three *pages* and includes citations from presidents of the United States and France, the Simon Wiesenthal Center, the Veterans of Foreign Wars, the United Jewish Appeal, the American Cancer Society. And last but not least, the Boy Scouts of America.

Even prenatally, his life had a karmic quality. Just three weeks before Gwyllyn was born, his mother survived a house fire. He became a "miracle baby," of whom great things were expected.

His father was a railway executive at a time when the province's Anglophone elite firmly held the reins of political and economic power. But the first watershed for young Gwyllyn came at the age of 4 when he was part of a local production of *Tom Thumb's Wedding* that seemed to leave a lasting impression.

First, he and his mother survived the fire, but the recurring health problems she suffered as a result dictated a move to a gentler climate. And so the family picked up and left the Canadian Shield on the north shore of the mighty St. Lawrence River for the warm, sandy beaches of Santa Monica, California, down the road from the movie capital of the world.

He practically lived on the stage at Santa Monica High. In 1934 he got his first job as a stage manager and soon he was acting in a West Coast company. Gwyllyn was discovered by 20th Century Fox and cast in his first film in 1939, *Heaven with a Barbed Wire Fence*. Fox let him get away, and he was signed by Columbia, where he remained happily for the next fourteen years.

Columbia's boss, Harry Cohn insisted that it was time for a complete name change. Gwyllyn was willing to give up Gwyllyn, but not the family name, which had a pretty grand tradition. His ever-so-clever compromise was a tribute to his father, who'd been born in a small town called Glenford Mills, Quebec.

Ford's good fortune would hold as the 1940s began. He was still on the New Guys' B-movie list. But in 1940, he teamed up for the first of several memorable collaborations with the beautiful, talented and soon-to-be-legendary Rita Hayworth in *The Lady in Question*. Then came a turn on the screen with established stars Frederic March and Margaret Sullivan. *So Ends Our Night* also brought him his first favourable review, in which he was singled out as "the juvenile find of the year." (The term juvenile must have acquired its negative connotation later because fellow Canadian Deanna Durbin had just been awarded a special Oscar for Juvenile Achievement.)

Ford enlisted in the Coast Guard Auxiliary even before the Japanese attack on Pearl Harbor brought the US officially into the war. He made his first Western, *Texas*, where he worked with William Holden, who remained his best friend for decades. The two rising young stars became notorious for never being short on female companionship. They were linked with just about every starlet in the Hollywood Hills.

The year 1942 saw him get his first starring role. He prepared for it meticulously, and while it was nowhere near his best work, it was a remarkable personal journey. *The Adventures of Martin Eden* was the film adaptation of the semi-autobiographical novel by one of Ford's all-time favourites, Jack London. He hung out at London's old waterfront haunts around San Francisco Bay. He went to the London ranch at Glenn Ellen, idyllically located in the Valley of the Moon. He listened to London's widow, Charmian, who was very skeptical of Hollywood types messing with her husband's work. She allowed him to listen to the dozen remaining cylindrical recordings of the author's voice. She was completely charmed by the young, focused actor and lent her enthusiastic support to the project.

The movie had to be shot inland as the American military forbade any seaside

*As Tom Corbett in **The Courtship of Eddie's Father** 1963 with Ron Howard as Eddie. Warner Brothers*

construction in fear of enemy attack. And just after the shoot ended, the Japanese struck at Pearl Harbor.

The studio chose an unlikely publicity campaign. They portrayed Ford as a muscular, bare-knuckled tough guy. And they decided to premiere the film, not in Los Angeles, or in London's San Francisco. Instead they chose to open it in what they considered Ford's hometown of Quebec City.

The Quebec press picked him up in Montreal and by the time he and his mother arrived at the old Quebec station, there were hundreds of fans carrying welcoming banners in English and French. A police escort with sirens wailing took them to the Chateau Frontenac, where civic leaders awaited.

It had been 20 years since he'd been there. His biography has him telling the Quebec papers, "Gosh this is the happiest day of my life. It's so swell, so wonderful when you've been away and come home. That's really something." Some tough guy. Mother and son were the pictures of sophistication at the *Martin Eden* premiere, she in mink, he in a tux and cashmere coat.

It was the next day that would remain one of the most moving of his life. Quebec's legendary Royal 22nd Regiment, the Van Doos held a special ceremony to present the Fords with the sword that Glenn's father, Newton, had carried while with the Regiment. Both struggled to hold back the tears. He set out for an afternoon of skiing but got caught in a heavy spring snowfall and was stranded. The press maintained an anxious vigil overnight, as the movie star failed to return. His rescue the next day by the Highways department was a big media event.

The film itself got mixed reviews. One who liked it was a reviewer in Washington, DC, the sister of an ambitious young naval officer named John F. Kennedy. Kathleen Kennedy called Ford's performance "topnotch."

After Pearl Harbor, Ford decided the movie-making would have to wait. He enlisted and served in the US Marines from 1943 to 1945. He mostly ran "safe-houses" for resistance fighters and Holocaust survivors fleeing the Nazis. He was one of the first US soldiers to enter the ghastly Nazi extermination camp at Dachau.

He returned to Hollywood to find he'd lost his place in Columbia's line and it's said that he almost took a job with Howard Hughes at Lougheed Company. Bette Davis saved his acting career, insisting that a war veteran of Ford's ability should not be unemployed. She had clout, and insisted he be given the male lead in *A Stolen Life* in 1946.

This brings us to *Gilda*, a film that film students write theses about. This is a film from a time before the explicit was allowed, where the two stars crackle with sexual chemistry just this side of spontaneous combustion. It's been written that millions of women fell in love with Ford as Johnny Farrell, a street-smart guy who's rescued from the gutter by a casino owner conveniently married to the sensationally sensuous Gilda, played by Rita Hayworth. Men still suffer shortness of breath at her spectacular entrance, flipping back her hair to reveal that perfect face, a whole handful of trouble. Ford later hinted the onscreen chemistry was helped by some off-screen chemistry. "I think the film remains so popular," he said, "because people realize it's a true story — that Rita and I were very much in love." It was a huge hit and is still considered a classic. They made three more films together, but none hit the Richter scale like *Gilda*. Ford was now at the top of the heap at Columbia along with his pal Bill Holden.

His next landmark was the noir classic *The Big Heat* in 1953. Directed by the legendary German expatriate Fritz Lang, it features Ford as Dave Bannion, a police detective as honest as the day is long. He has a lovely wife, played by Marlon's sister, Jocelyn Brando. Aside from them, pretty much everyone else is corrupt as they come, as Dave tries to solve a fellow cop's suicide. The *Times* critic heaped praise on Ford: "He is in fine style as the hero — as angry and icy as they come." Bannion pays a terrible price for his rectitude amidst the seedy, but the film "keeps you tingling like a frequently struck gong."

The 1950s were prime time for Ford. He had the gift of the ability to do everything (except dancing) well. *Blackboard Jungle* (1955) is his best-selling movie on Yahoo. It's one of his most remembered roles: the idealistic teacher with a roomful of thugs, including a searing performance of contempt and barely controlled rage by a young African-American named Sidney Poitier.

Ford was the biggest box-office star of 1958. He could play the tough guy, but he also shone in light romantic comedies like *The Courtship of Eddie's Father* in 1963, in which he plays a single father to an unbearably cute child actor named Ronnie Howard. And despite being pursued by rich socialites, he, of course, falls in love with the Girl Next Door, an astonishingly fresh-faced young beauty named Shirley Jones, who will forever be remembered as the mother of *The Partridge Family*.

He made some Westerns that are still considered classics in their genre: *The Fastest Gun Alive* and *3:10 to Yuma*, in which he actually plays the bad guy, but one so charming he almost gets away with it.

In 1968, he was sent to Vietnam for two tours of duty with the Third Marine Amphibious Force. This was no public relations job. It was real combat. And he would never discuss it in interviews.

The 1970s, the fifth decade of his career, saw him turn to television in two series, *Cade's County* and *The Family Holvak*. During the 1980s, film roles became sporadic and he worked in supporting roles, such as in *Superman*, in which he plays the Big Guy's earthly father.

Glenn Ford retired in 1991. He explained his success this way:

> On camera, I do things pretty much the way I do in everyday life. It gives the audience someone real to identify with. I'm not an actor I just play myself.

It's true that he wasn't the kind of star who jumps off the screen and alters the movie once he enters it. He had the common touch and never overplayed a scene. He compiled one of the most commercially and critically successful bodies of work ever to play on the silver screen. He was asked, late in life, what the secret was, how he could maintain that affable demeanour over fifty years in a vicious business. He replied,

> Never give up. Take what life throws at you and throw it right back. If life keeps throwing, then you have a tennis match. Learn to like tennis.

Hume Cronyn

B. LONDON, ONTARIO, 18 JULY 1911
D. FAIRFIELD, CONNECTICUT, 15 JUNE 2003

HUME BLAKE CRONYN WOULD NEVER HAVE TO STARVE FOR HIS ART. His mother was an heir to the fortune of the Labatt Brewing Company. His father was a highly regarded member of Parliament, as well as president of Canada Trust and the Mutual Life Assurance Company, a director of Labatt's, Bell Telephone and the National Research Council, and the governor of the University of Western Ontario. The young Cronyn wrote, in his self-mocking way, that he lived life "like any other over-privileged young man with roots in the Edwardian era" and would never be one to mope in a tenement room when times were bad.

At McGill, he anxiously awaited word from his fraternity of choice as to whether he would be accepted. To calm his nerves as he waited out the last day for invitations, he repaired to the bar at the Ritz Carlton on Sherbrooke Street. During a dry spell of unemployment in his twenties, there was no desperate search for menial jobs. He had the resources to weather the spell at operas and museums, in the gym and reading Strindberg and Eliot.

In any case, he wasn't supposed to be anywhere near a stage. He'd been dispatched to McGill to become a corporate lawyer. He soon discovered he much preferred the productions of the English Department and the *Red & White Revue* to attending classes, even those given by the likes of one of his favourite authors, Stephen Leacock. Cronyn was terribly disappointed by the Great Man's political economy lectures.

His parents were slightly appalled when he made his true ambitions known, but eventually agreed to send him to his drama school of choice. He chose the prestigious Academy of Theater Arts in New York City. He fled his freshman year at McGill as soon as he could and ended up in Washington, where a friend of a friend hired him for his first professional role, as a paperboy in a play called *Up Pops the Devil*. He was paid $15 dollars a week and had only one line. He rehearsed for days, then on opening night walked out to do his scene . . . and flubbed it.

In spite of the inauspicious debut, however, Cronyn soon got his wish fulfilled and submitted himself, at the Academy, to the tyrannical teachers who had terrified stars such as Rosalind Russell, Spencer Tracy, William Powell and Edward G. Robinson. He went on to more studies in Bath, England and Salzburg, Austria, where he was joined by his mother, who was devastated at the loss of her husband, Hume's father.

Hume returned to the US in 1934 to help found (and largely finance) the Barter Theater Company. Admission was 35 cents or its equivalent in food. It was nearing the depths of the Great Depression and cash was scarce. The actors literally ate the ticket price, and the Barter Theater Company didn't last long.

A 25-year-old man in the mid-1930s with no roles, no job and no prospects might have thought that things had gone wrong, that wrong paths had been chosen, that past indulgences must be atoned for. Not Cronyn. He enticed an old Academy friend to a dinner, somewhat lavish for an unemployed actor. Garson Kanin had been a couple of years ahead of Cronyn at school. He would later become a distinguished screenwriter, collaborating with George Cukor in the great Spencer Tracy/Katherine Hepburn romantic comedies *Adam's Rib* and *Pat and Mike*.

Kanin was then assistant stage manager in the wildly successful Broadway farce *Three Men on a Horse* by legendary producer George Abbott. It was like the happy script of a play. Failing actor begs old friend for audition, gets audition, wins part, lives happily ever after.

But Cronyn not only manufactured his own break through his old friends, he made the most of it under intense pressure. He was on his way, soon on stage with Burgess Meredith and Peggy (later Dame Peggy) Ashcroft in a Pulitzer Prize–winning play, *High Tor*.

At this point Hollywood came calling in the form of the formidable Harry Cohn, head of Columbia Pictures. He summoned Cronyn, who immediately disliked him. Cohn reminded him of Mussolini in the recent newsreels he'd seen. The two stubborn men locked horns. Cohn was exasperated by the young actor's refusal to do a screen test, and the impudent young actor suggested instead that the all-powerful mogul come and watch his stage production.

*As Herbie Hawkins in Alfred Hitchcock's **Shadow of a Doubt** 1943 with Joseph Cotten. Universal*

He did a test for Paramount, but turned down a contract because they wouldn't let him do theater work most of the year. The test film headed to the vaults. He returned to New York and between the spring of 1938 and the winter of 1940, he made seventeen plays in twenty-two months. More importantly he met and fell in love with an English actress named Jessica Tandy. The two would have a fairytale marriage and become one of the great acting duos of all time. At one disastrous dinner, he launched an ill-advised pontification on English manners. She replied with the brief but devastating putdown, "Well you *are* a fool." His great romance, like his film career, almost crashed on takeoff.

His family remained puzzled at his choice of career. He once asked one of his many uncles for an introduction. Uncle Edward replied "I knew an actor once . . . ," making it sound, Hume recalled, as if admitting "having been on good terms with a Ubangi tribesman."

But as often happened in his life, Hume got the girl and the prize role. Jessica agreed to go to Reno with him to get married. It was there that he got the call that would launch his film career. No less than Alfred Hitchcock wanted to see him. After a brief interview with the great director, he had his first screen role in *Shadow of a Doubt*, and a lifelong friend in "Hitch" to boot.

In the movie, the perfect American Newton family comes to learn that their visiting favourite Uncle Charlie is not such a nice guy. Cronyn plays Herbie Hawkins, the geekie neighbour and big-time crime buff. The *New York Times* called it "a bumper crop of blue-ribbon chills and shivers" and Hume's performance "a minor comic masterpiece." As soon as the filming was finished, he and Tandy finally married.

He made fifteen films between 1942 and 1948 of ever-increasing stature. He lamented that he hadn't yet become a star, "perhaps an asteroid," he wrote. But he was brilliant at the quirky art of character acting, the crucial supporting roles that movies can't succeed without. For him, a supporting role by no means meant a secondary presence.

In *The Postman Always Rings Twice* (1946), he grabs the attention away from accomplished attention-grabbers Lana Turner and John Garfield. He was noticed for his turn as "slyly sharp and sleazy as an unscrupulous criminal lawyer."

Even in Spencer Tracy's anti-Nazi tour de force, *The Seventh Cross*, Cronyn is "splendid" as the genial but conflicted Paul Roeder, who must choose between his family's safety and helping his old friend, Tracy, escape from a concentration camp. It was also Jessica's first film. She was praised for her "emotionally devastating portrayal" of Cronyn's devoted wife. And it won Cronyn an Oscar nomination for Best Supporting Actor in 1945. (He lost to Barry Fitzgerald in *Going My Way*.)

He got to work with an old friend and Hollywood powerhouse Joseph L. Mankiewicz on one of the greatest cinematic disasters of all time. *Cleopatra* set the gold standard for being overblown, overbudget and behind schedule. An epic flop, according to the *All Movie Guide*. The great scandal of the public affair between the stars, Richard Burton and Elizabeth Taylor, didn't help. Cronyn was cast as Cleopatra's adviser Sosigenes, or "Sausage Knees" as he came to be known. It was a good part, Cronyn wrote, "but as he wasn't present in any of the fighting or fornication scenes, he ended up mostly on the cutting room floor." Ten months work was reduced to about five minutes in the four-hour movie.

Despite the frustration, he was awed by Richard Burton, "one of the few actors touched by the finger of God." And though they finished *Cleopatra* with undeleted expletives, they worked together the very next year in the celebrated stage and film version of *Hamlet*. One of the most prestigious and unusual productions of the Shakespeare classic (the cast wears modern clothes, as if in rehearsal), it was directed by the great Sir John Gielgud. Cronyn's rendition of Polonius won him a Tony award.

He was firmly ensconced back in theatre, performing classics at the highly regarded Guthrie Theater in Minneapolis and the recently founded Stratford Theater in Ontario.

In 1965 he and Tandy were summoned to the White House to do a recital at a formal dinner for the upper echelons of President Lyndon Johnson's administration. He was flattered by the extended applause of such an august audience, but he worried about how one well-placed bomb that night could have blown away the entire government of the United States.

There were several more movies. *Cocoon* in 1985 was a feel-good commercial success. Almost as impressive was seeing co-star Don Ameche and Cronyn, at 74, having suffered the loss of an eye, in enviable physical condition as they swim in their fountain of youth from outer space.

He was made an Officer of the Order of Canada. After six Tony nominations (for *Big Fish, Little* Fish in 1961, *Slow Dance on the Killing Ground* in 1964, *A Delicate Balance* in 1965, *The Gin Game* in 1978 [for both Best Actor and Best Play] and *The Petition* in 1986) he and Tandy were awarded a special Tony Award for Lifetime Achievement in 1994. At an age when most would shut things down, Cronyn won three Emmys (for *Age-Old Friends* in 1990, *Broadway Bound* in 1992 and *To Dance with the White Dog* in 1994).

Tandy died in 1994. In 1996, Cronyn married Susan Cooper, the woman he'd worked so closely with on his later projects.

He was half of what was called "The First Couple of American Theater." The Law's loss was definitely Art's gain. Or maybe he would have been a heck of a corporate lawyer. As one fan said in a tribute posted on the web:

Versatility. Thy name is Cronyn.

Jay Silverheels

B. HAROLD J. SMITH, SIX NATIONS RESERVE, BRANTFORD, ONTARIO, 26 MAY 1912
D. WOODLAND HILLS, CALIFORNIA, 5 MARCH 1980

IT'S PROBABLY SAFE TO SAY THAT JAY SILVERHEELS is the only movie star to be discovered on a lacrosse court. He was a gifted athlete who excelled at lacrosse and boxing. But he was also a stunningly handsome physical specimen, with a presence and air of natural charisma about him. He caught the eye of big-time comic Joe E. Brown while playing an exhibition game in Los Angeles. Brown was so impressed that he suggested Silverheels take a shot at acting. Staying in Hollywood cost him a marriage. There were lean years of odd jobs and occasional stunt work. But more than a decade later he would beat out thirty-five other actors to win the role of Tonto in the TV series *The Lone Ranger*. He became a household name and icon to a generation of viewers. Silverheels' story was much more than one actor's career development. Mistreatment and discrimination against Natives permeated society to an even greater degree in the 1930s and 1940s. Hollywood was no exception, and had its own unsavoury brand. Silverheels had broken a colour barrier — he was the first Native to co-star in a TV series.

"Cowboy and Indian" movies were extremely popular in that era. Stars would make whole careers of them. The thing was, the "Indians" were seldom real "Indians" because Natives were so far off the social scale that Hollywood directors preferred to use white actors, often laden with very unconvincing greasepaint. In a pinch, they would use Mexicans or Italians, themselves victims of discrimination, but still, to many, preferable to an actual Native. Or the reverse might happen, equally contemptuous of cultural

The Legend of the Lone Ranger 1956. *Photofest*

heritage, and ironic if you think about it, an American Indian might be hired to play an Indian from India. In Silverheels' case, the proud Mohawk was once cast as an Inca prince in *Captain from Castile* and as Diego, a Mexican thug, in *The Feathered Serpent*.

Nevertheless, Jay Silverheels was a true trailblazer. He had one of those lives that was often hard but never dull. The Six Nations Grand River Reserve on which he was born had already produced several prominent First Nation overachievers: the renowned poet Pauline Johnson, the great long-distance runner Tom Longboat and Jay's own father, Major George Smith, the most decorated Native soldier of World War I, who returned with a chest full of medals but without his hearing, lost to a shell exploding in a nearby trench.

Harold Smith was one of eleven children. Early on, he became almost obsessed with athletics and bodybuilding. As a teenager, he joined an all-Mohawk lacrosse team, becoming an instant star. The team wore white shoes and Smith was so outstanding and quick, the team thought he deserved a nickname for the white blur his feet made flying down the court. "White Shoes" was not an option. Indeed "White" anything was hardly a complimentary epithet on a Mohawk reserve in the 1920s. So they chose silver and settled on Silverheels.

With the onset of the Great Depression, he joined the general exodus of Native and non-Natives alike who were leaving home to find work. His journey was a short one — to Buffalo, New York, where he signed onto a semi-pro lacrosse team. He joined a gym, befriended a boxer and came to master "The Sweet Science," as it was called, as well. There were photo spreads in the local paper with suggestions that he could become a matinee idol or model.

Then came the fateful trip to LA and the movie career. *The Sea Hawk* in 1940 starring Errol Flynn is acknowledged as his first film role, as an Indian scout. It's difficult to establish a complete filmography as he acted under several names (Harry Smith and Silverheels Smith, for two). And his parts were often so small that if you blinked you might miss them. Between his *Sea Hawk* debut and the start of *The Lone Ranger* in 1949, the *Internet Movie Database* lists twenty-four uncredited appearances. Still, he was working and, in time, the Gods of Tinseltown would smile on him.

One of his minor roles was in 1948, in the classic *Key Largo*, with a bevy of stars: Humphrey Bogart, Lauren Bacall, Lionel Barrymore and Edward G. Robinson, and directed by John Huston no less. He followed with the less memorable *The Cowboy and the Indians* (1949). That role changed his life — not because it was successful, but because he met an actor named Clayton Moore, who suggested that Silverheels audition for Moore's new TV series, *The Lone Ranger*.

The Lone Ranger had long been a hugely successful franchise on radio. Though

Signing autographs in Brantford, Ontario. Brant Museum

ostensibly set in the American southwest circa 1865–1890, the show aired from radio station WXYZ in Detroit every Monday, Wednesday and Friday night. It was the biggest hit of its day with an audience of 20 million listeners on 400 stations from Hawaii to Newfoundland. Its Motor City roots would account for a couple of small controversies surrounding the show. *Tonto*, in Spanish, presumably a common language in the series' setting, means "Stupid," which was a cruel thing to call your Indian co-star. Similarly, no one could find a language in the South that contained the word *Ke-mo-sah-bee*, Tonto's name for the Ranger. It struck an inauthentic tone. It turned out that the family of one of the show's producers ran a boy's camp in Michigan called Camp Kemosabee, which meant "trusty scout" or "faithful friend" in the dialect of the local Potowatomie tribe. And in the same dialect, *Tonto*, meant "wild one."

For a time, the show's opening was as familiar as the theme to *Hockey Night in Canada*: the *William Tell Overture* followed by the announcer intoning in celebratory voice, "A FIERY HORSE WITH THE SPEED OF LIGHT!!! A CLOUD OF DUST!!! AND A HEARTY HIII-YOOO SILVER!!! The show's back story began with the deadly ambush of six Texas Rangers, one of whom barely survives and is found and nursed back to health by his forever-after trusty sidekick, Tonto. Six graves are dug to hide his existence. He adopts his signature black mask and silver bullets to ride with Tonto on a two-man crusade against bad guys and frontier injustice.

When Episode 1, "Enter the Lone Ranger," went to air on September 15, 1949, there was no protest or fanfare to mark Silverheels' barrier-breaking achievement. It was unfortunate that the producers insisted on a fairly primitive portrayal of Tonto, the subservient savage with a demeaning vocabulary that made Silverheels and his family cringe. "Him send men to ambush me. But me take care of him." Two hundred and twenty episodes of that broken English that never improved was difficult for a proud, intelligent, articulate man.

But as it was for everyone who'd been scarred by the Depression, it was work. And Silverheels made it a cause as well. He eventually devoted much of his time to improving the lot of Native actors in the film and television industries. He was one of the forces behind the establishment of the Indian Actors' Workshop.

There were two movies based on the TV series as well. *The Legend of the Lone Ranger* in 1956 and *The Lone Ranger and the Lost City of Gold* in 1958, were likely the best, most complete Tonto that Silverheels ever got to portray. Some fan websites claim that the films were a remarkably sympathetic portrayal of the American Indian, for its time. There is no record of Silverheels sharing that view.

Other film roles came, though they were nowhere as big as Tonto. The air time was still brief, but his physical and now professional stature improved the quality of the roles. He played more great Indian heroes with much dignity. Geronimo (twice) and Tecumseh. But as *The Lone Ranger* succumbed to more sophisticated Western TV shows, the typecasting of Tonto hurt as much as helped Silverheels find other work. He played on many of the new generation of Westerns: *Laramie*, *The Virginian*, *Wagon Train* and *Daniel Boone* — even, once on *Love, American Style*. He played a thoughtful, articulate horse breeder in *Santee* (1973), with fellow Canuck Glenn Ford. He had a nice role alongside Burt Reynolds in *The Man Who Loved Cat Dancing* (1973).

Accolades began flowing. There is a painfully touching picture of the great athlete and imposing actor, dissolved in tears at the unveiling of his star on Hollywood's Walk of Fame. He was inducted into the Hall of Honor of the First American in the Arts. The National Center for American Indian Enterprise Development in Mesa, Arizona honours an actor each year with the Jay Silverheels Achievement Award given to an outstanding individual of Native American descent.

Tragically though, he suffered a series of strokes in 1975 that left him partially paralyzed. He died in Woodland Hills, California on March 5, 1980. His final resting place is back on the Six Nations reserve where his remains were scattered on the old family farm. He never got to hear but might have enjoyed the musical tribute from American singer Lyle Lovett in *If I Had a Boat*:

> *The mystery masked man he was smart*
> *He got himself a Tonto*
> *'cause Tonto did the dirty work for free*
> *But Tonto he was smarter*
> *And then said Kemo Sabe*
> *Kiss my ass I bought a boat*
> *I'm going out to sea*

Kate Reid

B. DAPHNE KATHERINE REID, LONDON, ENGLAND, 4 NOVEMBER 1930
D. STRATFORD, ONTARIO, 27 MARCH, 1993

KATE REID WAS ONE OF THE GREAT STAGE ACTORS of the 20th century. When a film with her came out, critics would fall to their knees at the opening credits, chant "We are not worthy" and begin the difficult search for synonyms for "gifted." Some of the most legendary playwrights of all time looked forward to collaborating with Ms. Reid. Tennessee Williams and Arthur Miller, no less, wrote plays especially for her.

Her awesome interpretive talents never really translated onto the big screen, which certainly doesn't detract from her artistic genius. There was just something about Kate Reid and making movies that didn't quite fit. In fact, perhaps her two best movie performances came in productions for television. She worked a lot in TV-land and was even a regular on the long-running series *Dallas*, which was a little odd for a classical actor. One wonders if Mr. Williams and Mr. Miller (her biggest fans) ever tuned in to catch her. The crossover to television is an unusual and difficult one for stage stars, but Reid made her living and considerable reputation mastering the biggest and most difficult of roles.

Daphne Katherine Reid was born in England, but moved to Canada before her first year on earth had finished, so she qualifies as a Canadian legend. Her stage debut came as a teenager at the University of Toronto in 1945. Her professional debut came a bit later in Muskoka, in the tony cottage country ninety minutes north of Toronto, with the Straw Hat Theatre troupe founded by Murray and Donald Davis. By 1956, she had hit the stage in her hometown of London, England in *The Rainmaker* and Chekov's

Three Sisters. Her three-decade-long connection with the Stratford Festival began in 1959 playing Celia in *As You Like It* and Emilia in *Othello*. In 1962 she had her first role on Broadway, not as supporting-cast member in the third row, but as Martha in *Who's Afraid of Virginia Woolf?* Her first appearance on TV (NBC to be precise) was as Queen Victoria in the much-acclaimed *The Invincible Mr. Disraeli* in 1963. She would make some eighteen TV movies and mini-series. So by her early thirties, Kate had thriving careers on stage, and in film and TV.

In *The Invincible Mr. Disraeli*, she was Queen Victoria to Leslie Howard's Emmy Award–winning Prime Minister Benjamin Disraeli and Greer Garson's Mrs. Disraeli in a drama centred on the relationship between the Empire's greatest Queen and "Dizzy," the colourful British author and politician who became prime minister in 1874 and endowed his Queen with the further title of Empress of India. In return she made him Earl of Beaconsfield. Reid's regal bearing was royally received with an Emmy nomination. (Ten years later she would again play Victoria, this time opposite Patrick Watson in the TV series *Witness to Yesterday*.)

The very next year she teamed up with Jason Robards, again on TV in *Abe Lincoln in Illinois* (a role made famous by Raymond Massey), as Mary Todd Lincoln. Now those are movies!

From there it was onward and upward to 1966 and a very nice turn in support of rising stars Natalie Wood and Robert Redford as Wood's control-freak mother in *This Property is Condemned*. Bosley Crowther, the *New York Times* redoubtable critic was in fine form after seeing this one, describing Wood as "the cutest thing that ever nibbled a piece of southern fried chicken." And he applauded Reid's rendition of an unsavoury character, Mama, "the boardinghouse keeper whom Kate Reid makes monstrously meaty and maudlin . . ." While she collected this one line of acknowledgment from the film critic, the adulation for her stage work was reaching a crescendo. This from *The Canadian Encyclopedia*:

> . . . there were Tony nominations for *Dylan* (1964), opposite Alec Guinness, and for her roles in Tennessee Williams's *Slapstick Tragedy* (1966), which the author wrote for her. Arthur Miller also penned The Price (1968) with Reid in mind, as did Edward Albee in *A Delicate Balance* (she performed the film version in 1973).

And from *Time* magazine for her performance in *Dylan*, with (Sir) Alec Guinness depicting the last chapter of the life of Dylan Thomas:

> It becomes the jabbing dance of the prize ring with Caitlin (Kate Reid),

his wife and sparring partner, as their savage domestic infighting vividly creates the image of a marriage where words not only lead to blows but are blows. Kate Reid is shatteringly good in portraying the kind of woman who marries her author ego.

While her stage work always earned lavish praise and her TV work was consistently well-received, the Big Screen was often less kind to her. Her very first film *One on One* (1961) was a film adaptation of the Kinsey Report, a ground-breaking study of human sexuality. *TV Guide* said it was "beyond bad" and the idea of making an academic report into a movie was "beyond reason."

1971 brought one of Reid's rare commercial successes, Universal Studios sci-fi thriller *The Andromeda Strain*. She plays Dr. Ruth Leavitt, a biologist who, along with fellow Canadian Arthur Hill, is trying to defeat The Mother of all Fungi From Outer Space that will surely destroy the planet. The critical thumbs-down, however, was widespread, though *Sci-Fi, Horror and Fantasy Review.com* found something of merit:

> What is also extremely interesting about the film is the casting of Kate Reid, who amid the mostly anonymous players gives an amusingly peppery performance. Most notably the difference comes in that in the book the character is male, while in the film she is a woman . . . Contrast Kate Reid to the usual women scientists cast in science-fiction films — one notable example being Raquel Welch in *Fantastic Voyage* (1966) who is cast as a scientific assistant solely for sex appeal — while here Kate Reid is just one of the film's players, not present as a function of the story's need to create token romance.

Next, she was the star of the CBC's alleged blockbuster TV series *The Whiteoaks of Jalna* (1972) as Old Adeline. But alas Whiteoaks was more like White Elephant and such a thundering disaster, it is rarely spoken of now.

When Ralph (now Sir Ralph) Richardson needed the perfect character actor to round out his ensemble for his 1973 American Film Theatre production of Edward Albee's play *A Delicate Balance*, he called on one of Albee's favourites, Kate Reid. She played Claire, the troubled alcoholic sister of Katherine Hepburn's Agnes. The all-star cast also included Paul Scofield, Lee Remick and Joseph Cotten. *TV Guide* found it a little stuffy but well-acted:

> Richardson's cast could hardly be better. I suppose KH and Paul Scofield will get the most notice for their Agnes and Tobias, and that's as it should be . . . But the supporting performances are what really

*As Dr. Ruth Leavitt in **The Andromeda Strain** 1981 with Arthur Hill. Universal*

make the play work. Joseph Cotten, whose acting ability hasn't been adequately used in the movies lately, is stunning as Harry; he describes the sudden terror that visited him, and we taste it. Kate Reid who plays the alcoholic Claire, also contributes a finely realized performance.

There were two more on screen triumphs for Reid, in 1980's *Atlantic City* and 1985's TV version of *Death of a Salesman*. And, of course, in the intervening years from 1973 to 1985, there were countless stage star turns and accolades. Her repertoire grew and matched anyone's for its depth and breadth. *The Canadian Encyclopedia* once more:

> Her range was impressive; from the cheap and brassy Big Momma in
> *Cat On a Hot Tin Roof* (1974) to the tyrannical queen Clytemnestra in
> *The Oresteia of Aeschylus.*

The great French director Louis Malle tabbed Reid for a sad but lovely little role in his 1980 commercially and critically acclaimed *Atlantic City*, starring Burt Lancaster (at his very best) and Susan Sarandon. Her character, Grace, a mobster's widow, is charmingly conceived. Roger Ebert said:

> . . . a widow named Grace who came to the city 40 years ago for a
> look-alike contest and depends on Lou to run her errands, some of a

*As Linda Loman in **Death of a Salesman** 1985 with Dustin Hoffman. Corbis*

sexual nature. She lives in an apartment so filled with photographs, stuffed animals, feather boas, geegaws, silk festoons and glitz that you might think it is a fantasy . . .

It was one of her most memorable of turns.

But none was more brilliant than her TV reprise of her stage performance of Linda Loman, opposite Dustin Hoffman as her husband Willy and with a young John Malkovich as Biff in Arthur Miller's classic *Death of a Salesman*. Malkovich and Hoffman both won Emmys for their work, but *Time* noted that Reid's performance was equally laudable as ". . . the patiently loving wife, played with unsentimental fortitude by Kate Reid in a performance in its way as awesome as Hoffman's."

And so to end this piece about a gifted, enigmatic actor who had a great career, but could have had a happier personal life. The demons that seem to be the artists' occupational hazard were Reid's constant companions. The amazingly accomplished performer even suffered from horrible bouts of stage fright.

Here is the eloquently simple tribute read as she was made an Officer of the Order of Canada in 1975:

Actress of international repute. For her contributions to the performing arts on stage and television.

Lorne Greene

B. OTTAWA, ONTARIO, 12 FEBRUARY 1915
D. SANTA MONICA, CALIFORNIA, 11 SEPTEMBER 1987

DUM-DA-DA-DUM, DA-DA-DUM DA-DA-DUM DA-DA DA-DA, end with flourish from the wind section, dissolve to special effects with the Ponderosa Ranch Brand searing the map of Nevada into flames, and there you have the delicious beginning to another episode of *Bonanza*, a weekly ritual for tens of millions North Americans, tuning in to see what the Cartwright boys were up to. There were actually lyrics to the instrumental theme sung by Greene, who would once have his very own hit pop song. The version was rarely heard. Even more rare was the version sung by the whole cast.

> *We chased lady luck till we finally struck — Bonanza*
> *With a gun and a rope and a hatful of hope*
> *We planted our family tree*
> *We got ahold of a potful of gold — Bonanza*
> *With a horse and a saddle and a rig full of cattle*
> *How rich can a fella be?*
> *On this land we put our brand*
> *Cartwright is the name*
> *Fortune smiled the day we filed*
> *The Ponderosa claim*
> *Here in the West we're livin' in the best — Bonanza*
> *If anyone fights any one of us*
> *He's gonna fight with me*

Everyone had their favourite. Little Joe was kind of cute for the women folk. Hoss, the big lug, was adorable in his own outsized way. Pernell Roberts was Adam. But people tuned in mostly to see how the family patriarch, the sadly thrice-widowed single father, Ben Cartwright, would resolve the latest crisis facing his clan. Within the hour, he inevitably settled everything amicably, teaching His Boys an invaluable Life Lesson, while advancing the cause of civilized behaviour on the American frontier of the late 20th century.

Greene's career strikingly resembles that of another TV legend described in these pages, Raymond Burr. A first job in radio, then, with both from families showing no genetic predisposition to performing, an unabashed addiction to serious stage work. Then a middling film career typecast as unsavoury types, emerging on television, across the character spectrum, as men of considerable virtue. Burr became the incorruptible, unbeatable trial lawyer in *Perry Mason*; Greene became the wise old rancher Ben Cartwright in *Bonanza*.

It's a very close three-way contest for the title in the College Degree Most Irrelevant to Acting Career category. William Shatner's Commerce degree from McGill is a contender. Arthur Hiller's Masters in Psychology is a strong entry. Shatner's Commerce has some budget-conscious resonance, and you could rustle up some weak argument that Hiller, a director, might have benefitted from his better understanding of people's psyches, though it's not likely anything in school prepared him for understanding let alone directing Ali McGraw. But for sheer uselessness, Greene's studies at Queen's in Chemical Engineering have to take the cake. Besides, how many engineers do you know who have had to choose between their profession and remaining an actor?

Greene began acting at Queen's University, then went on to study acting in New York for a couple of years, making that painful but mandatory discovery that your chosen profession in life has been very happily getting by without you and shows every intention of continuing to do so.

A tactical retreat to Toronto began a whole separate (though in Greene's mind, completely interim) career as a news reader. Or "announcer" as they were then called. The common TV word today is "anchor," truncated from "anchorman." Greene, though, had the booming bass voice, the kind that made Orson Welles sound like Tiny Tim and could put the Fear of God into you any time he wanted. Sadly, World War II would provide him with no shortage of worrisome copy and with his vocal qualities, he became known as "The Voice of Doom."

But by 1953, he was back in New York and on Broadway. He landed his first real movie gig, in the tedious Biblical drama *The Silver Chalice*, coincidentally debuting with another rookie named Paul Newman. In a way, you could say that Greene started at the

*Ben Cartwright in **Bonanza** 1959-73 with Pernell Roberts, Dan Blocker and Michael Landon.
Copyright c. 2006 Bonanza Ventures Inc/NBC Universal*

top, in that his first role was as St. Peter. But the product was so bad that *Wikipedia* alleges that when it started running on TV, Newman issued an apology and a request that his fans not watch it.

In spite of the film's quality or lack thereof, Greene was up again the next year in a star-studded and decently reviewed production of *Tight Spot*, alongside no less than Ginger Rogers, Edward G. Robinson and Brian Keith. According to the *New York Times*,

> Miss Rogers tackles her role with obvious, professional relish. Mr. Keith and Mr. Robinson are altogether excellent. Lorne Greene makes a first-rate crime kingpin and Katherine Anderson is a sound, appealing matron. If Academy awards aren't in order, neither are apologies.

His thuggish persona, however was firmly established and persisted through Robert Aldrich's 1956 offering *Autumn Leaves* with Joan Crawford. Then came two long-forgotten (and frankly except for those of us who are Greene-ologists, deservedly so) Westerns. *The Hard Man* (1957) and *The Last of the Fast Guns* (1958) cemented his reputation as a louse, although this time of the somewhat deadlier variety. Ironically, he usually resisted parts in Westerns because they were considered career-limiting. Yet, they set the stage, along with an appearance on the journeyman TV series *Wagon Train*, for his successful audition as Ben Cartwright and his status as immortal Screen Legend.

There are any number of websites now devoted to the cosmic significance of *Bonanza*, with its prescient handling of burning social issues and such, and maybe they're right to a degree. But icon status happens for many reasons. Some are simple: Lorne Greene was a really good actor who was perfectly cast. There were characters the viewing public adored, and Ben was one. But so was Hoss, and the series only briefly survived his unfortunate passing in 1972.

Some are more complex. In the preview of the 1959 TV season, *Time* magazine noted that NBC had the foresight to shoot 96% of its fall schedule in colour, while CBS shot only 58%. This may have been a major factor in the changing of loyalties. Ironically, *Bonanza* would play a major role in ending *Perry Mason*'s extremely successful run, in head-to-head competition. Greene's cowboy series was one of the first to be shot and shown in colour, trumping the black-and-white format of *Mason*. As well, *Bonanza* could boast that it was the training ground for future Screen Legends such as Robert Altman.

The last episode of *Bonanza* ran on January 16, 1973. It had registered enviable ratings for more than a decade. The long-running success of *Bonanza* soon invited the ultimate form of flattery:

> ABC also has a variant of *Bonanza* called *The Big Valley*; Barbara
> Stanwyck plays Lorne Greene, dispensing wise advice and stuff to her
> three sons and a daughter.

For a time, Greene was a much sought-after guest on celebrity talk shows, such as Carson, Merv Griffin, Dean Martin, and *Rowan and Martin's Laugh-In*. He starred in another seminal TV series, *Battlestar Galactica*, which *TV Guide* dismissed as *Star Wars ½*. He became an American celebrity, to the point of hosting the Macy's Thanksgiving Day Parade. Beyond that he has left the most intelligent perspective on the fleeting fame of Hollywood, in a classically self-effacing way. Here are Lorne Greene's Four Stages of Celebrity, from a Hollywood producer's point of view:

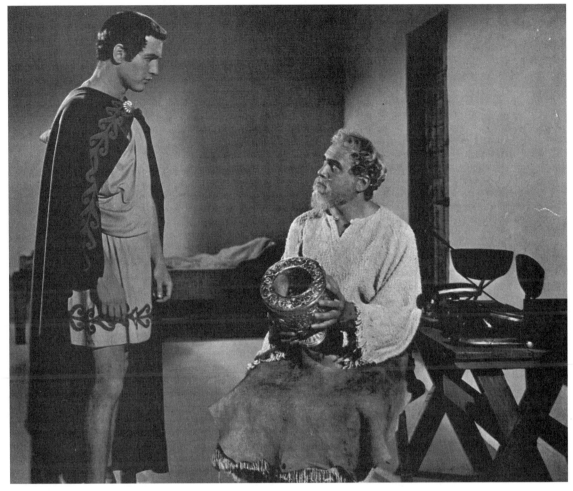

As St. Peter in **The Silver Chalice** *1954 with Paul Newman. Andrew J. Klyde Collection*

1) Who's Lorne Greene?
2) Get me Lorne Greene
3) Get me a young Lorne Greene.
4) Who's Lorne Greene?

Much to his credit, he spent his later years as an environmental activist, though the term had yet to be invented. He made a series of eloquent documentaries advocating protection of wildlife habitats.

He was about to embark on a reprise of his Ben Cartwright role when his health suddenly failed.

Louis B. Mayer

B. ELIEZER MAYER, MINSK, RUSSIA, 4 JULY 1882
D. LOS ANGELES, CALIFORNIA, 29 OCTOBER 1957

IN ONE SENSE, YOU'VE GOT TO TIP YOUR HAT TO LOUIS B. MAYER. There are many poor-kid-makes-good stories in these pages, but none of them compare to the heartbreaking adversity Mayer had to overcome. And let's face it. Anyone who goes from Minsk via a scrap-metal shop in Saint John, New Brunswick to become the head of the Rolls Royce of Hollywood studios and a place on *Time* magazine's list of the 100 Most Important People of the 20th century is one impressive guy.

But, especially in Mayer's case, impressive by no means translates to likable. Sure there were the usual garden-variety studio mogul stunts, like swindling rising stars out of hard-earned raises. All the studio moguls did that and those stunts have become Hollywood legend. The "problems" with Louis's legacy have more to do with events later in his life, and his appalling treatment of his own family and questionable political choices.

The story of Mayer's young life makes Horatio Alger look like a spoiled, third-rate slacker. Having seen enough of their Jewish community cut down by Cossack hordes in Czarist Russia, the Mayers somehow made it to New York and then on to Saint John, New Brunswick. Father Jacob had an unsuccessful scrap metal business. Mayer had changed his name to Louis around that time. He later added the "B" just because he thought it sounded classier. Life for the young Mayer in Canada was a step up from the Cossacks, but was still well within the realm of Hell. He despised his abusive father; the family's existence was barely above starvation level;

and there was still enough anti-Semitism for him to experience the occasional beating at school.

That he had leaving on his mind became apparent when he changed his birthday to July 4. He clearly had no long-term plans to stay in Canada, though he always had a soft spot for people from his hometown. He would later hire the young Walter Pidgeon just because they shared the same Canadian roots. When people tried to ingratiate themselves by alleging to come from the same town, he demanded they spell it. Few would know to spell out the S–a–i–n–t.

He moved to Boston in 1904 and did better on his own, well enough to marry the daughter of a kosher butcher and scrape up the cash to buy a rundown theatre (well, really an old burlesque house) in Haverhill, Massachusetts. He knew he had a product with a bright future and proceeded with the sureness and skill of an experienced acquisitions expert of a Fortune 500 company. He squeezed enough revenue out of his first theatre to buy another and soon controlled the largest chain in New England.

In 1915, he somehow cornered the market on distribution of the D. W. Griffith epic *The Birth of a Nation* and rode that blockbuster hit to a sizable fortune.

By 1918, he had the inclination and more than enough money to move to California and go into the production business with what later became Metro Pictures. Marcus Loew, who founded the theatre chain bearing his name, bought Metro as well as most of Samuel Goldwyn's company and the magical name was born. Metro-Goldwyn-Mayer opened for business in 1924 with Louis B. Mayer as vice president. He would rule the studio from that position with an iron fist for nearly thirty years.

His transformation was not quite complete. As if trying to hide his background as a poor Russian Jew who came of age in Eastern Canada, he became a hyper-patriot, wrapping himself in the American flag. He felt that his studio should make movies that reflected and refined American values, which he thought were the finest on earth. His view of that society was a mythical one, out of a Norman Rockwell painting with a prosperous family: Father smoking a pipe and reading the *Saturday Evening Post*, Mother in an apron and children being well-groomed and subservient. Budd Schulberg offered this example in *Time* magazine:

> With films like the Andy Hardy series, featuring teenage star Mickey Rooney, sage father Judge Hardy and charming mother, Mayer was defining American society according to his fantasies. He took his responsibility for American values so seriously that when Rooney, a precocious womanizer and partygoer, got out of hand, L.B. was overheard screaming at him, "You're Andy Hardy! You're the United States! You're Stars and Stripes! You're a symbol! Behave yourself!

Ben Hur 1959. *Corbis*

He considered himself to be a grandfather to the amazing stable of stars he was astutely compiling. "More Stars Than There Are in Heaven" was MGM's slogan — Clark Gable, Spencer Tracy, Norma Shearer (of Montreal), Katherine Hepburn, Marie Dressler (of Cobourg, Ontario), the Marx Brothers and, of course, his crowning achievement and personal discovery, Greta Garbo. It was, in fact, Mayer's idea to create the Oscar Awards that so many of his people would win.

Perhaps the most astute acquisition he ever made was Irving Thalberg. Thalberg was a genius of frail health but enormous creativity who oversaw MGM's record-breaking artistic achievements: *Ben Hur, Anna Christie, Grand Hotel, Mutiny on the Bounty* and

With Clark Gable and Carole Lombard. Warner Brothers

The Wizard of Oz. He became resentful when his efforts weren't rewarded with salaries and promotions. Mayer resented the widespread gossip that he, the highest-paid, most powerful mogul in Hollywood, was really just riding the brilliant coattails of his right-hand man. The team that had collaborated on some of the most profitable, artistic and memorable movies of all time ceased to speak to each other. Then Thalberg died tragically at the age of 37.

      Aside from his self-imposed mission to preserve truth, justice and the American way, Mayer was also known for acts of kindness. Especially toward older actors, down on or at the end of their luck. He would find them small roles, make sure they got paid for work, even if it ended up on the cutting room floor, sensitive to preserving their dignity.

Though none of the studio heads was above a little blackmail to keep stars' salary demands in check, Mayer played a serious game of hardball. When Clark Gable demanded a raise because of all the money that MGM was making off of his work, Mayer threatened to inform Mrs. Gable of the actor's affair with Joan Crawford. They settled on a fraction of what Gable had asked for. His own dear Garbo asked for so much money that Mayer threatened to have his "friends" in Washington deport her back to Sweden. When she said that was fine with her, the blackmailer had his tables turned.

The awards and classics, meantime, continued apace. There was an elegance and sophistication to MGM films that became part of its aura. *The Great Ziegfeld* (1936), *Boys Town* (1938), *The Philadelphia Story* (1940), *Mrs. Miniver* (1942) — overall, everything at MGM, down to the minutest production values, just seemed a cut above the rest.

There are supporters and biographies who insist that Mayer was a great man whom other people hated only out of envy. His greatness is undisputed, but how anyone can dismiss the bitterly vengeful acts in later life mystifies. He abhorred unions. His politics became increasingly, almost obsessively, conservative. Having supported the disastrous Herbert Hoover for president in the 1930s, he hung out with the likes of J. Edgar Hoover. In 1952, a dedicated Republican, he dismissed war-hero Dwight D. Eisenhower as too moderate. And in his darkest moment of all, he supported the notorious House Committee on Un-American Activities run by the fanatical, now-discredited congressman from Minnesota, Joseph McCarthy. McCarthy's shameful witch hunt for Communists destroyed careers and lives. And Mayer was right there naming names. It was a low point in American political history and Mayer was a part of it.

In fact, his militant right-wing views alarmed the rest of the studio's board of directors and the once-omnipotent studio head was deposed, voted off, as it were, the MGM island, the dynasty he'd built. Ironically, it was the same year that the Academy he'd founded chose to give him an Honorary Oscar for Lifetime Achievement.

When he died six years later in 1957, his will left the family in a state of shock. He disowned several family members, including his own daughter Edith because her husband was too liberal for Mayer's taste. Schulberg sums up the light and the dark sides of Mayer's legacy:

> He knew how to turn American life into pipe dreams. But give the
> devil his due: this self-inflated, ruthless and cloyingly sentimental
> monarch presided over the most successful of all the Hollywood dream
> factories, leaving a legacy of classic, inimitable films that defined
> America's aspirations, if not its realities.

Mary Pickford

B. GLADYS LOUISE SMITH, TORONTO, ONTARIO, 8 APRIL 1892
D. SANTA MONICA, CALIFORNIA, 29 MAY 1972

THERE ONCE WAS AN ADORABLE YOUNG GIRL who grew up to be a rich and famous actress by playing adorable young girls. Mary Pickford was a formidable woman who rose from near-destitution in Toronto to become the dominant figure of the Silent Film era. Hollywood's first superstar, she wrote, produced and had complete creative control of her films, negotiated her own contracts and was a founding member of United Artists. Adolph Zukor of Famous Players, no small rags-to-riches story himself, once said that if Pickford chose not to act she could have run US Steel.

Just about every book, article and web page written about her begins the same way. That (1) she was known as America's Sweetheart despite being born in Canada and (2) attempts to explain how unexplainable the extent of her fame at the time was. And her celebrity is a fascinating issue, one that's likely much more complex than it has been treated. In a world of comparatively primitive media, before studios had small armies of publicists, it is jaw-dropping to think what a universal phenomenon she became. In the 1920s, while touring Europe with her dashing husband, Douglas Fairbanks, the frenzy of a London crowd nearly crushed them to death. She was Elvis, Marilyn and Lady Di to the second power, all without the slightest hint of sexuality. It is difficult to refute the notion that Little Gladys Smith of 175 University Avenue in Toronto was the biggest star of all time.

Her reputation was essentially based, on playing one kind of role — the plucky little heroine who is much disadvantaged but triumphs over adversity and injustice to send everyone who'd spent their quarter on a movie home happy. She had proven her serious acting bona fides on stage, but her box-office success and her public adoration rested on endless variations on this theme. In a review of *The Pride of the Clan*, *New York Times* critic Mordaunt Hall wrote:

> One can almost sketch a Mary Pickford photoplay to the final fade-away, so closely do they all follow a formula. Make Miss Mary an orphan, give her some chickens, kittens or other livestock to mother, mix in some scenes that allow her to be wistful, petulant, and pouty—and there you are.

Perhaps the pain and loss of innocence that had set in during World War I made her perpetual innocence and purity safe haven for a weary world, just like her sometime rival and future business partner Charlie Chaplin's brilliantly simple slapstick antics.

Scott Eymans described her immense but puzzling appeal as follows:

> By 1916, Mary was 24, a married woman with at least one lover; making considerably more than the Presidentof the United States. But as far as the American publicwas concerned, she was somewhere between 12 and 16.

A more technical (and sympathetic) assessment from the *Times* reviewing *Tess of the Storm Country*:

> Mary Pickford makes her real. Much of the time, of course, she is just cute and curly-headed and comical, but much of the time, too, she is true. For Miss Pickford acts. She scampers and skips about in her old familiar way—which may be diverting but doesn't mean anything in particular—but she also acts. She has several scenes, a number of intensely human moments, in which she becomes a real Tess in a real world of troubles, and, sometimes, joys. Her pantomime is subtle and finished, individually and definitively expressive.

In a way her life story is like watching one of her movies. She, her two siblings and mother were left in a most precarious state when Mary's father died very young. "Little Gladys" was "discovered" by a stagehand at the Princess Theatre, which was within walking distance from the Smith home, where the Toronto Hospital for Sick Children now stands. The stagehand was either a fellow-boarder in a rooming house or someone Mary's mother Charlotte was doing some sewing for to try to make ends

With Douglas Fairbanks, Charlie Chaplin and D.W. Griffith.

meet. He suggested that Gladys looked like just the girl they needed for the play, *The Silver King*. So on September 19, 1898, at the ripe old age of 5, going by the name "Baby Gladys Smith," she won her first part — with a speaking line to boot: "Don't speak to her, girls. Her father killed a man." And with that the world's most famous actress began her ascent. Whether sheer financial desperation, precocious narcissism or a natural instinct for acting accounted for her apparently effortless entry into showbiz, we'll never know. But she loved everything about it.

By 1901, she was being singled out for promotion in playbills. One said, "The souvenir tonight will be of Gladys Smith, the little tot whose work has been so much admired." She was hired into a touring group at the age of 9. Charlotte, though initially apprehensive about exposing her daughter to the sordid world of showbiz, soon set aside her sewing basket to become the aggressive mother-manager.

By 1905, they were in New York City. Charlotte had become so accomplished in her new position that she found roles for all three Smith kids in a credible production. Gladys, at 14, had spent much of the previous six years on the road and was a young veteran. She laid siege to the renowned producer and impresario David Belasco. Refusing to take no for an answer, the feisty little teenager talked her way into an audience with the Great Man. Even in her youth, she could hold her own in the shark tanks of New York and Hollywood. And just as in one of those Mary Pickford movies, the plucky scamp auditioned, got the part in a major production, *The Warrens of Virginia*, for 25 dollars a week and changed her name to Mary Pickford.

This was a big break for an aspiring actor. Belasco's name carried a lot of weight and looked awfully good on a resume. He also mentored her, between his famous temper tantrums that didn't faze young Mary in the least. To her, he was the King of England, Julius Caesar and Napoleon, all rolled into one. For his part, the theatre veteran noted that Mary was the first to arrive and last to leave rehearsals.

Pickford held the emerging movie industry in some contempt — until she found out how much some people were making. She marched into a building on East 14th Street, and up to the offices of the American Mutascope and Biograph Company. She corralled a failed actor who would soon become one of film's most innovative directors, named D. W. Griffith, and lectured him on why he needed to hire her. And he did.

Pickford's first day on camera came on April 20, 1909, in the background of the comedy *Her First Biscuits*, coincidentally starring fellow Canadian Florence Lawrence. Her first favourable review came a few months later in *They Would Elope*, with one critic calling her "an ingénue whose work in Biograph Pictures is attracting attention."

Keep in mind, these films are short. *Elope* runs just six minutes. Here is the slight plot summary from the *Internet Movie Database*:

> Two lovers elope and expect to be pursued by her father. But the clever father has tricked them into running off, and celebrates their wedding when they return home.

She made eighty-one films for Biograph from 1909 to 1911, then jumped from studio to studio at evermore dizzying salaries. After her 1914 version of *Tess of the Storm Country*, she was billed as "America's Foremost Film Actress." She would periodically

The Royal Couple with Charlie Chaplin

attempt more "serious" roles, like *Stella Maris* and the well-reviewed box-office flop directed by the great Ernst Lubitsch, *Rosita*. But her fans wanted the same little girl with the golden curls. It got to the point that she was 27 and playing a 12-year old character in *Pollyanna*.

One way she tried to vary her repertoire was to play characters of different ethnicities. Rosita, the Spanish street singer, the Scottish Marget Mctavish in *The Pride of the Clan* and even Cho-Cho San in *Madame Butterfly*. Today, that kind of one-woman ethnic diversity would likely be crucified.

There are differing theories for her motivation in founding United Artists studio with Charlie Chaplin and Douglas Fairbanks in 1919. One holds that no one could afford her astronomic salary demands anymore. The other is that the astute business-woman wanted to keep the revenues that the old studios were getting from distribution. Either way, it is a clear measure of her power, her drive and how far ahead of her time she really was.

She and Fairbanks married in 1920 and were Hollywood's Royal Couple. Their legendary parties at their legendary house, called Pickfair, had the likes of Albert Einstein and Winston Churchill vying for invites.

There is a tiny gap in her filmography that few would notice but that, in truth, foreshadowed much. An amazingly prolific actor who had made some 250 films, she made none at all in 1928. That year her mother died at the age of 55 and Mary was devastated. Perhaps more importantly, the industry was reeling from the fallout of the success of the first talking picture *The Jazz Singer*. United Artists wasn't the only studio unsure of their next move. But to take a year off suggests the confusion that must have reigned.

Pickford made her sound debut in 1929 as the Southern belle Norma Besant in *Coquette*. It truly astonishes to watch the film today. Terrible production values, cliché-ridden dialogue, acting that seems like a parody of a real film. Yet the Academy (which she had just helped found) gave her the Best Acting Oscar, likely more for her body of work than that performance. She and Fairbanks followed with a film adaptation of *The Taming of the Shrew* that was good enough for the *New York Times* to put it on their Ten Best list (then again, they liked *Coquette*). But it didn't do much box office.

She won rave reviews for her performance in *Kiki*, but it flopped, though not as badly as *Secrets* in 1933.

And that was it. Her career was over.

Schadenfreude is a ten-dollar word that refers to the illicit joy people feel about others' misfortunes. There is no joy in recounting the end of Pickford's rainbow. From 1928, when Charlotte died, to 1936 when her brother died, she had lost her entire family, her fabulous career, the love of her life and her fabled marriage. She and Fairbanks divorced that year, after he'd run off to Europe with a new love.

It was a heartbreaking end to a charmed life. She began collecting prints of her films, intent on destroying them. Years later, she was persuaded not to, but many had nearly decomposed, which may partly explain why her celebrity has faded so much over time. A trip home to Toronto in 1934 raised her spirits. There was a Bay Street parade, and they said that the crowds were bigger than those attracted by the Prince of Wales, the future Edward VIII. She did some producing and charity work. But after she sold her stake in UA in 1953, she became a recluse, finding refuge, if not solace, in depression and alcohol.

The Academy gave her another Honorary Oscar in 1976, though they had to take it to her, unwell and bedridden. Before she died, she reacquired her Canadian citizenship, perhaps the only Hollywood expatriate to do so.

For almost a quarter century she ruled the film world. It is by no means a stretch to say, as the title of one her biographies does, that Gladys Smith is *The Woman who Made Hollywood*.

Walter Huston

B. WALTER HOUGHSTON, TORONTO, ONTARIO, 6 APRIL 1884
D. HOLLYWOOD, CALIFORNIA, 7 APRIL 1950

IT WOULD SEEM RARE AND GRATIFYING when one's professional and parental achievements intersect. So it must have been a sublime moment, and a memorable party afterward, when Walter Huston, age 64, got to pose with his brilliant son, John, with their Oscars for their collaboration in the 1948 classic *The Treasure of Sierra Madre*. There were many Oscar nominations for the two of them, but their only wins came for the same picture: The father, for Best Supporting Actor; the son for Best Director and Screenplay.

The movie posters called it "Greed, Gold and Gunplay on a Mexican Mountain of Malice." The critics raved.

> Walter . . . as the wise old sourdough is the symbol of substance, philosophy and fatalism as well as an unrelenting image of personality and strength. Mr. Huston plays this ancient with such humor and cosmic gusto that he richly suffuses this picture with human vitality and warmth.

Walter pretended to complain that "It may have been a good performance, but John has ruined my sex appeal with long underwear and no teeth." That this distinguished leading man of stage and screen, who had once been the choice of no less than D. W. Griffith to play Abraham Lincoln, had to lose his expensive dentures and stately appearance and dress in long-johns to win his award is a wonderful meditation on the price of fame. Humphrey Bogart untypically played a weak yet repulsive loser in what

Walter Huston: He gave to this craft a splendor it did not have before.

some called the finest performance of his career. He joked after the Awards that working with "one Huston was bad enough. Two are murder."

Huston had the worst possible combination of afflictions: an innate addiction to performing along with a chronic case of stage fright. As a boy, he would convulse the family with his impersonation of the local preacher. But when it came to act in a school play at age 8, he was paralyzed. He recalled:

I knew that by some freak of nature I wanted to be an actor. I lived in a stern family of hard-working men. To be an actor was like being a five-footed cow."

In his teens he literally ran off with a travelling road show. He worked nickel-and-dime stuff, mimicking the actors he used to see at Toronto's Shea Theatre, his boyhood second home. After some very lean years, he landed a part in New York at 18 in a production of *Julius Caesar*. The family biography said that it paid "the staggering, hunger-ending, rent-paying sum of $25 a week for just four lines." But again he froze and was summarily stripped of his costume armour and dumped in the back alley. It was the low point of his life.

He got a gig playing semi-pro hockey in Brooklyn. But needing to be around a stage, he also worked as an assistant stage manager. He was not up to facing an audience. He was reading some engineering books in the hopes of real work when his new wife's rich father summoned them to Missouri, where Huston was given work as a junior to the town engineer. At one point, he emptied the town reservoir for cleaning just hours before a fire broke out. He raced to the pumping station to get the pressure up to supply the fire department with enough water, only to blow the water main sky high. He said he had the impression his engineering career was over. But for the wrong turn of the wrong valve at the wrong time, Hollywood may never have seen one of its most accomplished leading men.

It was back to barnstorming. By 1915, his first wife had had enough and they divorced. In a fortuitous development, his sister had married money and still believed in his acting ability. She offered to bankroll his return to the stage and he jumped at the chance. For five years, three and sometimes five times a day, he would perform the same song and dance routine with his new wife, the memorably named Bayonne Whipple. Son John later recorded that

> I marveled that this was the same man who later became a close friend
> of Franklin Roosevelt, George C. Marshall and Arturo Toscanini. If
> there ever was a caterpillar who became a butterfly, it was my old man.

Afraid he was facing a bleak future, and it would be hard to argue that point, his brother-in-law's deep pockets came to the rescue, offering to finance a play, *Mr. Pitt*, on the condition that Huston was given the lead. The biographer noted the producer

> . . . did what any producer would do. He cashed the check and gave
> Huston a contract for $500 a week.

*Best Supporting Actor for **Treasure of Sierra Madre** 1948 with son John as Best Director for the same film. AMPAS*

For perhaps the first, but by no means the last time, he came through in the clutch. As if given one last chance, now age 40, he had the critics asking, "Who is this guy?"

Walter Huston, until last night, an obscure vaudeville actor, stepped forth in the role of Mr. Pitt as one of the biggest finds of the present season.

Yet more acclaim followed the next year with his performance in Eugene O'Neill's *Desire Under the Elms*. It was enough to win him an MGM screen test in 1927. True to form, he failed it. But he regrouped. All those years of slogging through vaudeville and stock theatre suddenly paid off and his fortunes soared.

He launched his screen career in 1929 with no less than six releases. He played a newspaper editor in *Gentlemen of the Press* and the bad guy in the classic Western *The Virginian*, with Gary Cooper and Richard Arlen. He caught the eye of reviewers with the 1930 release *The Bad Man*:

> Walter Huston, as the all-seeing bandit adds another good characteriza-
> tion to his already long string of impersonations . . . He plays the part
> of Pancho Lopez with a great deal of skill and seems to be giving his
> audience as well as himself an enjoyable time.

1930 would be quite a year. He went from playing the bandito extraordinaire to playing Abraham Lincoln in the film of the same name directed by the legendary D. W. Griffith. Huston had become a full-fledged star in what was only his sopho-more year. Griffith had been a giant of the Silent Film era but had fallen on hard times with the advent of sound. *Lincoln* was his comeback, his first "talkie." And he banked everything on Huston, wisely as it turned out. There was lavish praise. Hal Erickson in the *All-Movie Guide* writes:

> Walter Huston is a tower of strength, making even the most florid of
> speeches sound human.

And the *Times* said:

> It is quite a worthy pictorial offering with a genuinely fine and inspiring
> performance by Walter Huston in the role of the martyred President.

The movie has long since lost its regard. Huston was grateful for the reviews, but it was an unhappy marriage of cursory battle scenes with long florid speeches, and he wasn't happy with how it turned out.

The great directors now sought him out. He first teamed up with William Wyler in *A House Divided* in 1931. A bleak drama about a father and son in love with the same woman, the *Village Voice* called it "memorable for Walter Huston's ferocious perform-ance in the main role."

He returned to Broadway in 1934 for the stage adaptation of the Sinclair Lewis novel *Dodsworth*. It ran for over a thousand performances. Of his portrayal of the busi-ness tycoon and wronged husband, Sam Dodsworth, one critic wrote, "Among the virtues of Dodsworth, count Walter Huston foremost." When Wyler mounted the film version in 1936, Huston was the only choice. The film was nominated for seven Academy Awards, including Huston's first for Best Actor. He lost to Paul Muni for *The Story of Louis Pasteur*.

In *Dodsworth*, Sam finds salvation in the lovely arms of Mary Astor in her Italian villa. Who wouldn't? (The film also contains an uncharacteristic performance by a young David Niven as a cad, bounder and gigolo.) He and Astor would again work together in his son John's 1941 classic *The Maltese Falcon*. Huston Sr. had a bit part that lasted just a few seconds — falling though a doorway, dropping a precious package and dying. Son John decided to make his dad earn his day's pay, making him do twenty takes. The next morning, Astor, pretending to be John's secretary called Huston père, alleging the scene had to be redone. To which Walter replied, "I'm still sore all over. You can tell my son to get another actor or go to hell!"

In that same year, Huston had a grand time as the Devil in *The Devil and Daniel Webster*. Grand enough to be nominated again for Best Actor. (Gary Cooper won for *Sergeant York*.) As if to prove there was nothing he couldn't play, Huston took on the role of the father of renowned musical composer, playwright, actor, dancer and singer George M. Cohan in *Yankee Doodle Dandy*. He had worked for Cohan Sr. on Broadway. He sang and danced his way to another Oscar nomination in 1942 and yet more enthusiastic reviews:

> The intimate family story is appealing largely because of the warm-
> hearted portrayal of the elder Cohan by Walter Huston.

In 1938, he had also played the part of the Governor of New Amsterdam (New York City in the 17th century) in the musical comedy *Knickerbocker Holiday*. His heart-wrenching rendition of the ageless "September Song" was considered definitive and would reappear on the Hit Parade after his death in 1950.

The Treasure of Sierra Madre with its award-winning father-son collaboration will always be considered the pinnacle of his career, if not his life. No one knew that as he gave his acceptance speech, he had two years to live. He had done awfully well for a failed engineer with stage fright. From stage and film classics, and from searing drama to musical comedy, he truly did it all. At his wake, his good friend and fellow Oscar-winner Spencer Tracy delivered an eloquent eulogy:

> He was the best. He gave to this craft a splendor it did not have before.

Walter Pidgeon

B. SAINT JOHN, NEW BRUNSWICK, 23 SEPTEMBER 1898
D. SANTA MONICA, CALIFORNIA, 25 SEPTEMBER 1984

OF ALL THE HOW-I-GOT-DISCOVERED STORIES, Walter Pidgeon's is the most charming. The terribly handsome, multi-talented young stage actor had somehow gained an audience with Louis B. Mayer at MGM, the most powerful, perhaps most ruthless man in all of Hollywood. LB, as he was called, didn't seem all that interested in Pidgeon, despite the young man's solid credentials. Until, that is, it came up that Walter came from a faraway town called Saint John, New Brunswick. The Great Man fixed him with an icy stare and demanded that Pidgeon spell the name aloud. However bizarre it might have seemed, an aspiring actor wasn't going refuse LB, so he said, "S–A–I–N–T J–O–H–N." Mayer's face lit up as if he'd found a long-lost relative. It turned out that that's where LB had grown up. He thought the coincidence amazing: the only two men in all the Hollywood Hills from that same place. Pidgeon was hired on the spot at the handsome salary of $300 a week. Minions were dispatched to find the new recruit some work immediately. A little handshaking and backslapping and Mayer left for his next meeting. Who knows what kind of dance young Walter had broken into when the office door reopened, LB sticking his head in asking, "Oh, just one more thing, Pidgeon. You CAN act can't you?" MGM's newest and unlikeliest acquisition assured him he could, and one of film's most distinguished careers was launched.

At first glance Pidgeon's story seems much less exotic than just about any

Hollywood star's. He was a good kid with talent, worked hard, became successful. No starving, no misbehaving. His only obsession seems to have been with having perfect creases in his pants. His longtime co-star Greer Garson said she never heard him raise his voice in anger or say a bad word about anyone. All of which, truth be told, makes his story a pleasure to tell.

His father had a store at the corner of Main and Bridge Streets in Saint John, where Walter worked on weekends, as well as being the city's youngest paperboy. He enrolled at the University of New Brunswick in 1915, and joined the Royal Canadian Artillery the next year. He was injured in training and discharged.

He had a very fine voice and fully expected to have a career as a singer. He joined the Boston Conservatory of Music. The wholesome life goes on. He was discovered singing in the Boston Light Opera Company on a visit home to New Brunswick.

The theatre critic for the *Moncton Times* singled him out, saying,

> Mr. Pidgeon has a robust baritone voice that is enhanced by his masculine appearance and excellent stage presence. Mark my words, this young man will go far in the world of the theatre.

It is to be hoped that the perceptive, unnamed critic lived long enough to find out how right he was. Pidgeon kept the clipping in a scrapbook he would show old friends decades later.

He also played the lead in *Rose Marie*, as the singing Mountie Sgt. Bruce, a role Nelson Eddy would make legendary in the 1936 film with Jeannette Macdonald. Pidgeon would later tell the story that he loved wearing the uniform so much that he actually tried to join the RCMP, but was turned down because of his war injuries. He did, however, go on to be an excellent Dudley Do-Right in his own way.

A few years later, a then-unknown dancer named Fred Astaire heard Pidgeon sing in Boston and recommended him to a friend. In 1925 he was making $100 a week in a Broadway revue called *Puzzles*. Though a rich, well-trained baritone voice wouldn't seem to qualify him for silent movies, his matinee-idol good looks did, and the studios came calling. History records his first film came in 1926, *Mannequin*, with Warner Baxter and Zasu Pitts.

His voice was heard for the first time in Universal Pictures first musical *Melody of Love* in 1928. In the early thirties, he decided to return to Broadway for a spell to establish his credentials as a dramatic actor. It paid off in parts with big stars like Jean Harlow and Clark Gable in *Saratoga* (1937), and with the great director Fritz Lang in *Man Hunt* (1941). 1941 would be a pivotal year for Pidge, as he was now called by friends. It marked his first of eight movies with Greer Garson in *Blossoms in the Dust*.

And it was the year that he made the hugely successful *How Green Was My Valley* with director John Ford.

A beautifully painful epic depicting the dignified but inexorable decline of a Welsh coal-mining town, it earned ten Oscar nominations and firmly established him as a bona fide star. He plays the charming but star-crossed preacher, Mr. Gruffyd with his unrequited love for a miner's daughter played by a stunning 19-year-old Irish actress named Maureen O'Hara. Its Best Picture win was one of Oscar's most controversial, beating two other films now considered among the greatest of all time: *The Maltese Falcon* and *Citizen Kane*.

Pidgeon's own Oscar nominations for Best Actor would come over the following two years through his collaborations with Greer Garson. They made one of the screen's greatest film couples ever. *Mrs. Miniver* (1942) was released on the first anniversary of Winston Churchill's famous "We shall never surrender" speech. Directed by William Wyler, the film is a compelling study of the awful effects of the war on a privileged British family and their stoic efforts to cope. Garson as Kay, the title character, faces her own personal fight for survival in the face of the unwelcome arrival of a desperate, wounded German pilot who's stumbled into their country home. Pidgeon as Clem answers the call of duty without question, the picture of pipe-smoking fearlessness as he returns in his little boat from the desperate rescues off the beach at Dunkirk.

The *New York Times* said that it was perhaps too soon to call this one of the greatest films ever made, but

> It is hard to believe that a picture could be made within the heat of present strife which would clearly, but without a cry for vengeance, crystallize the cruel effect of total war upon a civilized people. Walter Pidgeon is a real inspiration to masculine stamina and resource as Clem.

The closing scene with the stirring sermon in what's left of a bombed-out church, with the Minivers and the rest of the village calmly coming to terms with their terrible personal sacrifices, remains a stirring one. Garson won Best Actress. Pidgeon was nominated but lost to Paul Lukas for *The Watch on the Rhine*.

Mrs. Miniver had influence well beyond the box office and Academy Awards. It was credited with making the American public more sympathetic to President Roosevelt's efforts to aid the British.

The following year, the Pidgeon-Garson team re-joined to make *Madame Curie*. The two actors portray the first family of science in their early days, leading up to the Nobel-Prize winning discovery of radium in 1903. A great period drama, it was nomi-

*As Mr. Gruffyd in **How Green Was My Valley** 1941. Corbis*

nated for seven Oscars, including Pidgeon for Best Actor. But for the second year in a row, Pidge lost out, this time to James Cagney's tour de force in *Yankee Doodle Dandy*.

Personally he thought his best work came in the 1948 production *Command Decision*, in which he played Major General Roland Kane, Clark Gable's commanding officer for a suicide mission deep inside Germany in World War II.

He then ventured into the dicey realm of science fiction making two cult classics that became TV series. In the true cult classic *Forbidden Planet* (1956), he played the scheming scientist Dr. Morbius, with his omnipotent robot. The standard depictions of robots in that era were like a combination of an industrial-strength vacuum and the Pillsbury Doughboy. The critics dismissed it as the Keystone Kops in outer space. More important, it was the inspiration for the legendary TV series *Star Trek*. (Inspiration may be an understatement. It WAS *Star Trek*.) Gene Roddenberry somehow made off with it lock, stock and phaser. The movie's plot is directly copied in an early episode of the famous TV series. There was a transporter room, and a handsome Captain of a "United Planets" ship played by a Canadian, Leslie Nielsen. The director Fred Wilcox died in 1964, two years before *Star Trek* appeared on the small screen. He never knew what he missed.

The second and less successful was 1961's *Voyage to the Bottom of the Sea*. The *Times* wrote Pidgeon was "aptly vigorous" as Admiral Harriman Nelson, skipper of the state-of-the-art nuclear submarine "Seaview." The film was produced and directed by Irwin Allen, who would later inflict such classics as *The Poseidon Adventure* and *Towering Inferno* on the movie world. It had a stellar cast: Peter Lorre, Joan Fontaine, Barbara Eden. In the TV version Richard Basehart took command.

Pidgeon remained handsome and became even more distinguished with age. He played the savvy Senate majority leader in *Advise and Consent* (1962), again with a gilt-edged cast; Henry Fonda, Franchot Tone and Burgess Meredith. In 1968, he played opposite Streisand as the great Flo Ziegfeld in *Funny Girl*.

His last screen appearance came at the age of 81 in *Sextette*. He had come a long way from Dad's clothing store at Main and Bridge in Saint John, NB.

His obituary began:

Walter Pidgeon, the courtly actor who distinguished his 47-year career
with portrayals of men who prove both sturdy and wise, died yesterday
at a hospital in Santa Monica, California.

Pidge's old colleague and friend, Greer Garson, called him "a 100%, solid gold gentleman."

Jack Warner

B. JACOB EICHELBAUM, LONDON, ONTARIO, 2 AUGUST 1892
D. LOS ANGELES, CALIFORNIA, 9 SEPTEMBER 1978

IN HIS AUTOBIOGRAPHY, JACK WARNER summed the high and low lights of his life.

> I have managed a wrestler, shot craps in a San Francisco clip joint,
> caught a fish from President Roosevelt's yacht, jerked a rabbi's beard,
> pawned a horse and belted a chimpanzee with a two-by-four. I shouldn't
> have hit the chimp.

Jacob Eichelbaum was the ninth of twelve children. He came from a family of unlikely visionaries who had fled the stifling anti-Semitism of Eastern Europe long before it flowered into Nazism. He and his brothers would persevere through desperate times long enough to become some of Hollywood's founding fathers. They jumped around trying to escape abject poverty, from New York to Baltimore, then to London, Ontario long enough to beget Jacob, lose another business and, more sadly, a young daughter. The parents, Ben and Pearl, were devastated. But the good people of London brushed aside the unfamiliar religion and thick Polish accents and came calling with food and sympathy.

Jacob would become Jack, the eventual power of the film studio, but it was elder brother Sam who made all the astute calls to get there. First, he induced the family to move to the tough but booming industrial town of Youngstown, Ohio. There were better prospects there and they opened a grocery/butcher shop. Jack would get up at 4:00 a.m.

to make deliveries, but otherwise his family found him to be a problem child. And when he was older, some of his Hollywood peers thought so too.

In his youth, he was a lousy student, flunking Hebrew and messing with the rabbi's beard. His brothers were busting their butts to keep the wolf from the door; Jack styled himself the class clown. The brothers slogged at shoeshines, bowling alleys, ice cream parlours, and as carnival barkers.

Jack had been blessed with a gorgeous boy-soprano voice and got a job singing at the local nickelodeon for $18 a week. He hired out to sing at special occasions, like a wedding singer, and changed his name to Leon Zuardo because Italians got paid more. He indulged in a brief but brutal spell on the vaudeville circuit. This was all bizarre behaviour to his old-world family. His eldest brother, Harry, despised Jack until the day he died. To Harry, the younger brother was an embarrassing buffoon who would disgrace a good Jewish family.

It was Sam who recognized the opportunity that led to the family dynasty. He'd seen the hardworking people of the industrial heartland flock to see Thomas Edison's amazing new invention, the kinetoscope. The early prototype of the projector, it played flickering images that actually moved.

When a secondhand kinetoscope came up for sale for $1,000, an urgent family meeting was held. All the Warners agreed that this was a gamble worth taking to finally end their hand-to-mouth existence. Jack's junior vote counted for little. Besides, everyone knew that if it had to with showbiz, Jack was all for it. They totalled their collective assets and came up short. Family legend has it that selling Ben's gold watch and the grocery delivery horse "Old Bob" put them over the top. Talk about humble beginnings.

The first show given by a family that would become a Hollywood dynasty took place in the backyard of a ramshackle house in Youngstown, under a homemade black tent, with a junkyard auto body as a stage and a bed sheet as a screen. No small part of the deal was the inclusion of a print of the wildly successful early film *The Great Train Robbery* (1903). The prized kinetoscope acquired for the entire family fortune betrayed its second-hand status and could barely project a decent image. The event was less than successful. But after a little basic maintenance on Sam's part, it was fine. They took their show on the road to a nearby carnival and cleared $300 in a week. They were off. Somehow they knew that their rickety little machine was the emerging version of the kind of diversion that from ancient time had led people to trade bread for circuses.

In one of the early convulsions that the new industry endured, a huge legal dispute over patents decimated small independent companies like the Warners'. They were forced to sell the family business, but came away with what was, in those days, a

With Marilyn Monroe March 2, 1956. Corbis

sizable fortune. The boys rolled back home with wads of cash in a new Buick White Streak, the likes of which Youngstown had never seen.

The brothers soon decided the key to financial success was making the films themselves. So they joined the many others, who would be far less successful, on the trail of dreams that led to Hollywood. Their first film, *Passions Inherited* in 1917, failed miserably. They followed that flop with the less-than-epic *Open Your Eyes* for the Army, about the dangers of venereal disease.

Again it was Sam who found a winner. *My Four Years in Germany* was the memoir of the US ambassador to Berlin who had watched the military buildup and tragic drift to war first-hand. It was a hit and it made them a lot of money. But far more important, it brought the brothers a measure of respect among the early moguls who had regarded them as little more than hick-town hucksters.

In 1923, twenty years after they rolled the dice on their first kinetoscope, they officially opened Warner Brothers Studios. It was built in a field, not of dreams, but of weeds. Jack was a vice president in charge of production, along with Sam. Harry was president.

If selling a horse had helped them get started, it was casting a dog that gave them their next big break. Jack signed the original Rin Tin Tin to a three-picture deal at $1,000 a week. The wonder dog's debut, *Where the North Begins* was a box-office phenomenon, as was the sequel, *Find Your Man.* Jack called Rin Tin Tin the "Mortgage Burner" and said that the dog was his favourite actor — always on time, a dependable performer who never asked for a raise. Rin Tin Tin had Chateaubriand every night.

Their next big step, and the studio's legitimate piece of history, came with its daring leap into the emerging realm of sound. They put *The Jazz Singer* into production in early 1927 with Al Jolson as the star. Those early talkies were crude, and very difficult to produce. The film had to be synchronized to the recorded sound. Those recordings, then done on wax, had to be shipped to a lab in Oakland to be covered in graphite and plated with copper. The edited film and the record were delivered to a theatre newly equipped with a sound system. The sound and image were played in exact tandem. Sam oversaw his futuristic vision so obsessively that he literally worked himself to death, succumbing to pneumonia the day before the premiere in October 1927.

The critics saluted the business acumen of the brothers as much as their artistic achievement. Sam's death had been devastating, especially for Jack, who adored him. But as they grieved their personal loss, they celebrated their professional triumph. They'd unquestionably become Hollywood's first family.

In 1929 they bought up a failing rival, First National Pictures, and Jack, at age 37, presided over two huge studios that sailed into the Great Depression. Everyone at the studio claimed credit for making *Little Caesar* with Edward G. Robinson as the Mob boss in 1930. Regardless of who actually deserved the credit, it was the first of three landmark films that established the WB "brand."

Jack had signed James Cagney after seeing him in a New York play. The actor

A duet with Al Jolson circa 1950. Corbis

became an instant star in 1931's *Public Enemy*. The two gangsters' classics gave the studio an "edge" to its image, one that fit with the gloom of the Depression.

And then as if stumbling onto the public's new appetite for extravaganzas, they
made *42nd Street* in 1932. Musicals had been so common and so overdone since the
advent of sound that everyone was sick of them and Jack had personally banned any

from production. But the brilliant, young Darryl Zanuck brought in the equally brilliant choreographer Busby Berkeley to make it. The art form of the movie musical had been reinvented. And Warner Bros. had the best performers to do it: Ginger Rogers, Dick Powell and James Cagney, not to mention Ruby Keeler of Dartmouth, Nova Scotia.

By no means did success and acclaim cause Jack to mellow. The drive and ego that had pushed him to the top were not about to roll over and lie down. He had never been or ever would be an angel. To work at Warner Brothers, in good years or bad, was to live in constant fear of being fired. Jack made Donald Trump look like an old softie, as he enjoyed laying waste to hundreds of WB and First National jobs. And Rin Tin Tin, the "mortgage burner? Movies can talk now. Dogs can't. You're fired! Ernst Lubitsch, the magical German director brought in to lend prestige to the fledgling studio? Fired. John Barrymore, one of the greatest stars of all time? Let go. An ordinary employee who forgot to turn off a light before leaving? Fired. All the while wearing his famous smile. Douglas Fairbanks called Jack a "sinister clown."

He fought ongoing wars with his stable of stars. Cagney would just put on his hat and walk out when Jack yet again turned down his raise. Bette Davis sued. Humphrey Bogart called him a jerk. But however he mistreated people, it's astounding to think how a failed singer with a Grade 4 education assembled a roster of superstars and genius directors to create what are really lasting works of art.

WB's first best picture Oscar didn't come until 1936 for *The Life of Emile Zola*. The masterpieces that bear his name as executive producer are on everyone's best-ever list: *The Roaring Twenties, Yankee Doodle Dandy, The Big Sleep, The Treasure of Sierra Madre, Casablanca.*

This is not to credit Jack with infallible judgment. He castigated his protégée Hal Wallis for wasting $500 on a film test for "that big ape," who turned out to be the young Clark Gable. He said Lana Turner "just doesn't have it." He axed future stars Debbie Reynolds and Grace Kelly and said Mario Lanza was "too fat." He blasted the director of *PT-109*, a two-hour-plus epic about John F. Kennedy, dismissing it as a "three-piss picture."

He stayed active longer than almost all his peers, still deal-making into the 1960s and 1970s. Most notable of those years were *My Fair Lady* and *Camelot*. His longevity won him the epithet "The Last Mogul." When he did sell to Seven Arts, he said, "Who ever thought a butcher's son would end up with 54 million smackers?"

His creative and financial legacies are impressive. His personal one is less so. He is remembered for being tough and astute, part mogul and part monster for sometimes revelling in vulgarity. He made a huge faux pas in his speech at an evening honouring Mrs. Chiang Kai-Shek in the Chinese community. Rising, looking out at the audience, he said, "That reminds me. I have to pick up my laundry." He publicly humiliated his best producer, Hal Wallis, by beating him to the podium to grab the Best Picture Oscar for *Casablanca*, when custom dictated that the producer accept.

Jack Benny once said that Warner would rather make a bad joke than a good movie. At a Warner roast in 1965, Dean Martin sang this for the great man, to the tune of "Old Man River":

> *Jack L Warner*
> *That Jack L Warner*
> *He don't know nuthin'*
> *But he must say sumthin'*
> *So he just keeps yakkin'*
> *He just keeps yakkin' along.*

That's Jack L. Warner of London, Ontario.

Geneviève Bujold

B. MONTREAL, QUEBEC, 1 JULY 1942

THERE WAS, TO BE SURE, MUCH TURBULENCE in Montreal in the late 1960s and early 1970s. But for young men coming of age, there were also things too sublime to really describe.

Smoked meat and beer at Ben's after midnight pickup hockey. Two tickets behind the plate at Jarry Park to see the Expos and the San Francisco Giants with Willie Mays. *Willie Mays*!

And then, there was the face of Geneviève Bujold.

Before this seems too shallow, it wasn't just the delicate perfection of her features, those incredible eyes that still amaze. Bujold was more than that. She was one of those "happenings" that were suddenly making the world sit up and finally take notice of Montreal. We'd had Expo 67, Pierre Trudeau, a major league baseball team and then we had Geneviève. She was part of the New Canadian Cool that went way past watching Wayne and Shuster on the *Ed Sullivan Show*. She'd worked for the legendary French directors that young people idolized. She was a Hollywood Star. Already she'd almost won an Emmy *and* an Oscar. She had been on the cover of *Time* magazine.

Bujold endured a strict Catholic upbringing as long as she could, but eventually got tossed from the Hochelaga Convent. It was the first sign of the renegade in her, the defiance of authority that would later influence her career. She went straight to acting school, the Conservatoire d'Art Dramatique. Having trained in classic French drama, she played in her first film in 1964, *Fleur de l'age*. Small as the film was, *Time* magazine noted:

*As Martha Hayes in **Act of the Heart** 1970 with Donald Sutherland. Universal*

the Canadian [Bujold] walks off with the show . . . Bujold at 24 displays a confident talent and a pert, dark beauty that suggests the imminent emergence of a star.

She worked in France in a travelling production, playing Puck in *A Midsummer Night's Dream*. It seems that either Alain Resnais or his mother saw her, and either way, the renowned director signed her to co-star opposite the yet-more-renowned French actor Yves Montand in 1965's *La guerre est finie*. Only 25, she would soon dazzle another clutch of legendary film makers. She was starting at the top, in the vanguard of the leading edge.

She played an asylum inmate and the love interest of Alan Bates in the love-it-or-hate-it cult classic *The King of Hearts*. 1967 brought *Le voleur*, a film for the great director Louis Malle, with the French living legend, Jean-Paul Belmondo. She was awarded the Prix Suzanne Bianchetti, France's equivalent of "Star of the Future." It was an honour that had been granted to Simone Signoret and would later go to Isabelle Huppert, Isabelle Adjani and Audrey Tatou. An auspicious honour, indeed.

Bujold made her American debut as St. Joan in a 1967 NBC *Hallmark Hall of Fame* rendition of the George Bernard Shaw play. Again, *Time* was most impressed with her choice of technique:

> She settled instead for her own ability to move between ingenuous youth and wide-eyed fanaticism as the script demanded. The sight and sound of her snapping the weakling Dauphin (Roddy McDowall) into action—"I shall dare, dare, and dare again, in God's name! Art for or against me?"—was a remarkable demonstration of her stage presence.

Her performance was remarkable enough for an Emmy nomination.

She returned to Quebec, to the craggy coastline of Gaspé to make *Isabel*, the first of a series of films with her new husband, Paul Almond. Foreign critics were disappointed with it. She was " a lovely actress and a dutiful one," but the plot "is as tangled as the seaweed on the Gaspé shore."

She headed off to England to make *Anne of the Thousand Days* with Sir Richard Burton no less as the murderous Henry VIII. Bujold's performance as the feisty, though doomed Anne Boleyn more than matched the superstar Burton's scene for scene. It is still a remarkable sight to watch the two compete for the camera, with the young ingénue usually winning. Burton later bemoaned being upstaged, saying "Bring me back the unknown actresses." Bujold won a Golden Globe and was nominated for a Best Actress Oscar, losing to Maggie Smith for *The Prime of Miss Jean Brodie*. As the critics noted, "The performance establishes the star."

She was a bona fide star not yet 30, on the cusp of great celebrity, wealth and artistic achievement. A contract with Universal Pictures came along. And the renegade returned. She refused to play Mary Queen of Scots, fearing typecasting, and rather than pay the $750,000 the studio sued her for, she fled to Greece in 1971 to play Cassandra in *The Trojan Women* with a decent little ensemble of Katherine Hepburn, Vanessa Redgrave, and Irene Papas. Roger Ebert wrote that it would just not be possible to assemble a better cast. She was electrifying. In the *New Yorker* Pauline Kael foresaw "prodigies ahead."

On set of **Anne of The Thousand Days** *1969 with Richard Burton. Universal*

Then came a third film with Almond, *Journey* (1972), which was not very well received.

Next up was Claude Jutra's Quebec epic *Kamouraska* (1973). The critics liked her more than the film.

She made up with Universal in 1974, returning to make the "blockbuster" disaster epic *Earthquake*. The critics called her "brisk and beguiling." She made only eight more films in the rest of the decade. One of them, *Obsession* (1976), a noirish effort by Brian

De Palma with a screenplay from Paul Schrader, stands up extremely well, was well received and revived her career. At least until her next movie, *Alex and the Gypsy* (1976) with Jack Lemmon, which bombed. But who would turn down an opportunity to work with Jack Lemmon? *Coma*, which she made in 1978 with Michael Douglas was a hit thriller.

The 1980s brought better roles. Director Alan Rudolph's quirky *Choose Me* is still well worth a look. It features Bujold at her most sensuous, though Nancy, her character, by day an on-air radio relationship counsellor, was badly bent out of shape. And Canadian director David Cronenberg's films are not for everyone, but Bujold excelled in his creepy 1988 production, *Dead Ringers*, with Jeremy Irons. The charming 1989 film *Les noces de papier* (*The Paper Wedding*), directed by the Quebecois great, Michel Brault, again put her back on the critical radar:

> *A Paper Wedding* is simply directed and holds little surprise, but it is given considerable substance by the performance of Miss Bujold, a stronger and more persuasive actress in each new role.

Her next, likely unwanted burst of celebrity came in 1997, when she signed onto the latest *Star Trek* incarnation, *Voyager*, as the distaff version of Jean-Luc Picard, Nicole Janeway, Commander of the Starship Enterprise. After just a few days of television's unrelenting shooting schedule, she walked away from her latest shot at fame and fortune.

It's hard to tell if it were she who deserted conventional Hollywood stardom or vice versa. She seemed to march to a different drummer, distrustful if not distasteful of conventional "Julia Roberts" kind of acclaim. She remains a curious contradiction. She moved to Malibu in the 1970s because "scripts in Montreal do not fall like snowflakes." Her choices speak not so much of bad judgment as a loyalty to a set of priorities she has kept to herself. She established a career with brilliant promise and chose, instead, a path to pursue on her own terms.

But then, the Montreal boys who adored her from afar always knew that was her most attractive feature. This was not ever a woman to be taken lightly.

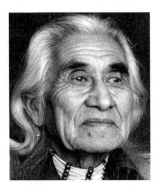

Tes-Wah-No
(Chief Dan George)

B. BURRARD RESERVE #3, VANCOUVER ISLAND, BRITISH COLUMBIA, 24 JULY 1899
D. VANCOUVER, BRITISH COLUMBIA, 23 DECEMBER 1981

How long have I known you, oh, Canada? A hundred years? And many,
many seelanum more. And today when you celebrate your hundred years,
oh, Canada, I am sad for all the Indian people throughout the land.

DAN GEORGE WAS A PRINCE AMONG CHIEFS, a wonderful man of many talents. The opening quote is from his legendary "Lament for Confederation," spoken at Empire Stadium, Vancouver to mark the country's hundredth birthday. It's one of the most moving, eloquent, soulful passages you'll ever read. To have heard him deliver it must have been an amazing experience.

The son of a Chief, he got his anglicized name at age 5 when he entered mission school. He had a number of occupations: longshoreman, construction worker, school bus driver. He was Chief of the Tsleil-Waututh (known then as the Burrard Band) from 1951 to 1963. Chief Dan George was 61 years young when he fell into a TV show on the CBC and discovered he was a natural actor.

The point is that you just never know. That series, *Cariboo*, could easily have been the end of it, and the Chief left in eternal obscurity. But, and it's a big but, someone from

Disney saw and optioned it, and decided that it would make a nice wholesome star vehicle for their nice, wholesome (and Canadian) star Glenn Ford. And before you could say Indiana Jones, George's film career was assured. He made *Smith* (1969), his first feature film, at the age of 70, reprising his *Cariboo* role as Ol' Antoine. In the film version, he's the kindly native who raises the orphaned Glenn Ford character. Well past retirement age, George was just beginning. His performance led to a part opposite Dustin Hoffman in *Little Big Man* (1970).

Many of the native parts in the film were played by members of the Indian Actors' Workshop founded by another Canadian, Jay Silverheels, who also had small part in the film. It was a cause for Silverheels, to end the tasteless practice of using Mexicans or heavily made up white actors to play Indians. Sure enough there's Warren Oates as the top-billed Indian in the cast. The studios were still discriminating against Native actors, but perhaps it could be said that between Dan George and Jay Silverheels they finally put the final nail in that well-deserved coffin.

> *I have known you when your forests were mine; when they gave me my*
> *meat and clothing. I have known you in your streams where your fish*
> *flashed and danced in the sun, where the waters said come and eat of my*
> *abundance. I have known you in the freedom of your winds. And my spirit,*
> *like the winds, once roamed your good lands.*

Little Big Man, directed by American heavyweight Arthur Penn, is a kind of precursor to *Dances With Wolves* (1990). The interesting premise is that there may have been one unknown survivor at the battle of Little Bighorn, a.k.a. Custer's Last Stand, where Lt. Col. George Armstrong Custer and 264 men of the Seventh United States Cavalry were wiped out by Sioux and Cheyenne warriors in the rolling hills of what is now Montana.

The film opens with Dustin Hoffman under layers of fake wrinkles as the 120-year-old Jack Crabbe, alleging that as a young man he'd escaped the carnage that day of June 24, 1876. The plot circles and circles in a widening gyre, the centre barely holding. Hoffman-Crabbe is captured by Cheyenne as a boy and raised as a brave. Then he's re-captured by the US Army, goes on to Little Big Horn and then back to the Cheyenne, referring to Old Lodge Skins (George) as "Grandfather."

Opinions about it vary greatly. Roger Ebert thought it "endlessly entertaining" and praised "the folksiness of the film." Pauline Kael was deeply critical of the excessive depiction of violence, and Vincent Canby in the *New York Times* did find it a tad pedantic. Vincent and Pauline might have a point. The movie's true delights are in wonderful supporting roles: Faye Dunaway as the oversexed wife of a preacher, and above all; way

*As Old Lodge Skins with Dustin Hoffman in **Little Big Man** 1970. Photofest*

above all, is Chief Dan George, the 70-year-old with exactly one film under his belt.

There was much reviewer discussion of the disrespect shown in having Indians speak English, but even speaking English, Dan George as Old Lodge Skins brings a touching, dignified presence to the proceedings. Ebert calls the qualities "serenity and conviction."   One of his classic one-liners from the film comes when he is trying unsuccessfully to exercise his fading powers. He shrugs and says, deadpan, "Sometimes, the magic just doesn't work." In short, he is wonderful. That performance earned him an Oscar nomination for Best Supporting Actor. (John Mills won for his work in *Ryan's Daughter*.)

> *But in the long hundred years since the white man came, I have seen my freedom disappear like the salmon mysteriously out to sea. The white man's strange customs pressed down on me till I could no longer breathe. My nation was ignored in your history books. I was ridiculed in your plays and motion pictures. Oh Canada, how can I celebrate with you this centenary, this hundred years?*

In 1974, he cracked them up in a little scene with comic legend Art Carney in *Harry and Tonto*.

> Harry is tossed into a cell already occupied by an ancient Indian (Chief Dan George) who has been arrested for practicing medicine without a license. The two old men gravely discuss recent television shows and the problem of bursitis, and the chief cures Harry's aching shoulder in return for an electric blender. Chief Dan George is so solemn, so understated, with Mazursky's dialogue that the result is a great comic scene.

He began getting regular gigs on TV shows: *Bonanza, The Incredible Hulk, Marcus Welby, M.D.*, and various Disney programs.

> *Shall I thank you for the reserves that are left to me of my beautiful forests? For the canned fish of my rivers? For the loss of pride and authority?*

Clint Eastwood directed *The Outlaw Josey Wales*, released in 1976. It's another whopper at 137 minutes, and just like *Little Big Man*, it has many flaws that are redeemed by George's performance. In fact, Eastwood seems to have had the foresight and security to share the limelight with his septuagenarian co-star, making it a most unusual kind of buddy movie with Chief George getting all the punch lines.

In the film, Clint is a simple Southern family man who loses his wife, child and

Tes-Wah-No (Chief Dan George)

*As Lone Watie in **The Outlaw Josie Wales** 1976. With Clint Eastwood. Photofest*

several close friends to atrocities committed by the Union Army in the Civil War. He sets out to extract revenge as only he can do, but along the way acquires an entourage he cares about and that need protecting. His dream is of putting the past behind and living out his days in what little peace than can be salvaged. Said entourage includes the terribly vulnerable and fetching Sondra Locke. They find a beautiful old farm that they fix up, rout the bad guys a-gunnin' for Clint, and make peace with the local Natives who could snuff them out in a heartbeat if they wanted to.

George's character, Lone Watie (and he has second billing behind Eastwood) has a series of great lines that he delivers with great aplomb. It is a treat to watch a no longer young man suddenly discover he's really Jack Benny. He insists that he personally never surrendered to the White Man:

> I didn't surrender but they took my horse and made him surrender.
> They probably got him pulling a cart somewhere out in Kansas.

Ms. Locke's pain-in-the-butt grandmother, just before the big shootout, rails against Josey and George shuts her right up.

> *Granny:* This Mr. Wales is a cold-blooded killer. He's from Missouri, where they're all known to be killers of innocent men, women and children.
> "*George:* Would you rather be riding with Comancheros, Granny?"

Like *Little Big Man*, *Josey Wales* was a critical split-decision. The *Times* dismissed it with barely concealed contempt with hardly a mention of George:

> Each time Clint Eastwood, in *The Outlaw Josey Wales*, kills someone, or is about to kill someone, or is on the verge of some other major policy decision, he spits. This is to establish the character.
>
> Mr. Eastwood has established several pints of character by the time he rides off into the sunset fully two hours and seventeen minutes after the movie begins. A number of other characters are established by devices every bit as worn and dribbly.

On the other hand Ebert loved the movie and *especially* George's performance:

> Chief Dan George brings an aura to his role that audiences seem to respond to viscerally. He has his problems (he's humiliated, as an Indian, that he's grown so old he can no longer sneak up behind people), but he has a humanity that's just there, glowing. He's as open with his personality as Josey Wales is closed; it's a nice match.

Josey Wales seems infinitely more watchable than *Little Big Man*. The Hoffman-George collaboration is good, but the unlikely chemistry between Eastwood and George is way more interesting. In fact, Ebert suggests quite rightly that George's portrayal of Lone Watie was the more deserving of an Oscar nomination. *Josey Wales*'s two hours plus moves along with agility, more storytelling and much less moralizing. A really fun evening.

Tes-Wah-No (Chief Dan George)

O God in Heaven! Give me back the courage of the Olden Chiefs.
Let me again, as in the days of old, dominate my environment.
Like the Thunderbird of old I shall rise again out of the sea; I shall grab
the tools of the white man's success — his education, his skills, and with
these I shall build my race into the proudest segment of your society.

The Chief Dan George Centre in Vancouver, a collaborative effort between George's son Leonard and Simon Fraser University, is now working towards fulfilling the Chief's dream. The Centre explains its mission this way:

> Building on the life of the late Chief Dan George, the Centre is a place to celebrate Aboriginal culture and achievements through education and lifelong learning.

Kate Nelligan

B. PATRICIA COLLEEN NELLIGAN, LONDON, ONTARIO, MARCH 16, 1951

IN HER TEENS, TRISH NELLIGAN was a top-ranked amateur tennis player. But it would be at centre stage, not centre court that she would make her mark. Her eclectic Irish family included a dancer for a father and a father for a brother, at least once he was ordained. Her acting career started at the age of 16 at university in a campus production of *Hamlet*. She liked it, and did well enough to apply to and be accepted at the London (England) Central School of Speech and Drama.

Graduating at 21, she went straight to the Bristol Old Vic Theatre Company. She moved to London the next year, joined the National Theatre Company, then the Royal Shakespeare Company. She'd gone from student to star in six years. By the age of 27, she'd distinguished herself in enough classics and received enough acclaim for almost a whole career, and she had Broadway and Hollywood still to come.

In 1975, she made her first feature film, *The Romantic Englishwoman*, with no less than Brit heavyweights Michael Caine and Glenda Jackson. You'll never forget Nelligan's first, screen-filling entrance, oozing the female equivalent of suave. She walks up to Caine and Jackson(in the middle of some serious mouth-to-mouth marital combat) as if they were her oldest friends in the world and sharing, if not stealing the screen, from the two greats like water off a duck's back. It's utterly riveting.

She then landed the much-coveted lead role in *Plenty*, the new play by the renowned English dramatist, David Hare. Both play and player were smash hits and the film career she'd been thinking about was wheels up and airborne, though turbulence lay ahead. She was still this side of 30.

Maybe the 1979 version of *Dracula* with Frank Langella was worth it for her in terms of demonstrating an ability to come down from the classic dramatic clouds where she dwelled and handle commercial material. She certainly did herself no harm in playing Lucy, the love of Dracula's life. Or lives. *Time* magazine applauded her but little else:

> Kate Nelligan, as Lucy, the young woman who enthralls him and is herself enthralled, is superbly spirited. In the film's early scenes, she plays the part as a liberated lady, turn-of-the-century variety. Once Dracula has begun to work his will on her, she becomes a resourceful woman fighting boldly for her forbidden love.

But neither was there much glory as critics had a field day (excepting her) in ridiculing the film.

She hung around London long enough to make one more film, *The Eye of the Needle* (1981), a truly harrowing thriller set in World War II, with Donald Sutherland at his evil worst. The intriguing premise is that Sutherland is The Needle, a crack German spy who has got the goods about D-Day. Knowing the British are onto him, he flees for home by boat, but shipwrecks on the isolated island where Nelligan and her husband live. From *The Apollo Movie Guide*:

> This is a gem of a movie — one that never got the credit it deserves. In addition to Sutherland's convincing performance, Nelligan is also very good as the lonely and ultimately desperate Lucy. It's spine-tingling to watch as she gradually figures out the awful truth about what she's gotten herself into, and it's terrifying to watch as she tries to protect herself and her son from the calculating killer.

The *New York Times*, whose reviewers, young, old, male and female, never had an unkind word to say about Nelligan, singled her out;

> Lucy, as played with enormous passion and intelligence by Miss Nelligan, accomplishes the unimaginable when she begins to distract Faber from his mission . . . Miss Nelligan invests Lucy with a fullness and warmth far beyond anything the screenplay calls for.

By 1981 Nelligan had set her sights on a career in film and headed to Los Angeles in search of work and encountered her first bout of turbulence, in that no one in LA seemed to care. Thankfully, some big-time New York types, namely Broadway great Joseph Papp and film director Stanley Jaffe, still had her in their legendary Rolodexes and enticed her back East with a pair of leading lady opportunities. On stage, Papp wanted her to reprise her triumphant portrayal of Susan Traherne in a New York production of her breakthrough gig in *Plenty*. And Jaffe wanted her for the starring role in his upcoming movie *Without a Trace*.

The stage play had critics wearing out their thesauri for superlatives. The winning entry is from *Time* magazine:

> Though the play has flaws, Nelligan seemingly has none. Her performance is so unique, mesmerizing and shattering at the same time, that it is hard to imagine anyone else in the role. She plays Susan Traherne, who as a girl of 17 was dropped behind German lines in France to work as a British courier. The character is never able to recapture the purity of her wartime zeal. As the play follows her through the next 20 years, shifting backward and forward through time, her personality hardens into madness, and she brings ruin not only to herself but her husband.

She followed that grand success with another as Josie Hogan in Eugene O'Neill's classic *Moon for the Misbegotten*, all the more impressive in that she was taking over for fellow Canadian stage great Colleen Dewhurst, considered *the* authoritative O'Neill interpreter. Again, from *Time* magazine:

> For this Broadway revival, the usually cool Nelligan has turned up the heat to blistering levels. Raucous, tender and compelling, she is an astonishment, the perfect instrument for young English Director David Leveaux's energetic and often surprisingly humorous conception of the play.

The thing about air pockets is that, like black ice, you can't see them coming. So who would have expected trouble after a set of reviews like those?

Trouble presented itself in the form of a starring role in a film called *Eleni* (1985), the biographic rendition of the life of a *New York Times* reporter obsessed with discovering why his mother was executed by firing squad during the Greek Civil War in the late 1940s. The critics seemed stunned and a bit puzzled about what to say, but ultimately absolved her (and young co-star John Malkovich) of any responsibility for the cinematic result.

There seemed to be some concern that the damage cause by *Eleni*, coupled with the box-office failure of *Without a Trace* could be career-ending. Real work dried up. It

Kate Nelligan: "A thing of beauty."

certainly caused her to lose the role of Susan in the film adaptation of her own stage
hit, *Plenty*. It went to Meryl Streep with John Gielgud. For a time it seemed the film
career had not just hit the Mother of all Air Pockets, but it had actually crashed and
burned. Nelligan even took to doing volunteer work.

There was, however this praise of her stage work in *Time*:

TIME BEST OF 1988
SPOILS OF WAR In Michael Weller's poignant memoir, off-Broadway and briefly on it, Kate Nelligan gave the performance of the year as an Auntie Mame mom, mingling furtive boozing and strutting glamor, dignity and desperation.

Offers started to flow in again in 1990 and in that wacky way that fate works, the following year brought her two of her best roles. Barbra Streisand cast her as Lila, the troubled mother of the totally dysfunctional Wingo clan in *The Prince of Tides*. The film is dominated by the outstanding performance of Nick Nolte as Lila's son trying to figure out his sister's attempted suicide with Streisand as Dr. Lowenstein, the uptown Manhattan shrink.

Nolte was robbed of a much-deserved Oscar by Anthony Hopkins' Hannibal Lecter in *Silence of the Lambs*. Nelligan is much more interesting, in much less screen time. Who can forget her in that great scene when her cretin of a husband complains the food is too Frenchified and why can't a hungry man get some real home cookin'? Her face is a study in hate, contempt and world weariness as she heads to the kitchen, gets the kids to chop onions, opens a can of dog food, adds some hot sauce and serves it to her fine figure of a husband, mighty satisfied, as the dog whines by the side of the table. She earned an Oscar nomination for Best Supporting Actress, which was won by Mercedes Ruehel in *The Fisher King*.

In the same year, Garry Marshall (*Pretty Woman*, *Happy Days*) put her in his 1991 hit *Frankie & Johnny*, with Michelle Pfeiffer and Al Pacino in the title roles. Marshall does know comedy, but who knew Nelligan did? She played Cora, a foul-mouthed, gum-chewing waitress of easy virtue with a Brooklyn accent. The *Times* applauded heartily the classically-trained actress slumming and apparently loving it:

> Kate Nelligan, nearly unrecognizable, is outstandingly enjoyable as the gum-chewing, man-crazy one. "You see something cute in every guy," she is told. "I know," she beams. "I'm lucky like that."

Garry Marshall reportedly offered her the highest praise in his inimitable way:

> Anyone who can play Nick Nolte's mother for Barbra Streisand and a slut for me has quite a range.

She did some nice comic turns for Woody Allen in *Shadows and Fog* (1991); and Carl Reiner in *Fatal Instinct* (1993). And there was more praise for her roles in *Margaret's Museum*, *Up Close and Personal* and *How to Make an American Quilt*.

*As Lucie Steward in **Dracula** 1979 with Frank Langella. Universal*

But to end with a story far better told by Patrick Watson, the Creative Director of the Heritage Minutes and these Screen Legends. He cast Nelligan as the redoubtable Emily Murphy, one of the great activists in the First Wave of Feminism around the time of World War I. When he actually saw a picture of Emily Murphy, he realized he'd hired one of the most beautiful women in the world to play one of the least photogenic women in the history of photos. There was some anxiety on the set as the minute-long script timed out to less than 40 seconds. What could be done? Watson said, "Just sit back and watch." Nelligan took the short script, added a pause here, a gesture there, worked a little of her magic and there it was, exactly to time, and like the actor herself, a thing of beauty.

Leslie Nielsen

B. REGINA SASKATCHEWAN, 11 FEBRUARY 1926

IN HIS AUTOBIOGRAPHY, *The Naked Truth*, Leslie Nielsen seems to thoroughly enjoy turning his entire life into another zany episode of his now truly legendary *Naked Gun* series. Telling fact from comic invention gets to be easy with a well-trained, highly attuned sense for these things. For instance, one suspects one is having one's leg pulled when he says, "We lived in an unheated log cabin not far from the Arctic Circle." And what are we to make of his claim that he and his brother played all the normal childhood games like "Cowboys and Eskimos"? According to Nielsen, his father told him the Facts of Life he would need to become a man:

> Never run holding a sharp pencil. Never piss into the wind. And you
> can never have too much starting pitching.

But it can be confirmed that he spent some early years in what was then Fort Norman in the Northwest Territories (now Tulita "where the rivers meet," population 473), which is not all that far from the Arctic Circle; that his father was a real, live Mountie and that he did have a brother, Eric, eventually the Honourable Member for Yukon, once Deputy Prime Minister of Canada and known on Parliament Hill as old Velcro Lips for his powers of discretion, which clearly passed his sibling by completely.

Leslie enlisted in the Canadian Air Force in what he called "The Deuce," i.e., World War II, at the age of 17. He came home to unemployment and found a job in radio. Next he enrolled in the Lorne Greene Academy of Radio Arts. Greene, an Ottawa native is described elsewhere in this volume as a Legend in his own right who emerged from his war years as a newsreader on CBC radio with the nickname "The Voice of Doom."

From there Nielsen went to New York for serious training in two of the most renowned acting schools in the world: The Neighborhood Playhouse and The Actors' Studio. Intense work on method acting, mime, even dance with the great Martha Graham, were all to build on his "leading-man" looks. He set his sights on a serious acting career. Though according to *The Naked Truth* one of the best of his early roles was as Richard III in a kosher Manhattan deli. With those impressive credentials on his resume, he soon forged an extremely prolific career, first in the great series of TV's so-called Golden Age: *Dr. Kildare, The Wild, Wild West, MASH* and *Bonanza* (with his old mentor Lorne Greene), and eventually in film.

He was first noticed in the movies by the *New York Times* in the 1956 thriller *Ransom*, with Glenn Ford and Donna Reed (Mel Gibson did a much less effective remake in 1996):

> Leslie Nielsen is professionally outrageous as the newspaper reporter
> who practically takes command.

In that same year, Nielsen starred in the sci-fi cult classic *Forbidden Planet* as the dashing Commander John J. Adams of United Planets cruiser C-57-D, on a mysterious rescue mission in the 23rd century to the planet Altair–4.

Now, granted, one usually needs to be a member of the cult to enjoy one of its classics, but it's not too much to say that *Forbidden Planet* is a groundbreaking artifact. It established science fiction as a legitimate film genre. And if you're into arguing about this sort of thing, you could argue it begat a film and TV lineage of decidedly mixed pedigree, from *Lost in Space* to *Star Trek* to *Star Wars* and maybe even *2001: A Space Odyssey* depending on your stamina. It is fascinating to watch (once) not, alas, because of Nielsen's performance, but because of how much of it was, shall we say, borrowed for the cult series of all time, *Star Trek*. The creator of *Forbidden Planet* died two years before *Star Trek* went to air and Leslie Nielsen was the prototype for James T. Kirk, Captain of the Starship Enterprise.

Nielsen landed another starring role the very next year in *Tammy and the Bachelor*, featuring the impossibly adorable Debbie Reynolds and that wretchedly cloying theme song that makes you want to floss. The plot, such as it is, is so thin you could spit through it. But Nielsen is very engaging as the wealthy bachelor who crash lands his plane in the bayou, and is rescued by Tammy/Debbie, the poor southern belle who nurses him back to health and sends him on his way back to his mansion where we find another Canadian Legend, Fay Wray, in one of her last film roles. When Tammy's Daddy, played by the also adorable Walter Brennan gets nabbed for brewin' up a little corn whiskey, she seeks out her flyboy for help. It was a nice part, played well and handsomely by our erstwhile leading man, but it wasn't exactly Oscar material.

It would be easy here to fast-forward to his later success and virtual franchise status in the sometimes inspired silliness of his later comedies. Recount the memorably insane punch lines and all that. After almost 25 years in the business, at age 54, this kind of material didn't seem to promise Great Things. Might have been a time to think about packing it in. But in 1980, his career was rescued, relaunched and resurrected with a goofy role in the classic comedy *Airplane!*, an early creation of the unstable and astute minds of David and Jerry Zucker with Jim Abrahams. It was a hysterically funny send-up of the disaster movies that sprang up like topsy in the 1970s, in the air, on the ground and at sea respectively: *Airport*, *The Towering Inferno* and *The Poseidon Adventure*. (Actually Nielsen had been the captain of the doomed ship *Poseidon* in the film.)

The production team loaded up on TV Golden Age talent: Robert Stack and Lloyd Bridges were cast as the hopeless emergency management types. Nielsen played the vaguely competent Dr. Rumack with a comic tour de force that no one knew he was capable of until then. He discovers the reason almost everyone on the plane is falling deathly ill, including the flight crew. Janet Maslin in the *Times* approved of the lowbrow humour and Nielsen's proficiency,

> *Airplane!* is more than a pleasant surprise, in the midst of this dim movie season. As a remedy for the bloated self-importance of too many other current efforts, it's just what the doctor ordered . . . Mr. Nielsen, who does a delightful job as the doctor on board, tells Striker, "Good luck, we're all counting on you," so many times that he's still saying it after the plane is down.

This is nice for Nielsen but misses the best line in the film entirely, also Nielsen's.

> *Dr. Rumack:* You'd better tell the captain we've got to land as soon as we can. We've got to get this woman to a hospital.
> *Flight Attendant:* A hospital? What is it, Doctor?
> *Dr. Rumack:* It's a large, brick building where they keep sick people. But that's not important now.

To this day, people will answer the challenge "Surely you're not serious" with "I AM serious. And don't call me Shirley." And so a legend, career and fortune were born. The

As Commander John J. Adams in **Forbidden Planet** _1956. Corbis_

movie was made for an estimated US$3.5 million and grossed US$83 million plus another US$40 million in rentals. It was the movie motherlode. The lucrative Zucker-Abrahams-Nielsen connection would continue for 25 years in one combination or another. Lucrative seems an understatement — this was more like a licence to print money.

   Police Squad ran for just seven episodes on ABC in 1982. But when it became _The Naked Gun: From the Files of Police Squad_, a feature in 1988, Nielsen reprised his immensely successful take on the Inspector Clouseau, Maxwell Smart type of bumbling detective, the now immortal Frank Drebin. There was more highbrow praise for the lowbrow masters. Vincent Canby said in the _Times_:

As Lt. Frank Drebin with Priscilla Presley in **Naked Gun 2 1/2: The Smell of Fear.** *Photofest*

The summer is saved. Lieut. Frank Drebin is back and Leslie Nielsen is again playing him in David Zucker's delirious new comedy, *The Naked Gun 2½: The Smell of Fear,* solemnly described as "more than a sequel."

The trilogy (*Naked Gun 2½: The Smell of Fear, Naked Gun 33⅓: The Final Insult*) grossed about a quarter of a billion dollars in US theatrical release alone. *Naked Gun 2½* is widely regarded as the funniest of the trilogy, with Drebin saving the free world from a cartel of bad guys nicely led by fellow Canuck Robert Goulet, who also has taken over Drebin's usual girlfriend played by Priscilla Presley. The opening sequence takes place at a White House luncheon honouring Drebin for killing his 1,000th drug dealer. With amazing lookalikes for the President and First Lady, the oblivious, deadpan Drebin repeatedly and accidentally knocks the stuffing out of the ersatz Barbara Bush, opening doors in her face and repeatedly beating her with lobster parts. It doesn't matter if you're Republican, Democrat, Marijuana Party or a PhD in Russian Literature, you cannot, try as you might, stop laughing at each new sight gag. Then he makes his speech and admits that for the 1,000th, he just backed his car over someone who just happened to be a drug dealer.

The over-the-top-roles rolled in, in various cracked-out incarnations: Dick Steele, Agent WD 40 in *Spy Hard*, which Nielsen executive produced. With a budget around $18 million, it took in $98 million on its first weekend in 1996. It co-starred future Desperate Housewife Nicolette Sheridan. Then he played Colonel Chi in *Surf Ninjas* and Dracula for Mel Brooks in *Dead: And Loving It*.

When David Zucker needed a doofus as president of the US in his horror movie parody *Scary Movie 3*, he called his old pal Nielsen, by then something of an elder statesman of comedy, with a net worth approaching Exxon-Mobil. There is a notable scene in *Scary Movie 4* when Nielsen spoofs the scene on 9/11 when President Bush was reading stories with schoolchildren. The *New York Post* applauded the scene:

> The movie scores a rare bull's-eye when the dimwitted president (who
> else but Leslie Nielsen?) literally has to be torn away from a children's
> story about an animal to cope with the national crisis.

But they panned the movie with perhaps the greatest New York putdown ever written of the fourth installment of a movie series: "4GEDDABOUTIT!"

As a sideline, Nielsen has done books and videos about his obsession with golf. ("They called it golf because all the other four-letter words were used up.") According to the *Internet Movie Database*, Nielsen has had 228 film and TV roles and counting. All that work. All the big roles in small films, the small roles in big films. It's the old Hollywood story. It took him only thirty years or so to become an overnight success.

Do not call him Shirley.

Denys Arcand

B. DESCHAMBAULT, QUEBEC, 25 JUNE 1941

DENYS ARCAND "BURST" ONTO THE INTERNATIONAL FILM SCENE in 1986, with his huge Oscar-nominated hit *The Decline of the American Empire*. In fact, serious critics and film buffs had been seeking out his usually intense works at festivals for more than decade. Arcand had made his first film in 1961, so like Leslie Nielsen and so many other screen legends in this book, he spent almost twenty-five years becoming an overnight success.

He was born in small-town Quebec. His father had been a sailor, but settled into a career as a marine pilot who helped ships navigate the treacherous waters of the mighty St. Lawrence. He was named "Queen's Pilot" in 1959 when he guided Her Majesty's Royal Yacht *Britannia* from Quebec City to Montreal.

Denys was sent to Jesuit school and university in Montreal. His biographer describes the young man as "the embodiment of artistic passion." A brilliant student, he was given access by his Jesuit teachers to books usually considered too controversial by both the Catholic establishment and the reactionary provincial government of Maurice Duplessis — Malraux, Gide, Camus, Sartre. It explains the feeling one gets watching his films, that he's quoting someone you might vaguely have heard of whom he knows like the back of his hand. Ironically, considering the number of shots he would later fire at organized religion, Catholicism in particular, the first first prize he won was in religion. He excelled at elocution and oratory, wrote learned articles and was given the nickname "Little Voltaire."

With his intellect and creativity, he could have chosen any number of paths to artistic self-expression. He pondered his future after the Université de Montreal. He considered a diplomatic career in External Affairs or a graduate degree at the University of California at Berkeley, one of epicentres of the counterculture quakes soon to come. He chose film, beginning with a subversive little effort at cinema verité in the fall of 1961 called *Seul ou avec d'autres* (*Alone or With Others*).

From the very beginning for Arcand, a movie just wouldn't be a movie without thumbing his nose at some form of authority, in this case the Church. The enigmatic title, the biography says, "refers to the question asked by the Priest in the confessional when a sin of the flesh is confessed." The first-love-on-campus story is full of Monty Python-esque barbs, the best being the faux radio show Soirée de Culte, for "all you rosary fans out there" hosted by Father Paul-Emile and sponsored by Dow Breweries and The Casgrain Rosary Company. The Father's favourite beer is one of Dow's best-sellers, Red Cap Ale, a play on the scarlet hat of Cardinals, and the film is terribly witty and avant garde in its representation of a society that in many ways was just joining the 20th century.

He later recalled meeting the famed Italian director Roberto Rossellini at the home of his colleague and idol, Claude Jutra. The great man left a great impression on the young film maker with his affirmation that what a director needs to be successful is a really good tailor, to look respectable while begging for money to make films.

Avec d'autres opened the door at the National Film Board for him and his career and his full-blown passion for film making began in earnest. His new heroes were Bunuel, Fellini, John Ford and Kurosawa.

It was near the height of the political and artistic ferment of the Quiet Revolution, that many historians date from the deposing of Duplessis and the repressive Union Nationale and the election of the Liberals under Jean Lesage (and senior cabinet minister René Levesque. (Though some others date the seeds of revolution from the Hockey Riots of 1955, when the National Hockey League suspended Quebec idol and Montreal superstar Maurice Richard for punching a referee.) By the mid-1960s the FLQ had begun their bombing campaign. In the midst of this exciting near-anarchy, Arcand was at the barricades in the intellectual firefights. He began work on historical documentaries and the trouble began almost right away.

His brutally realistic biography of Samuel de Champlain appalled the Film Board. *Le Devoir*, the intellectual voice of journalism in Quebec for decades called it "too intellectual" and relayed misgivings about portraying so much in terms of Champlain's sadism. *La Presse* wrote:

> The director's scalpel slices into a cherished Legend, exposing wounds
> . . . and leaving us with the skeleton of a cherished French God.

This is probably exactly what Arcand set out to do.

His reputation as the angriest of the angry, gifted young men taking over Quebec film making was set in stone with *On est au coton*, an excellent pun in French. The literal translation is "We are in cotton," apt for a documentary about workers in Quebec's textile industry. As a slang expression, the title is best translated as "We are pissed off," as the documentary also examines the closing of the mills, laying waste to an already exploited work force.

In the tense and tragic context of the October Crisis, *On est au coton* seemed like a raving Marxist, anti-business, anti-English, worker-to-the-streets diatribe. It must have landed on the desks of senior NFB officials like an improvised explosive device. So they banned it, then ordered a tamer re-cut. They banned that too. Bootleg copies circulated under the amusing title *The Life of John A. Macdonald*. *On est au coton* wasn't officially released until 1976.

Perhaps neglecting Rossellini's sartorial advice, Arcand was by now pretty much broke and would stay that way until *The Decline of the American Empire*, 15 years later. But he graduated into features, making what he called his "Gun Trilogy." All bleakly cynical, these were definitely films made by the same person who made *Au coton*. *La maudite gallette* (*Dirty Money*) is about crooks and greed; *Gina* involves a stripper and a film unit making a documentary about the textile industry; and *Réjeanne Padovani* is about greed and corruption.

The trilogy propelled him to the front ranks of Quebec artists. *Padovani* drew some interest from abroad, especially in the *New York Times* in October 1973:

> Denys Arcand, its 32-year-old director and a newcomer to the United States movie scene, maintains a good deal of suspense as his group of bigwigs dine at the plush Montreal home of Jean Lajeunesse on his completion of a superhighway. Corruption among its effete, influential Canadian wheeler-dealers, politicos and their ruthless hirelings is made shockingly obvious . . .
>
> As a sobering drama, *Réjeanne Padovani*, shown last night as the Canadian feature entry at the New York Film Festival, is, like its venal principals, fascinating but imperfect.

Gina flopped so badly in 1975, Arcand spoke of "knocking at the door of the Salvation Army or worse still become a professor at the University of Quebec in Montreal."

It would be a long dark fallow period relieved only with some TV work (*The Crime of Ovide Plouffe*) and some theatre. The personal trauma of the Referendum defeat was no small part of the malaise. In a 1982 interview Arcand said:

Oscar Night February 29, 2004. Corbis

That's just my problem at the moment. I have no dreams. I don't see a dream for Quebec anymore . . . the Parti Quebecois was the last dream. Their practice of power killed the dream of an entire generation."

In 1984, with a grant from Telefilm, Arcand began writing a script for a film tentatively titled *Racy Conversations*. It would become *The Decline of the American Empire*, which some critics called a French version of *The Big Chill*. Eight friends meet, eat, drink and talk smartly about the delights and problems of sexuality. That's it, that's all. American critics were enthralled and a little confused:

> *The Decline of the American Empire* is an unusual film on several counts: intensely personal in its vision, it was made for very little money by American standards — $1.3 million — and it eschews virtually all the trappings of most successful movies. There are no car chases, no explicit sex scenes, no one-liners — only a group of affluent, middle-aged people sitting around talking about their sexual experiences and opinions.

The venerable Vincent Canby was lavish, describing it as:

> . . . a comedy that so entertainingly and successfully expresses itself through intelligent characters defined entirely in their talk. Mr. Arcand's dialogue is not didactic. It's spontaneously funny and rueful and full of oblique revelations. Though highly intelligent, his characters are prone to self-delusion. They're nothing if not civilized, but they don't hesitate to lie and cheat in their own interests.

As the critics raved and the box-office rolled in Arcand made it sound simple:

> We do not have the kind of budget to compete with Hollywood — there's no way we're going to make *Indiana Jones and the Temple of Doom* — so we might as well make an entirely different kind of movie — one where people talk all the time, for example.

There was an Oscar nomination for Best Foreign Film for the director who'd fallen on hard times.

There was a second Oscar nomination in 1989 for *Jesus of Montreal*. Struggling actors mount a blasphemous production of a Passion Play (i.e. a play depicting the struggles, death and resurrection of Jesus). It is an indictment of a Church Arcand felt no longer understood or taught the true meaning of the Gospels. One Montreal paper called it "The Gospel According to St. Arcand." His worldwide celebrity led to the nickname "Denys of Montreal."

Now with a devoted following two more films didn't help his reputation, but neither hurt it much. *Love and Human Remains* (1993) and *Stardom* (2000) sank quickly from view, save for some dedicated enemies in Quebec who whispered about the films made "in English" and with "Toronto money."

The Barbarian Invasions, Arcand's third nomination, won the Oscar for Best Foreign Film. As bombs, babes and computer-generated graphics filled the multiplexes, this sad, cerebral film more than held its own. It tracks the slow painful death of a cancer victim in a morbid reunion of the gang from *The American Empire* wrapped around the events of September 11, 2001. It's like a film version of Yeats' *The Second Coming*: In this film, *nothing* holds. The Church, Canadian medicine, Quebec independence, American supremacy, the unions he once championed. Name it and it's dysfunctional. The profound disillusionment with everything is astonishing. It is all very powerful:

> *The Barbarian Invasions* is a film that effortlessly makes you laugh with delight, cringe with pain and weep for life's inevitable end . . . Together again, they face something more palpable and fearsome than the revolution they sought in youth. Now life recedes before them — in the person of Remy, the lustiest, most incandescently alive of them all."

It's never clear exactly who the barbarians are. American reviewers assume they are the hijackers of 9/11. His biographer suggests they are the forces that prevented Quebec separation. Others see a sort of plague of moral locusts destroying society's spirit and integrity. After all the intense intellectual speculation, Arcand admitted after shooting it that it was all about himself and his father:

> I accompanied, to our hospitals, my grandfather, father and mother, who all died of cancer. I never told them, especially my father that I loved them. I should have.

His biographer Réal La Rochelle says Quebec retains a love-hate relationship with its most famous enfant terrible. He's received rave reviews and many awards along with a "closetful of harsh invective from all sides: Marxists, Parti Quebecois members, feminists," all allies of a fellow traveller one would have thought. La Rochelle calls Arcand the "most enigmatic figure in the intellectual and cultural life of Quebec." Though it's hard not to like an Oscar-winning director who describes his philosophical view of the artistic medium of film in two words: "Pure Poker."

John Candy

B. TORONTO, ONTARIO, 31 OCTOBER 1950

D. DURANGO, MEXICO, 4 MARCH 1994

WHEN COMPILING THE LIST OF SCREEN LEGENDS, John Candy was an obvious one to include, as one of Canada's best-loved, best-known screen exports. Candy was without question a brilliant comic on stage and television, but his movie career, sadly spanned less than two decades. Truth be told, he was sought after by directors as accomplished and disparate as Steven Spielberg, John Hughes and Oliver Stone. He could count living legends like Bill Murray, John Belushi and Steve Martin as co-stars, friends and mentors. His oversized puppy dog persona, the lovable schlub with a big heart won him a devoted following and star billing. True, he was a major comic well before he hit the big screen but, if it's not too corny, maybe "Legend" status can be measured, not in the number of awards and reviews, but in the number of hearts touched.

The defining moment in John Franklin Candy's life came when he was just 5 years old, when his father died of a heart attack at age 35. Cardiac problems had plagued the family for generations. The trauma and insecurity caused by the loss haunted him the rest of his life. The devastated little boy would take refuge in the many characters he would invent and portray so memorably. In his biography, *Laughing on the Outside*, Martin Knelman quotes him recalling, "The loss of my father left a great emptiness in my heart." Far from being the ebullient class clown, he was introverted and beset by the responsibilities that come to young men of fatherless families.

He was a gentle giant from early on. His first recorded ambition was to play football, which he did with great passion. He overwhelmed his smaller high school opponents until a knee injury closed that window for good. It actually came in handy later, causing him to flunk the physical when he impulsively tried to enlist in the US military. He was drawn to a theatre course in high school, and enrolled in journalism in college before switching back to theatre and then dropping out altogether. He had a series of menial jobs, mixing paint, selling sporting goods, working as sales clerk at Eaton's department store.

In the early 1970s he lucked into some work doing commercials. Whatever had lit the desire to perform, he had completely come out of his shell in his teens, though always self-conscious about his size. Knelman recounts a Candy comeback line that cracked up the crew while shooting a toothpaste commercial with big-time TV host (and fellow Canadian) Art Linkletter. When Linkletter rebuked him for smoking, he replied, "Yeah, it'll stunt my growth."

Though barely holding his own doing children's theatre, two important things happened over the next couple of years. The first is that he met a lifelong friend in Dan Aykroyd, an Ottawa native who would go onto his own memorable comedy career. And the second is that he got to audition for the Toronto offshoot of the famous Second City comedy troupe of Chicago. They loved him. They hired Aykroyd and others for Toronto, but, deeply impressed with Candy's presence and potential, they sent him straight to the Big Leagues in Chicago.

In 1974, he was sent back to help the floundering Toronto venture. There was TV work to boot, when Second City morphed into a television series called *SCTV*. Two years later, Candy became part of a remarkably talented cast that included Andrea Martin, Eugene Levy, Catherine O'Hara and eventually Dave Thomas. He sent up over-size celebrities (Luciano Pavarotti, The Incredible Hulk) and created a surreal stable of original characters; sleazy talk-show host Johnny LaRue and, one of the Polka-playing Schmenge brothers. Collectively, the ensemble cast of *SCTV* won two Emmy Awards for Outstanding Writing in a Variety or Music Program.

His reputation was such that he attracted the attention of an up-and-coming Hollywood director named Steven Spielberg. Spielberg was then riding the wave of acclaim that followed his success with *Jaws* and *Close Encounters of the Third Kind*. He met Candy at a party and offered him a part in his next project, a comedy. Candy apparently thought it was just a patronizing "Let's have lunch" kiss-off and declined. But Spielberg persisted by phone and eventually Candy was on set as Pvt. Foley in *1941*. The movie attempts to tell the story, in the wackiest of ways, of the post-Pearl Harbor hysteria in California caused by a lone Japanese submarine off the coast.

The cast was brilliant, as if Spielberg had visited the Comedy Hall of Fame in the future. Dan Aykroyd, John Belushi, Penny Marshall, Joe Flaherty along with Mickey Rourke, Ned Beatty, Robert Stack and James Caan. For Candy, it was a mixed bag. He had been pursued by and blessed with the opportunity to work with a Great Director. But it unluckily came in one of the Great Director's rare critical and commercial flops. But he added John Belushi to his list of pals. He would be invited to be in the film reprise of the Belushi/Aykroyd *Saturday Night Live* skit, *The Blues Brothers*. Candy was almost buried by the amazing list of cameos (Ray Charles, Aretha Franklin, James Brown), but it was at least a hit at the box office.

In 1981, there was progress in his role as Dewey Oxberger in *Stripes*, starring his old friend from Chicago, Bill Murray. Serious critics, like Vincent Canby, got him on their radar:

> Another nice surprise is John Candy as a 350-pound recruit who plans
> to become a "lean and mean fighting machine."

Attempts to maintain a healthier lifestyle never seemed to take hold for long. His now-hectic performing career was fueled by nicotine, alcohol, drugs and junk food. John Belushi was one of Candy's role models. When, in 1982, the "Blues Brother" died of a drug overdose that spoke of years of excess, Candy was devastated and resolved to clean up his own act.

On the screen, good things were happening. The path to stardom seemed to be getting clearer. He was noticed in *National Lampoon's Vacation* in 1983. More important, he met the movie's producer and writer John Hughes. Hughes would become one of those hugely successful directors critics love to loathe for his lowbrow output (*Animal House*, *Mr. Mom*, *Beethoven*, *Flubber*). After he did *Home Alone* in 1990, he became one of those directors with a bank account so large, critics really didn't matter. Whatever Hughes else inflicted on the movie-going public, he would be the one who somehow drew out Candy's best work.

In the meantime, 1984's Tom Hanks/Darryl Hannah hit *Splash!* seemed to bring the brass ring within reach. Hanks plays Alan Bauer, saved from drowning by a mermaid (Hannah) who comes to look for him in New York. They fall in love, with Hannah withholding the crucial secret of what happens to her bodacious human form when touched by saltwater. Word of the whole fish out of water romance gets out. Candy got rave reviews as Jack's brother Freddie. Everyone mentions the famous racquetball scene where the brothers play each other, Freddy managing to handle a racquet, a drink and a cigarette at the same time. It looked like something straight out of his old *SCTV* days. Janet Maslin in the *New York Times* came to praise. But the gratuitous reference to Candy's size must have wounded him deeply:

*As Del Griffith in **Trains, Planes and Automobiles** 1987. With Steve Martin. Photofest*

The film would not be nearly so successful without the bulldozing presence of John Candy, as the hero's hilarious brother. The mere sight of the tubby Mr. Candy is funny enough (the spectacle of him playing racquetball really is something to see). But he also gets most of the better lines in the screenplay.

He followed with *Brewster's Millions* with Richard Pryor, and then his first starring role in *Summer Rental* (1985). Candy plays a burnt-out air traffic controller who takes the family on a beach holiday which predictably ends up in shambles. Reviewers found it a tad thin but observed that, "Mr. Candy is fun to watch under any circumstances." He had proven he could flat out act and play a normal human being. It was also a seminar on film making from the legendary Carl Reiner, who played the character Allan Brady on *The Dick Van Dyke Show* that Candy loved to watch growing up.

Re-enter John Hughes with a slight premise and a big star for a film. The premise consisted of throwing together two guys who could not have less in common, and adding an inconceivable string of misfortune that prevents their return to Chicago for Thanksgiving. The star of *Planes, Trains and Automobiles* was Steve Martin as Neal, an uptight, contemptuous advertising executive whose plans to fly in and out of Manhattan for a meeting (quickly returning to his perfect family, in his perfect house in the perfect suburb) go badly awry. Candy was signed to play Martin's bête noir, a lovable loser named Del , an itinerant shower-ring salesman who, when the flights start getting cancelled, sticks to Neal like a bad rash. Where Neal is sort of prissy and wears expensive suits, Del is an annoying slob who cracks knuckles, snores, smokes, talks too much and has a wardrobe of mismatched clothes from Goodwill.

As piles of snow cover Chicago, close the airport and back up air traffic for days to come, the New York to Chicago flight is diverted to Wichita, Kansas and the plot's point of departure unfolds: How to get back to Chicago for Thanksgiving while having a life-changing experience leading to a happy ending. Roger Ebert describes the tenor of the proceedings:

> Fate joins their destinies. Together they will endure every indignity that
> modern travel can inflict on its victims. What will torture them even
> more is being trapped in each other's company. Del wants only to
> please. Neal wants only to be left alone.

Otherwise adult, sophisticated people have been reduced to bowls of lime Jell-O, laughing at Candy removing his shoes and saying, "Oh, my dogs are really barking today."

And after Neal's contretemps with a surly cab dispatcher, Del deadpans, "I've never seen a man picked up by his testicles before."

He can be quite witty in a way, as in his reality check in the Wichita airport: "Come on, Neal. We've got a better chance playing pickup sticks with our butt cheeks than getting a flight out of here."

And he can be touchingly sad. Sitting, freezing in the snowstorm in the burnt-

*As Buck Russell with Macaulay Culkin in **Uncle Buck**, 1984. Universal*

out shell of a car he set on fire, he talks to himself: "I am the biggest pain in the butt that ever came down the turnpike."

It's not the only eerie moment when you feel like you're watching John Candy, not Del Griffith talking to himself. A warm and friendly disposition, easily hurt and suffering from paralytic self-doubt all sound like Del and/or John.

In one last motel room together, as Neal has passed the point of wanting to strangle his travelling companion, they are attempting Death by Minibar. Neal puffs up his pillows and tells Del he is a most unique individual. Del drains the little bottle of rum and replies, "Unique? What is unique? Latin for asshole?"

Some dismiss *Trains, Planes and Automobiles* as a one-trick pony. Others consider it a minor classic. Either way it'll make you laugh.

Candy's career survived dreadful choices like *The Great Outdoors* (1988), *Who's Harry Crumb?* (1989) and *Delirious* (1991). But back with Hughes again, he had great

chemistry with young Macaulay Culkin in *Uncle Buck* (1989) and his small role as the
Polka King brightened *Home Alone* in 1990. Of his portrayal in *Only the Lonely* (1991)
of an adult son desperately trying to escape a suffocating mother in Maureen O'Hara,
Janet Maslin wrote:

> Thanks in large part to Mr. Candy, who gives an honestly touching per-
> formance in what might have been a cloying role, this story does have
> its simple charms. Mr. Candy succeeds not only in bringing some depth
> to the mother-son struggle, but also in making the film's love story gen-
> tly credible.

Leonard Maltin called his 1991 cameo as Dean Andrews in Oliver Stone's *JFK* "surprisingly effective."

1991 was a terrific year for John Candy — good roles, good reviews, good
money. He had season's tickets for the NHL's Los Angeles Kings. He was impressed
with Bruce McNall, the team owner, financial wizard and The Man Who Bought Wayne
Gretzky from Edmonton for $15 million. The trio, Candy, Gretzky and McNall, bought
the actor's beloved home football team, the Argos. Candy revelled in hands-on managing of the team's affairs. They even won the Grey Cup that year. But it was too good to
last. It soon became obvious that McNall's "empire" was smoke and mirrors, perhaps the
first of the epidemic of financial frauds to come.

He was credible as the coach of the true story of the oxymoronic Jamaican bob-
sled team in *Cool Runnings* (1993), but his time had run out. Despite all kinds of health
problems, he went to Mexico to shoot *Wagons East* and died there in his sleep at age 43.

Roger Ebert was captivated by Candy and Martin in *Planes, Trains and
Automobiles*:

> Like certain other popular entertainments *(It's a Wonderful Life, E.T.,
> Casablanca)* it not only contained a universal theme, but also matched
> it with the right actors and story, so that it shrugged off the other
> movies of its kind and stood above them in a kind of perfection. This is
> the only movie our family watches as a custom, most every
> Thanksgiving.

Ebert tells a story about meeting Candy in a hotel bar, indulging in his too-familiar hob-
bies, smoking and drinking:

> He was depressed. People loved him, but he didn't seem to know that,
> or it wasn't enough. He was a sweet guy and nobody had a word to say

against him, but he was down on himself. All he wanted to do was make people laugh, but sometimes he tried too hard, and he hated himself for doing that in some of his movies.

In *Planes, Trains and Automobiles*, Neal takes Del home to Perfectville where Neal's family reacts like he's done six tours of duty in Iraq. He has a too-long embrace with his astonishingly beautiful middle-aged wife as Del looks on. The movie ends with a medium close-up of Candy, watching all the wonderful things his friend has and he doesn't, with that still youthful face smiling. At least, on the outside.

Douglas Shearer

B. MONTREAL, QUEBEC, 17 NOVEMBER 1899
D. CULVER CITY, CALIFORNIA, 5 JANUARY 1971

THERE'S NO QUESTION AT ALL THAT THE SHEARER CLAN'S glamorous genes ended up with Douglas's younger sister Norma. She was the quintessential leading lady of the 1930s and one of the great glamour queens of all time, with a Best Actress Oscar to her credit. Douglas, on the other hand, was quiet, prim, level-headed, plain-looking (the term geek had yet to be invented). But he was an absolute genius with sound. In terms of awards, influence and importance his career dwarfs that of any Canadian that ever hit Hollywood.

The Academy of Motion Picture Arts and Sciences counts things in finicky ways, but any way you slice it there are *fourteen* Academy Awards with Douglas Shearer's name on them, and another eleven nominations. Most likely he was second only to the Granddaddy of Oscar collectors, Walt Disney. To put another way, Shearer won more Academy Awards than the rest of Canada has won all together, to date.

History records Universal Studio's *The Jazz Singer* as the first talking picture in 1927. It was really a silent film with a few minutes of Al Jolson talking and singing at the end. In truth Shearer had had film with sound in theatres two years before. And afterwards, Shearer's constant innovation and invention not only put MGM at the head of the pack, but moved the whole industry forward into the new worlds of sound and widescreen film projection. The great Spencer Tracy paid him tribute once, in 1963:

> Douglas Shearer is the only person I know who has received twelve Academy Awards without ever having been seen on the screen.

He knew about sound when sound hadn't been invented. He has made many stars by his achievements in the development of sound equipment. I wonder where I'd be today if it wasn't for the genius of this man. He's a star himself, but he'll never admit it.

Shearer grew up with his sisters in the Westmount mansion they would lose in the depression of 1919. Though the family fell on hard times, there is still a Shearer Street in Montreal that any working-class Montrealer knows well. The lumber yard with which Grandfather had built the family fortune was on a lane over near the Lachine Canal in what became known as Point St. Charles. The city let them call it Shearer Lane, eventually a street where Northern Electric built a huge plant employing many of the residents of "The Point." It was where Douglas got his first job. He was so proficient in mathematics and so set on becoming an engineer that he dropped out of high school and got hired on the spot.

According to Charles Foster in *Stardust and Shadows: Canadians in Early Hollywood*, Douglas's idea of a good time was to race over to the local power plant after school to harass the plant engineers into detailed explanations of what he called "the seemingly unlimited miracles of sound and light." At 18 he somehow wangled a way into McGill University without a high school diploma, and studied engineering and physics. He also enlisted in the Royal Flying Corps, but never served, having been felled, as countless millions around the world had, by the Spanish Flu in the 1918 pandemic. While his mother and sisters were gallivanting around New York and LA launching Norma's film career, Douglas stayed behind in Montreal as a salesman of industrial power plant equipment, bringing him into contact with the leading engineering firms of the day. He also bought a stake in a Ford dealership, fixing cars in his spare time.

He visited his sister Norma in New York in 1921 where he discovered an aptitude for improving lighting on movie sets. In 1924, he sold his stake in the dealership for a healthy chunk of change and bought a return train ticket, Montreal to Los Angeles. He never used the return. Norma was well on the road to stardom when he arrived and at a party, he was offered a job by (fellow Canadian) Jack Warner. He had the unglamorous, unscientific jobs of looking after props and babysitting one of Warner Brothers early stars, Rin Tin Tin.

Still, he was an engineer, and one of the early prophets of the possibilities of sound and of movies with talking and singing. This was a concept that even the daring entrepreneurs who ran the big studios in the silent era regarded as an expensive, dubious passing fad. At that point, in 1926, he was one of the few people in the world who could (and did) actually make it happen.

It's a fascinating, almost unknown story told well by Charles Foster. It must have been quite a scene when Douglas, a 26-year-old ex-prop manager and high school dropout, told his new bosses at MGM that he could and they should make talking movies. He proposed to take two minutes of footage from one of sister Norma's long-forgotten films, *Slave of Fashion*, separately record the actors speaking their lines from those excerpts, and play the film and record together, synchronized. According to Foster, Douglas Shearer later recalled that

> . . . the results were startling. When Louis B. Mayer saw the results he stopped work on every set and invited everyone to see what we'd created. He warned the whole group that if they mentioned what they'd seen they'd be fired. There was great applause and we felt as though we'd cleared a major hurdle toward the creation of talking pictures.

At the time, even the most basic details were daunting technological challenges. Being the greatest sound technician of all time meant changing *all* the equipment used to make movies.

Early cameras were so large and noisy that the microphone could pick up the whir of the film rolling. Putting the camera and operator in a soundproof box tended to suffocate the cameraman, so Shearer tinkered with the camera innards to make them quieter. Microphones were too bulky to embed in actors' clothing and if someone was even a bit too far away from a mike stand, the voice would sound like it was coming from next door. Shearer developed the overhead boom microphone and methods of using it without casting shadows across actors faces.

Early efforts centered on synchronizing separate sources so that the sound on the record matched the mouthing of the words in the film. With the help of RCA Victor, Shearer later came up with the modern day technology of "sound-on-film" in which the audio and visual elements are physically played back on a single reel.

For *Slave of Fashion*, though, he tried to find a way to get enough equipment and reliable technicians to run the synched, separate reels in all fifteen theatres in which the movie was playing. He couldn't, but he hit on the ingenious alternative of taking the audio disk and a suitcase full of cash to a local radio station. He arranged to broadcast the sound playback cued to the second the film rolled in the theatre. He didn't need thirty technicians and sixty machines. He just needed fifteen radios plugged into the theatres' speakers. It was perfect. The audience was incredulous, demanding to see the two-minute trailer again and again. Shearer left in triumph, so he missed the commotion that followed when an enraged audience loudly protested the silence of the film that followed. They felt duped into thinking the whole film

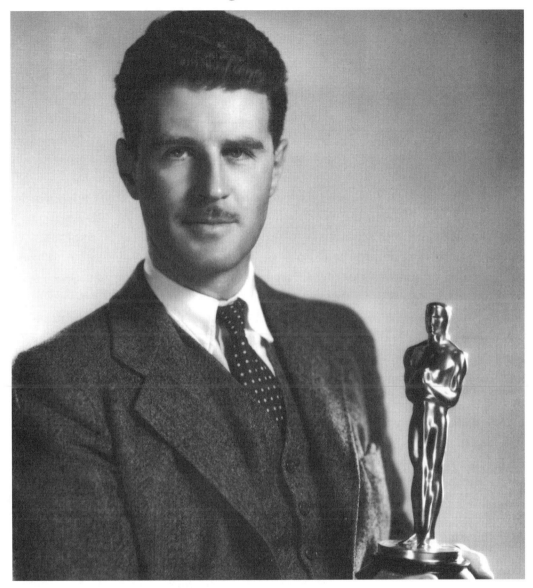

Douglas Shearer with Oscar. One of many. Photofest

would speak, and theatre owners had to quell minor riots.

Shearer was given a big raise and a fancy title, Director of MGM's Sound Research Department, which he found quite amusing, since at the time he was the *entire* Research Department. Oddly, his first attempt to tinker with a full-length feature was deemed a failure by the *New York Times*. In 1928, he tried to introduce sound and musical tracks in *White Shadows of the South Seas* and the *Times* was deeply unimpressed.

He was then made Lighting Director as well, and teamed up with Art Director Cedric Gibbons. They would do hundreds of films together and give MGM the look and sound that made it known as "The Rolls Royce of Studios."

One of their biggest triumphs came in 1929 with *The Broadway Melody*. They obviously overcame whatever problems had caused *White Shadows* to flop. MGM promoted it heavily as "Metro-Goldwyn-Mayer's TALKING SINGING DANCING Dramatic Sensation!" The movie opens with dramatic but surprisingly shaky aerials of Manhattan. But your toes are already tapping and you're humming along with the title song, George M. Cohan's "Broadway Melody." The first scene, at the Gleason Music Publishing office, appears ordinary to the eye, but to the ear, especially an ear in 1929, it's quite audacious. It's as if the cocky audio virtuoso was showing off. There are four different acts rehearsing in separate, not quite sound proof rooms . . . a soprano, a jazz quintet, a flapper duo, and the star up front doing "Broadway Melody." And you can hear them all in brilliant cacophony never before achieved, layer upon layer of sound all mixed together. It's as if Shearer was saying, "You want sound? I'll give you sound."

The *All Movie Guide* calls it the "landmark MGM musical." Pauline Kael recalled, "When talkies were new, this was the musical everyone went to see." The *Times* deemed it "a tour de force with which its producers here hope to rival the ten-month run of Jolson's *Jazz Singer*." It was the first musical to win Best Picture. The *Classic Movie Guide* notes:

> Though MGM was late to the "talkie" revolution, the production quali-
> ty of this musical, a popular early genre after the advent of sound, was
> so superior to the rest of the industry that it won the Oscar.

Shearer worked more Oscar magic in 1930 in the Wallace Beery prison drama *The House*. Again the sound quality was enough to make even the *Times* sit up and listen as never before:

> In some sequences one not only hears the principals carrying on a conver-
> sation, but there also come from the screen the undertones of the voices
> of other prisoners. The rat-tat-tat of machine guns, the sudden entry of a
> couple of tanks add to the stirring quality of the closing scenes.

The Shearers lived a quiet home life, rarely indulging in the ongoing party that was Hollywood. That quiet life was shattered in 1931. Douglas's wife never recovered from the death of her mother, and committed suicide horribly in front of hundreds at a shooting gallery on the Santa Monica Pier. Foster cites his testimony at the inquest: "We all tried very hard, but she was unable to recover from the shock of her mother's unexpected death."

He'd had neighbours keep an eye on her while he was at work. As horrific as the trauma must have been, it might have been something of a relief, the end of so much pain and suffering. Besides, Shearer was a man of few emotions. In forty years of pressure-packed work in a crazy business, no one ever recalled him losing his cool. That he went straight from the funeral back to the lab seems like something that a traumatized widower might do to bury the hurt with work.

In his quest for sound perfection, Shearer became a master of all trades, refining cameras, lighting techniques, film stock quality, and one of his all-time favourites, upgrading theatre speakers with a kind of precursor to modern stereo sound.

> His proudest accomplishment did away with the sound distortion troubling the MGM-controlled Loew's theatres. The two-element "Shearer horn" — tried out first at Loew's theatres in Montreal and New York in 1936, and used at the opening of *Romeo and Juliet* (with sister Norma) helped earn Douglas Shearer and the MGM sound department a scientific/technical award from the Academy's Board of Governors.

He also won the Best Sound Recording Oscar for *San Francisco*, an epic about the 1906 earthquake that destroyed the city. The star, Clark Gable thought it was a dull movie until he heard Shearer's audio mix that left him "gasping for breath with its realism." He had been a double winner the year before as well. The first award was for Sound in *Naughty Marietta*. Oft-repeated legend has it he "fixed" the, shall we say shortcomings, in the voice of the star, Jeannette Macdonald, who would go on to make those mediocre but famous Mountie movies with Nelson Eddy. Shearer's MGM team also won a Technical Achievement Award "for their automatic control system for cameras and sound recording machines and auxiliary stage equipment."

Other films that Shearer won Oscars for were:

Strike up the Band (1940) by Busby Berkeley with Judy Garland and Mickey Rooney.

30 Seconds Over Tokyo (1944) This was the first portrayal of the famous Doolittle Raid mounted by the US in retaliation for Pearl Harbor.

For Special Effects in *Green Dolphin Street* (1947), with Lana Turner.

One online fan wrote:

the story is told against a backdrop of native uprisings, tidal waves and earthquakes that are all realistically depicted. No wonder the film won an Oscar for its startling Special Effects.

And lastly, *The Great Caruso* (1951) with Mario Lanza.

There were also numerous Technical Achievement Awards, Awards of Merit, and Scientific and Engineering Awards. Mentioning just a few of them will give you a general idea of what a multifaceted genius Douglas Shearer was:

1964   For the engineering of an improved Background Process Projection System

1960   For the development of a system of producing and exhibiting wide film motion pictures known as Camera 65.

1942   For pioneering the development of fine grain emulsions for variable density original sound recording in a studio production.

1938   For a method of varying the scanning width of variable density sound tracks (squeeze tracks) for the purpose of obtaining an increased amount of noise reduction. Technical Achievement Award.

For the design of the film drive mechanism as incorporated in the ERPI 1010 reproducer.

For the development of a practical two-way horn system and a biased Class A push-pull recording system.

He was secretly seconded to the military in World War II at the request of Churchill and with the blessing of Roosevelt. Foster quotes him as saying, matter-of-factly, "We were able to perfect the radar that I believe helped shorten the war." Declining a civilian citation for his contribution, he was said to have kept a personal letter of thanks from Churchill framed in his study.

He had two other amazing accomplishments: He created the famous Tarzan yell for Johnny Weismuller, and gave Leo the MGM lion his roar.

According to the *Internet Movie Database*, he did 801 films. More than any other man, he was responsible for the perfection of motion picture sound. He contributed greatly to the Allied cause in the war. His is a wonderful story that is known only to a few — at least until now. A true giant, he was likely Canada's most influential, prolific and decorated export before Wayne Gretzky, and surely the only person to go from owning a Ford dealership in Montreal to revolutionizing an entire medium.

Michael Sarrazin

B. JACQUES ANDRE MICHEL SARRAZIN, QUEBEC CITY, QUEBEC, 22 MAY 1940

THE GOLD STANDARD OF CELEBRITY HAS SHIFTED OVER TIME. For Florence Lawrence, it was merely having her name mentioned in movie reviews. RCAF flyboys painted Deanna Durbin's likeness on the nose of their planes in World War II. Some of the actors in this book have had their face on the cover of *Time* magazine (Alexis Smith and Geneviève Bujold). There are of course the traditional awards, the Oscars, Emmys and such. In the latter part of the 20th century, though, the truest measure of being hot in Movieland was to be invited to be the guest host of *Saturday Night Live*.

And there was Michael Sarrazin on April 15, 1978, hosting the ne plus ultra of contemporary fame with jazz wiz Keith Jarrett as musical guest. This was the show's heyday, and the episode featured Ottawa native Dan Aykroyd and his famous impersonation of Jimmy Carter. Gilda Radner played her "Dolce Gilda" bit ("I *love* to play. Ciao") and as usual appeared on "Weekend Update" as Roseanne Roseannadana ("Never mind").

The week before, the show had been hosted by Michael Palin of *Monty Python* fame, and a week later by comic legend Steve Martin. Steve Martin would set records for the number of appearances on *SNL* over three decades.

For Sarrazin, whose name is misspelled on the SNL website, this was his ninety minutes of fame, a step up from Andy Warhol's classic limit of fifteen. After some short films at the National Film Board and parts in solid TV series (*The Virginian*, *Wojeck*), Michael Sarrazin burst onto the Hollywood scene with eight films between 1967 and

*As Leland Stamper in **Sometimes a Great Notion** with Paul Newman 1971. Universal*

1969. Fame was instantaneous, though looking back at his filmography, it's not easy to see what the big deal was. Still, he almost always had the most glamorous of leading ladies. Must have been those eyes.

He began with a small role in *Gunfight in Abilene* with Bobby Darin, but was first noticed in support of George C. Scott in *The Flim Flam Man*. In 1968's *The Sweet Ride*, he played a beach bum at Malibu with a mostly unemployed actress girlfriend, Jacqueline Bisset. A cautionary tale for would-be Age of Aquarius rebels and ne'er-do-wells, it was produced by a man named Joe Pasternak, who, thirty years earlier, had launched Winnipeg's own Deanna Durbin in *Three Smart Girls*. Sarrazin won a Golden Globe and Bisset's affections, while Bisset was named Most Promising Newcomer.

In 1969 he had the starring role in the Stephen King thriller *Eye of the Cat* ("Terror that tears the screams right out of your throat!"). Then came the completely

As Robert Symington with Jane Fonda in 1969's **They Shoot Horses Don't They?** *Photofest*

unintelligible *In Search of Gregory*, a psychological Italian co-production in which Sarrazin has the pleasure of co-starring with Julie Christie at the height of her considerable fame and beauty in the late 1960s. She plays a woman in love with Gregory, a man she's never met. Sarrazin is a famous athlete she uses to bide her time until she finds Gregory.

Then came the role for which he is perhaps best known, as the gawky out-of-work actor Robert Syverton in *They Shoot Horses Don't They?* He is the partner in a 1930s dance marathon of a brilliantly bitter and twisted Jane Fonda. She was nominated for Best Actress. The film received eight other nominations and Gig Young, as the marathon's carney-man emcee ("Youza, Youza Youza") won for Best Supporting Actor. Sarrazin's ultimately tragic character is an actor who seems proud of his most recent credit as a dead French soldier.

At the time it made sense as a dark, Vietnam-era look at the human indignities inflicted on people by society in the Great Depression. Fonda argues with a fellow contestant, a sailor wonderfully played by Red Buttons (just one of those who die by film's end). Her character from dustbowl Texas and says that cows in the slaughterhouse have it better than people. At least they don't know they're going to die and they get fed. Vincent Canby in the *Times* said

> The movie is far from being perfect, but it is so disturbing in such important ways that I won't forget it very easily, which is more than can be said of much better, more consistent films.

Sarrazin's best reviews came for *Sometimes a Great Notion* in 1971, an adaptation of a Ken Kesey novel directed by Paul Newman. He's the rebel of the Stamper family, which consists of Newman, Henry Fonda and Lee Remick, who are trying to keep the family logging business from going under. The *Times* applauded the ensemble:

> As he showed in *Rachel, Rachel*, Mr. Newman knows how to direct actors, and he has obtained lovely performances from Mr. Fonda, Michael Sarrazin and Richard Jaeckel (as two of the younger Stampers), as well as from Lee Remick.

Newman was impressed too because Sarrazin was cast in a small role in *The Life of Judge Roy Bean*, again starring Newman, and directed by the great John Huston. Sarrazin played the husband of Rose Bean, coincidentally played by Jacqueline Bisset. It was quite a cast, and included Anthony Perkins, Ned Beatty, Stacey Keach, Roddy McDowell and Ava Gardner. Newman plays Bean, a legendary lawman who metes out justice frontier style. He's what they would have called "a hangin' judge."

Sarrazin played a well-received *Frankenstein* on TV in 1973 and Barbra Streisand's husband in *For Pete's Sake*. He had a nice little turn as the ill-fated golden boy of the Hornby clan in the 1985 Ted Kotcheff-Mordecai Richler charmer *Joshua Then and Now*. In fact he made several movies in Canada, including the pretty funny 1993 Quebec comedy *La Florida* along with Margot Kidder and Remy Girard.

The initial flash never got turned into long-term stardom, but Sarrazin has never wanted for film or TV work. He certainly had a penchant for unusual roles in unusual films. A career that has roles with Streisand, Bisset, Fondas (Henry and Jane) Christie, Scott and Newman is one of legitimate Legend status.

Arthur Hill

B. MELFORT, SASKATCHEWAN, 1 AUGUST 1922

ARTHUR HILL HAD A LONG CAREER OF DISTINGUISHED stage performances, film supporting roles and even his own television series. He wasn't George C. Scott or Robert Redford — he was that old pro Canadian guy you wanted in your foxhole when the dramatic firefight broke out.

Melfort, about 175 km northeast of Saskatoon, was founded in 1902. The Canadian National Railway asked Mrs. Reginald Beatty, the first woman in town, to name it and she chose the name of her Scottish birthplace. It is in one of the most fertile areas on earth, the Carrot River valley, which is said to have rarely, if ever, suffered from drought or severe crop failure. And it's only fitting that it should have bred a man of fertile imagination and considerable talent.

Yahoo Movies describes Arthur Hill as:

> A sturdy leading man of stage and TV, and key supporting player of the screen. He has consistently delivered thoughtful, well-modulated work that lacks the pyrotechnics that often get an actor noticed. Hill has brought reliable intelligence to his portrayals of doctors, lawyers, judges, professors, military officers, concerned fathers or corporate executives.

A perfect illustration of this point is his inclusion in the cast list for the epic World War II drama *A Bridge too Far* (1977), about the Allies' disastrous attempt at an airborne landing behind enemy lines in Belgium:

Lieut. Gen. Frederick (Boy) Browning . . . . Dirk Bogarde

Staff Sgt. Eddie Dohun . . . . James Caan

Lieut. Col. (Joe) Vandeleur . . . . Michael Caine

Maj. Gen. Robert Urquhart . . . . Sean Connery

Col. Bobby Stout . . . . Elliott Gould

Maj. Gen. Stanislaw Sosabowski . . . . Gene Hackman

Lieut. Col. John Frost . . . . Anthony Hopkins

Dr. Spaander . . . . Laurence Olivier

Brig. Gen. James M. Gavin . . . . Ryan O'Neal

Maj. Julian Cook . . . . Robert Redford

Lieut. Gen. Wilhelm Bittrich . . . . Maximillan Schell

Kate Ter Horst . . . . Liv Ullmann

Tough colonel . . . . Arthur Hill

Let's see now — there he is with some multi-Oscar winners, a few who've been knighted, some living legends. It's sort of like cracking the lineup of the 1927 New York Yankees with Ruth, Gehrig at al.

Hill's career path may have been professionally conventional, but the geographic progression was not exactly a straight line. He began acting at the University of British Columbia, and then went on to Seattle before moving to England in 1948 to make his London stage debut in *Home of the Brave*, a controversial play at the time about racial discrimination in the US army. He made his (tiny) English screen debut in a small role in *Miss Pilgrim's Progress* (1950). In 1955 he moved on to Broadway, where he performed in such classics as Thomas Wolfe's *Look Homeward, Angel*.

His real breakthrough role came in Edward Albee's great work *Who's Afraid of Virginia Woolf?*, as the hard-drinking, misery-loves-company college professor George caught in an incessant marital war with wife Martha (played by the legendary Uta Hagen, who mentored, among many others, our own Kate Reid). The role won him the prestigious 1962 Tony Award for Best Actor.

He had already caught the attention of TV producers, with some fifteen appearances between 1960 and 1962 on series that were the cream of the prime-time schedule: *Dr. Kildare*, *The Untouchables*, *Route 66*, *Ben Casey* and *Alfred Hitchcock Presents*. But he barely had time to set his Tony on the mantelpiece before movie offers started rolling in.

In 1963, in *The Ugly American*, Hill played the aide to the swaggering, commie-

*As Grainger in **The Ugly American** 1963. With Marlon Brando. Universal*

hating American ambassador (played by a swaggering Marlon Brando) to a fictitious southeast-Asian country that strongly resembles Vietnam. It was pretty impressive company for a boy from the Carrot River valley, and the company he kept would continue to be top-drawer.

Another steady stream of TV work followed in series such as *Mission Impossible, Voyage to the Bottom of the Sea* and *The Fugitive,* in which he displayed both stamina and an ability to master a range of roles not so surprising from a man who had cut his acting teeth on Wolfe and Albee.

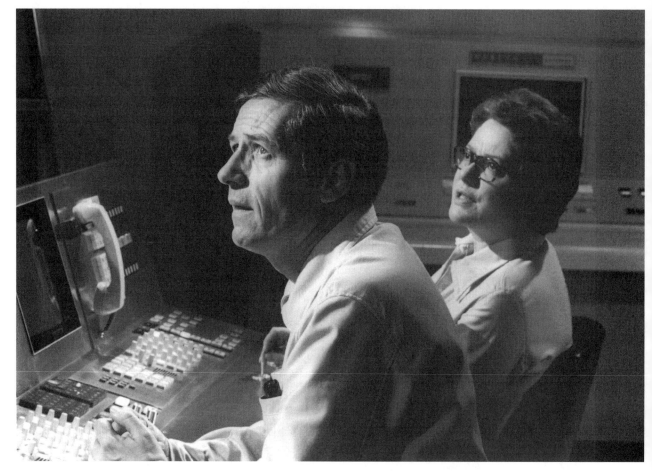

*As Dr. Jeremy Stone in **The Andromeda Strain** 1971, with Kate Reid. Universal*

By 1968 he was keeping the not-too-shabby company of actors George C. Scott, Richard Chamberlain, Joseph Cotten and Julie Christie, director Richard Lester and cinematographer Nicholas Roeg in *Petulia*. It's a 1960s classic with Christie in the title role. Hill has a nice time as Scott's old pal Barney, whose mission is to get Mr. Scott to forget Petulia and reconcile with his wife.

Hill himself would squire some of Hollywood's most accomplished and beautiful women on screen. In 1955, he was Vivien Leigh's boyfriend in *The Deep Blue Sea* and Jane Fonda's kind but jilted husband in 1963's *In the Cool of the Day*. His signature, low-key style as Sam Bonner in the latter was noted approvingly in the *New York Times* as the perfect counterpart to the apparently much-agitated Peter Finch. In 1979 he played both Faye Dunaway's spouse, again kind and jilted, in Franco Zeffirelli's *The*

Champ and Sally Kellerman's husband and the father of very young rising star Diane Lane in George Roy Hill's *A Little Romance*.

He also made two science-fiction movies — *The Andromeda Strain* (1971) with Kate Reid, and *Futureworld* (1976) — before taking on the role of evil head chauvinist in *The Revenge of the Stepford Wives* in 1980. The film wasn't exactly a success, but it does feature future stars Sharon Gless (*Cagney & Lacey*), Don Johnson (*Miami Vice*) and Julie Kavner (Marge Simpson).

By that time, Hill was an established TV commodity. In 1971, he starred in the pilot movie for *Owen Marshall: Attorney at Law*, playing the lead character who acts on behalf of a hippie accused of murder in a California town. He had some very capable help with Vera Miles and Joseph Campanella and William Shatner as District Attorney Dave Blankenship.

The pilot sold and the series ran for sixty-nine episodes on ABC until 1974. One of its creators was also the brains behind another immensely successful series, *Marcus Welby, M.D.*

James Doohan

B. VANCOUVER, BRITISH COLUMBIA, 3 MARCH 1920
D. REDMOND, WASHINGTON, 20 JULY 2005

SCREEN LEGEND STATUS CAN COME IN THE STRANGEST OF WAYS. James Doohan was a journeyman actor, who was born in Vancouver but grew up in Sarnia, the youngest of four children. His father was a dentist, veterinarian and pharmacist. Irish through and through, his family were Catholic refugees from Protestant Belfast.

Cut from there to one day in Hollywood, when he pulled up alongside a Cadillac that he noticed was having tire problems, to warn the driver to get to a garage right away. It was Elvis Presley, who replied, "Sure thing, Scotty." Even the King respected "Scotty's" advice.

Googling "James Doohan" today produces ninety-seven pages of hits.

In one way or another, Doohan gladly played the role of Lieutenant Commander Montgomery Scott for the last forty years of his life. On television, in movies and then, as cult status grew, at countless Trekkie conventions. For hard-core Star Trek fans, he *was* Scotty.

He had a difficult young life that included a near-fatal bout of diptheria and an abusive, alcoholic father he never forgave. He went to school, did a little acting and some singing as a boy soprano, and early on developed his career-making knack for mimicking other people's voices and accents.

When World War II started, he enlisted in the Royal Canadian Artillery, seeing little action until D-Day, June 6, 1944. He was given command of Winnipeg Rifles'

D Company in the assault on Juno Beach. He lasted the day before a German machine gun raked him with bullets, blasting most of his middle finger off. He took four more bullets in the leg and two in the chest, where only a silver cigarette case prevented his certain death at age 24. The finger had to be amputated, its absence hidden throughout his *Star Trek* run.

To his war wounds, he added a broken heart, as he received a Dear John letter from the girl he'd left behind, explaining that she'd become involved with another man. He returned to postwar life alone, unemployed and with a very uncertain future. At a friend's urging, he enrolled in a Veteran's School in London, Ontario, to follow his interest in chemistry.

The story of his unlikely transition into showbiz is told in his autobiography, titled, as you might guess, *Beam Me Up, Scotty*. One night, listening to the radio, he became so annoyed at the amateurish quality of the show that he gathered up some Shakespeare, marched down to the local station, CFPL, and read it to tape. The technician, whose name is lost to history, praised it and mentioned that a brochure from the Academy of Radio Arts in Toronto had just arrived and that young Doohan should apply. So he did. He went on to win the Academy's top prize, a scholarship to the renowned Neighborhood Playhouse in New York. There he befriended fellow Canadian and future star Leslie Nielsen, whom he described as "funny, crude . . . and a solid human being."

He did well, and began commuting from New York to Toronto and the CBC. By 1958 he had become much in demand, with some 450 live shows to his credit. His first film role came in *The Wheeler Dealer*, with James Garner (whom he recalled very fondly), Lee Remick and Jim Backus. The director was yet another Canadian, Arthur Hiller.

In the mid-1960s, Doohan followed his friend Leslie Nielsen's advice to head west to Hollywood. Nielsen even put him up at his house while he looked for work. According to Doohan himself, it was he who convinced Gene Roddenberry that the Chief Engineer of the *Enterprise* should be Scottish. They shot the pilot in 1964 and waited for months to hear whether it had been picked up.

Star Trek's initial run was from 1966 to 1969. But reincarnated in reruns and films, it became TV's most successful franchise. Doohan's portrayal of the redoubtable Mr. Scott was single-handedly credited with increasing enrolment in engineering schools, to the extent that he was granted an honorary degree from the Milwaukee School of Engineering. Scotty would always be at the controls in key situations of the transporter room, a device that could scramble human beings into molecular energy and "transport" them across vast distances to be reconstituted on board the *Enterprise*.

More often than not, it was the intrepid Captain James T. Kirk giving the

Lieutenant Commander Montgomery Scott, the USS Enterprise. Corbis

command. But it's to Doohan the phrase "Beam me up, Scotty" has become indelibly attached. And like Humphrey Bogart's famous "Play it again, Sam," it was never actually said. "Two to beam up, Mr. Scott" was common. Or "Energize." But "Beam me up, Scotty" is a line that even the most devoted "Trekkie" can't place.

Most of the other *Star Trek* characters had signature lines. Mr. Spock's "Most illogical" was one. Dr. McCoy can still be heard explaining "It's life, Jim, but not as we know it." Even Sulu's warning of "Klingons off the starboard bow" signalled a death-defying scene. But Scotty's real signature line was the oft-uttered one from deep inside the ship's warp-drive engines, tools in hand, with oblivion a heartbeat away, the bridge pleading for more power to the protective shields or to power up the ship's constantly damaged lithium crystals. A wild, panicked look in his eyes, he would reply, "I canna change the laws of physics, Captain." But few people remember that.

The TV series lasted only three seasons, and at first Doohan considered it to be an albatross that would make it difficult for him to find further work. But then he realized "how far that albatross would fly." A string of movies, spinoffs and a huge cult following that still defies explanation followed *Star Trek*. Beyond that, what must it have been like to work with a cast who achieved stardom in middle-age and remained together through old age and death? Doohan's best friend was George Takei, "Sulu." He was also very much enamoured by the affable personality of DeForest Kelly, "Doctor McCoy." He deeply admired Leonard Nimoy, "Mr. Spock." He wasn't as crazy about "Captain Kirk," William Shatner.

Scotty was, though, the most affable and perhaps most loved *Star Trek* character. He revelled in the Trekkie conventions and the adulation that followed the rediscovery of the series in the 1970s and 1980s. He was one of the few Enterprise originals to appear with and approve of *Star Trek: The Next Generation* and the ship's new Captain Jean Luc Picard, played by Patrick Stewart. He artfully described the difference between the two versions, and why the original characters remain so near and dear:

> Let's say the engines are in trouble. Geordie, the new Chief Engineer
> would say, "If I can reroute the isometric ion pulse through the engine
> core, then maybe I can backload the matter-antimatter resonance."
> Scotty would say "Ah'm holdin' 'em together, Cap'n, with spit and bail-
> ing wire, but it won't last for long."

Even though he suffered terribly through later life from a stroke, Parkinson's and Alzheimer's, he was a constant, cheery presence at public events. His star on the Hollywood Walk of Fame came in 2004. It's a shame he couldn't have been beamed up, but at least his ashes, thanks to NASA, have been fittingly launched into space, The Final Frontier, where no man had gone before.

William Shatner

B. MONTREAL, QUEBEC, 22 MARCH 1931

IT IS A VERY SCARY PLACE OUT THERE ON THE WEB looking up things relating to *Star Trek*. A Google search for James T. Kirk produces 11 *million* hits. (Winston Churchill, by comparison, produces 7,590,000.) Surely this is more than anyone could possibly want to know about a television show that, after all, ran for just three seasons three decades ago. Here is part of an entry for Captain Kirk:

> James Tiberius Kirk (Tiberius 2nd Roman Emperor 14 AD)
> Born: March 22, 2233 Riverside, Iowa, Earth
> Graduates Starfleet Academy 2254
> Promoted to Captain of Federation Starship Enterprise 2264, after
>   serving on the Republic and Farragut. The youngest to achieve
>   that rank in Starfleet history.
> Dies: 2293 and 2371 (see below)
> Not to mention the Prantares Ribbon of Commendation AND the
>   Karagite Order of Heroism.

As William Shatner, the actor who played him, once asked, "What is it about a long-dead TV series that still inspires seemingly normal grownups to paint themselves green, wear pointed polyvinyl ears and glue brown rubber omelettes to their foreheads?"

And just as puzzling: how did a classically-trained Canadian actor who began on stage at the prestigious Stratford Festival in classics like Shakespeare's *Henry V* and

Marlowe's *Tamburlaine*, who was well-reviewed in his first real film, *The Brothers Karamazov* (1958) and again in the 1961 epic *Judgment at Nuremburg*, end up as Captain Kirk in a science-fiction TV series and an icon of the 20th century? It's even more surprising because his early life didn't seem like the classic training ground for a macho Starship Captain who would get all the girls while winning the award for single-handedly saving the universe 6,439 times.

The son of a Ukrainian Jewish family, he attended the Harvard Law of Montreal's inner-city Jewish community, Baron Byng High School, whose illustrious alumni include famed writer Mordecai Richler. He then went on to graduate from McGill with a Bachelor of Commerce. But somewhere along the way, the acting bug bit and never let go. Repertory work in Montreal led to Stratford. Stratford led to Broadway, and for Shatner that led to television more than film.

The road to celebrity could scarcely have begun in humbler circumstances than in 1954, as Ranger Bill on NBC's children's series, the *Howdy Doody* show, a show that also featured another future Canadian star, Robert Goulet, as Trapper Pierre. He later appeared on just about every hit series of that era: *Dr. Kildare, Route 66, 77 Sunset Strip, Gunsmoke,* and *The Twilight Zone.*

After *Nuremburg*, he acted in the long-forgotten experimental film *Incubis*, in which the dialogue was entirely in Esperanto. Though he was much in demand, everyone, especially actors, likes a regular gig and the opportunity for that came in 1966. Casting calls went out for a new prime-time science fiction series. Winning the role of Captain Kirk was the break of a lifetime, though it didn't seem that way at the time.

Shatner described working on *Star Trek* as toiling in the salt mines of television production, slaving away in stifling, antiquated studios twelve to fifteen hours a day. Mediocre ratings, budget problems and cast infighting made it a less than idyllic experience. It's hard to believe that what would become a multibillion dollar "franchise" was, at first, just an expensive prime time flop. Though the series' creator Gene Roddenberry would seem, at this distance, to have brilliantly cast the show to boldly go where no man had gone before, the ratings never even got off the ground. It struggled from the moment the first episode, "The Man Trap," went to air on September 8, 1966. *Variety* dismissed it as being "in an incredible mess of dreary complexities at the kick-off . . . It won't work."

Only seventy-nine episodes were ever made. In his autobiography, Shatner asserts that the show's cancellation, after just its third season, was the best thing that could have happened. Though truth be told, at the time, that wasn't immediately apparent to him. The Shakespearean thespian, the TV star, thanks to the cancellation and an expensive, acrimonious divorce, was reduced to living with his dog in an aluminum camper, travelling around the country doing summer stock theatre just to get by. Feeling that he'd been typecast as Kirk didn't help. He did, however, get excellent reviews in the PBS film *The Andersonville Trial*, directed by George C. Scott, in 1970.

But two events, obscure at the time, were laying the basis for the eternal fame of the crew of the good ship *Enterprise*. First the network sold syndication rights immediately and at bargain rates, to recoup some of its intergalactic investment. It may have been the constant barrage of episodes all day, every day, or it may have been some sort of second look, because suddenly ratings rocketed.

Secondly, on a snowy January night in 1972, at the Statler Hotel in New York, a group of fans held the first *Star Trek* convention and the Trekkie phenomenon was born. The entry on the résumés of the original cast that had been an embarrassing dud, overnight became the roles they would play for the rest of their lives. Shatner shunned those conventions until the 1990s, even though they had become ubiquitous and lucrative.

In 1979, they all reunited to save the galaxy yet again, this time on the big screen in *Star Trek: The Motion Picture*. But it, too, crashed and burned. At 143 minutes in length, they took themselves far too seriously. The BBC said, "The *Enterprise* may be back at warp speed, but nothing in the movie moves more quickly than glacial." The *New York Times* called it "overblown silliness." But the box-office and especially video rentals were strong enough to prompt studio executives to dream up sequels and other Generations.

The 1982 sequel, *The Wrath of Khan*, was much more successful. "Now that's more like it!" wrote the venerable Vincent Canby of the *New York Times*. "A sequel worth its salt." In it, Kirk, now an Admiral, flees his tedious desk job to do battle with the delightfully evil Khan, played by Ricardo Montalban. Canby notes that Shatner "makes the grandest of entrances and proves he has regained his dry sense of humor markedly absent last time around." He would in time become amusingly self-deprecating about his success and style. He rocked the Trekkie Universe in a 1986 *Saturday Night Live* skit, telling actors playing weird Star Trek fans to "Get a life!" which also became the title of his autobiography. He mocked his own Kirk-like delivery, honed at countless conventions where people would insist on trying out their impersonation of him on him : I–I–I! SPEAK! as IF! Every! Other! SYLlable WAS! of DIRE! ImPORtance! And his other familiar cadence: "They-y-y-y-fireduponus . . . W-e-e-e-e returnedthat fire!"

Whatever the up-and-down reviews of the seven *Star Trek* films, they revived his career. He got a successful police series, *TJ Hooker*, and began writing and directing

Captain James T. Kirk, Star Trek. Photofest

TekWar, based on the Trek-like novels he'd written. He even directed *Star Trek V: The Final Frontier*. One reviewer wrote,

> Scene for scene, Mr. Shatner's direction is smooth and sharply focussed. He has a sure feel for keeping Star Trek just this side of camp, and for the slightly tacky, artificial look that lets us know this is all a game.

The production led to a lampoon on one of the many websites about Kirk and Shatner. Most revere him. Some eerily treat him as a real person. One, *The First Church of*

Shatnerology, as he cheerfully shares in his book, is a site that "roasts and skewers me and teases me without mercy every day of the year. It's also incredibly funny." Here is the Church's "Ode to the Final Frontier" (sung to the tune of "Rudolph the Red-Nosed Reindeer"):

> *Then one foggy Christmas Eve*
> *Roddenberry said,*
> *Shatner with your toupee so curly,*
> *Let us make a* Star Trek *movie.*
> *Then all the actors loathed him*
> *And they all began to scream*
> *Shatner the toupeed actor*
> *Cut us out of every scene.*

In No. 6, *The Undiscovered Country*, Kirk battles a Canadian-bred evil Klingon duo of Christopher Plummer and Kim Cattrall. One review said that though the cast had reached "Hairpiece Heaven . . . the dependably wry William Shatner and Leonard Nimoy are a welcome sight." Shatner loved the movie and was taken aback when the call from the studio executive came about it being time to kill off old Kirk to make way for the new, successful version starring Patrick Stewart as Captain Jean-Luc Picard. He talked to his friend Nimoy, who recalled being surprised at how difficult it was to let Spock die. Shatner reflected that he'd spent half his lifetime with Kirk. He considered fighting it, but realized the jig was up. In a plot twist only a true Trekkie can fathom, Admiral Kirk retires, and at the ceremonial christening of the new *Enterprise*, disappears into one of those holes in the Universe that had plagued the crew for decades. He's pronounced dead, but through the efforts of Captain Picard and Whoopi Goldberg, he's found and brought back to help save the crucial planet Veridian 3 from the clutches of the demented madman, played convincingly by Malcom Mcdowell. In the struggle, Kirk is finally killed and buried. The franchise "torch" had been officially passed on.

Yes, there would be more work. In *Miss Congeniality* (2000) and the sequel (2005); as a slightly bent lawyer in *The Practice*. He would even finally win an Emmy for his work on *Boston Legal*.

But he never forgot attending his first Trekkie Convention in Alberta in the early 1990s, and the feeling that he and Kirk weren't really gone after all.

Margot Kidder

B. YELLOWKNIFE, NORTHWEST TERRITORIES, 17 OCTOBER 1948

MARGOT KIDDER HAD THAT KIND OF SENSUAL CHARISMA born of the 1960s and 1970s. She could also portray in an accomplished manner a convincingly lovely vulnerability. She was so cool, she was cast in the role of a lifetime as Superman's girlfriend, Lois Lane. It is one of the most memorable scenes in film — Lois falling off a skyscraper, screaming helplessly, and suddenly grabbed in midair by the Man of Steel, the late Christopher Reeves, who says, "Don't worry. I've got you." Lane/Kidder replies, "I know you've got me. But who's got you?"

Margot Kidder was born in Yellowknife, Northwest Territories, the daughter of a mining engineer. She began acting at the University of British Columbia and was soon appearing on the CBC. With no theatrical training, she performed in numerous Canadian TV shows as a teenager before being cast in *Gaily, Gaily* (1969), an early effort by director and fellow Canadian Norman Jewison, starring Beau Bridges, Melina Mercouri and Hume Cronyn

Due to her natural talent, she paid her dues, not starving in summer stock theatre or in marginal roles. She played in substantial TV series like *Mod Squad*, *Banacek* (with George Peppard) and *Barnaby Jones* (what Buddy Ebsen did after *The Beverley Hillbillies* and *Breakfast at Tiffany's*). She did amazingly precocious work in undeservedly forgotten films like *Quackser Fortune has a Cousin in the Bronx* with Gene Wilder, and starring twice in dual roles, in future husband Brian De Palma's thriller *Sisters* (1973) and in the hard-to-find but eminently worthwhile *A Quiet Day in Belfast*

(1974). She would first play Lois Lane in 1978's *Superman: The Movie*. The *New York Times* had reservations about the film, but none about Kidder's performance:

> Margot Kidder is also most charming, revealing (is this for the first time?) that Lois Lane is the sort of newspaper reporter who puts two p's in rapist.

A series of successes followed. She hosted *Saturday Night Live*, and starred in *The Amityville Horror* in 1979. She had a very nice turn in Paul Mazursky's 1980 feature *Willie and Phil*, an American version of Francois Truffaut's French classic *Jules et Jim*.

> Much more successful is Miss Kidder, whose Jeannette, though no match for Jeanne Moreau's Catherine, is a young woman of substance and humor and even mystery, someone you can believe without ever understanding completely.

She reappeared as Lois Lane in *Superman 2* in 1980, then did acclaimed work in *Heartaches*, directed by Don Shebib, who brought us the quintessential Canadian classic *Goin' Down the Road*.

She hooked up with Richard Pryor for *Some Kind of Hero* in 1982. Again, there was more praise from the *Times*:

> Miss Kidder is direct, funny and charming as the somewhat idealized prostitute Mr. Pryor falls in love with.

She was part of the smash Quebec hit film *La Florida*, directed by George Mihalka and written by Suzette Couture.

She had already overcome many of those difficulties that life throws at us all. Fame and artistic gifts combined with bad marriages and financial problems must present a daunting set of problems. *The Canadian Encyclopedia* has this brief summary which speaks volumes:

> Kidder's career has undoubtedly been affected by personal problems and setbacks. Marriages to prominent men such as American author Thomas McGuane and French filmmaker Philippe de Broca have failed. In 1990 she was seriously injured in a car accident on the set of a TV series, which kept her from working and left her bankrupt. In 1996 she suffered a highly publicized nervous breakdown. In 1997 Kidder resumed her career with a return to live theatre.

*As Maude in **The Great Waldo Pepper** 1975. With Robert Redford. Universal*

Some believe the truest picture of a person's character doesn't come at the peak of success, but rather in the trough of their despair and how they respond. Margot Kidder recalls another formidable Legend in this book, Bea Lillie, herself no stranger to sad turns in personal fortunes. "Avanti", Lillie always said. "It's always better down the road." And Ms. Kidder has, as Joni Mitchell once wisely wrote, seen life from "Both Sides Now." And she has persevered through it all.

John Elmer Carson

B. CARMAN, MANITOBA, 27 OCTOBER 1910
D. ENCINO, CALIFORNIA, 2 JANUARY 1963

HE'S KIND OF FORGOTTEN NOW, but back in the 1930s, 1940s and 1950s, Jack Carson was one of the funniest people alive. The critics were never very kind and his jovial, oval face precluded any thought of leading man roles. But he may have the most astounding filmography of anyone in this book. He was an elite member of the underappreciated club of supporting actors. He performed in varying degrees in a lot of serious films. His wit and charisma merited star status on his own network radio shows and, for a time, his own variety show in the early days of television. He was amazingly prolific, appearing in fifty-seven movies from 1937 to 1941.

Just look at this list of films he appeared in:

Bringing Up Baby (1938), with Katherine Hepburn and Cary Grant, directed by Howard Hawks.

Mr. Smith Goes to Washington (1939), with Jimmy Stewart, directed by Frank Capra.

Arsenic and Old Lace (1944), with Cary Grant, Raymond Massey and Peter Lorre, again directed by Capra.

Mildred Pierce (1945), with Oscar-winner Joan Crawford, directed by Michael Curtiz.

*As Matt Libby in **A Star is Born** 1954 with Judy Garland and James Mason. Corbis*

A Star Is Born (1954), with Judy Garland and James Mason, directed by George Cukor.

Cat on a Hot Tin Roof (1958), with Paul Newman and Elizabeth Taylor, directed by Richard Brooks, who among many other things wrote the screenplays for *In Cold Blood* and *Elmer Gantry*.

This is just a six-pack of some of the greatest films of the 20th century. Sure, some roles were tiny, and he may have been batting ninth in the order as it were, but these were the big leagues to be sure.

Jack Carson proved his bona fide acting credentials with good performances in *Pierce*, as the icky real estate agent Wally Fay, and in *Cat* as Burl Ives' son, Gooper Pollitt.

He suffered no shortage of celebrity in his time, but the dramatic promise shown in his later films, alas, would not be fulfilled. His life was sadly cut short by cancer at the early age of 53. There is still a website, in a technology invented long after his passing, that lobbies for a Lifetime Achievement Oscar in honour of his career. That would be a nice thing to have happen.

Monique Mercure

B. MONIQUE ÉMOND, MONTREAL, QUEBEC, 14 NOVEMBER 1930

THE ZANY ANTICS OF HOLLYWOOD are always fun, but it is a genuine pleasure to consider the career, careers really, of one of the most distinguished artists Canada has ever produced; someone who has actually made significant contributions to the cultural life of her country. Quebec author Michel Coulombe writes that "few actresses have had a career as rich as that of Monique Mercure. She debuted in the 1950s and she's been part of all the great moments in Québécois and Canadian film."

Monique Mercure has had an internationally renowned reputation since her stunning win for Best Actress at the Cannes Film Festival in 1978. She was made an Officer of the Order of Canada as a result:

> Montreal actor whose reputation and popularity extend beyond
> Canada's borders. She has performed on stage, on television and in
> film–her performance as Rose Aimée in the movie *J. A. Martin pho-*
> *tographe* earned her the Palme d'Or for best actress at the Cannes Film
> Festival of 1978.

By 1994, she had earned the prestigious upgrade to the Order's Companion rank:

> A renowned actress and comedian, she has proven her talents in all
> forms of theatre. She continues to give award-winning performances,
> notably a supporting role in *Naked Lunch*, for which she won a Genie
> award in 1992. Director of the National Theatre School since 1991, she

continues to oversee the future of the School in its newly-renovated site, the Monument National, in Montreal. This is a promotion within the Order.

Her mother was an accomplished pianist. The young Monique Émond mastered the cello, married the composer Pierre Mercure at a very young age, had children, separated in 1958 (almost unheard of in the Quebec of the era) and studied drama in Paris and Montreal. Her Anglo equivalents were the likes of Kate Reid and Colleen Dewhurst, accomplished stars of the stage who film makers couldn't resist casting in movies. Mercure has played everything from Euripides to Brecht to Genet to Michel Tremblay.

This is from the *Canadian Theatre Encyclopedia*:

> . . . she has become one of the country's great actors of the classical and modern repertory. She has performed at most of the major venues in Quebec as well as performing in France and in English in England and the United States and across Canada.

J.A. Martin photographe (1977) is a stunning visual and dramatic achievement, and the happy and memorable collaboration of an All-Star team of Quebecois film makers. The director, Jean Beaudin, who was also the lead writer, would go on to make such outstanding films as the huge TV mini-series *Les filles de Caleb* with Marina Orsini and Roy Dupuis in 1990, the film adaptation of Yves Beauchemin's lovely novel *Le matou* (*The Alley Cat*) in 1995, and *Souvenirs intimes* (1999) with Pascale Bussiéres. The cameramen, as you might expect in a film about a photographer, were topnotch.

Pierre Mignon worked with legendary American director Robert Altman on *Come Back to the Five and Dime Jimmy Dean, Jimmy Dean* (Cher, Karen Black, Kathy Bates) in 1982. He was the Director of Photography on Gille Carle's not-so-minor 1983 classic *Marie Chapdelaine*, and remains a force in Quebec film. He was cinematographer for 2005's offbeat hit celebration of sexual ambivalence *C.R.A.Z.Y.* Pierre Letarte would be tabbed to shoot *The Boys of St. Vincent* in 1992, *Dieppe* in 1993, 1995's Michele Pfeiffer hit *Dangerous Minds*, and Jennifer Love Hewitt's tribute to her heroine, *The Audrey Hepburn Story* in 2000.

Produced by the National Film Board, *J.A. Martin photographe* tells the story of the Martins. Every now and then, Mr. Martin loads up his camera equipment and travels about the province taking and selling photos. After fifteen years of marriage and five children, Mme. Martin decides it's time to get reacquainted and she sets out with him. There are places in the movie where the past seems so present that you can almost reach out and touch it. In rural Quebec, there remain scenes right out of the paintings of Clarence Gagnon, A.Y. Jackson and, for that matter, Cornelius Krieghoff. The film captures that romantic sensibility of 19th-century Quebec. It was *J.A. Martin* that began the Toronto International Film Festival's tradition of kicking off the festival with a Canadian-made film. Mercure has everything that a director could ask for in an actor — charisma, wit, unconventional beauty.

Her film career would remain almost an adjunct to her life in theatre. But her filmography is really interesting. It seems as if each part was carefully chosen for a perfectly good reason. The impressive crew in *J.A. Martin*; the intellectually provocative, as in the work of Quebecois film genius, Claude Jutra and the more controversial David Cronenberg; working with one of the masters like Robert Altman; or just having a good time as *Deux femmes en or* in 1970, where she and Louise Turcot play two bored suburban wives ordering out for more than pizza. The pizza guy, the milkman, mailman, phone repair guy all come away happy, happy. It was a pretty big hit and though it is now a bit dated is still fun to watch.

Mercure went effortlessly from French to English and back on both screen and stage. Her first collaboration with Jutra was on his most avant garde work, *À tout prendre*, in 1964, a sombre piece of guerilla film making, critically well-received. It's the one that ends on a scary note as the lead character, played by Jutra himself, walks off a pier and drowns. This is nearly the same way that Jutra would commit suicide 25 years later. They worked together again on his masterpiece *Mon oncle Antoine* in 1971, then again in 1975 in *Pour le meilleur ou le pire (For Better or Worse)*.

Martin followed, but before the Cannes Jury could hand her the Best Actress award, she made a quirky film called *The Third Walker* for Canadian director Teri McLuhan (daughter of Marshall McLuhan) with fellow Canadian stage great Colleen Dewhurst and William Shatner, still in comeback mode after his Captain Kirk days on *Star Trek* were cancelled.

She went from that to Altman's *Quintet* (1979), an end-of-the-world sciencefiction piece with Paul Newman. The title refers to the game that survivors play almost to the exclusion of everything else. It ain't online poker, though. The stakes are a tad higher. You lose, you die. The ultimate reality show. Altman had an eye for Quebec talent and though this wasn't his best effort, it is still another of those interesting choices Mercure had the wisdom to make.

In 1982, Mercure made another offbeat but interesting fantasy called *The Emperor of Peru* starring Mickey Rooney. As if to prove her linguistic adaptability, she played a Peruvian character named Aunt Elsa.

Monique Mercure: "But above all else, one needs to persevere."

She jumped at the chance to work with French film great Claude Chabrol and emerging American star Jodie Foster in 1984 on *The Blood of Others*, set in the French Resistance of World War II.

She won her Best Supporting Actress Genie for David Cronenberg's bizarre 1992 film *Naked Lunch*.

As if to remind us of her ongoing membership in the upper reaches of Canada's film aristocracy, in 2005 Mercure played Malvina in rookie director Robin Aubert's snappy, homage to the David Lynch thriller *Saints-Martyr-des-Damnés*.

Mercure still made movies (like the acclaimed *The Red Violin* in 1999) while serving as Director General of the prestigious National Theatre School from 1991–1997, and then as Artistic Director until 2000, overseeing the training and graduation of the next generation of Canadian Screen Legends. Just for example, the NTS has already produced Sandra Oh, found elsewhere in these pages, and Colm Feore, whose voice you hear on the TV vignettes on which this book is based.

For such a refined and accomplished woman, Monique Mercure has a remarkably simple philosophy, related in *The Canadian Encyclopedia*:

> Talent is one thing. So is luck. But above all things else, one needs to persevere.

Donald Sutherland

B. SAINT JOHN, NEW BRUNSWICK, 17 JULY 1935

IT MIGHT BE HARD TO TELL, but each chapter of this volume is the product of a little film festival, seeing or revisiting the movies made by our subjects. It was obvious that some would be wonderful. Norman Jewison and his great work; Glenn Ford, one of Hollywood's most accomplished leading men. Some were nice surprises: Marie Dressler in classics like *Dinner at 8* and *Min & Bill*; Catherine O'Hara in the very satisfying but acquired taste of *Waiting for Guffman* and *Best in Show*. But if the weather's bad, or you're just looking to chill, try the Donald McNichol Sutherland Film Festival.

Mr. Sutherland is a distinguished artist, an Officer of the Order of Canada, with solid intellectual and political activist credentials. He has Emmys and Golden Globe awards to his credit, along with decades of lavish praise from the crème de la crème of film critics. But there are two more aspects to his many talents to point out. For all his acclaimed interpretations of characters from comic to classic, he excels at embodying sex and evil.

Cases in point: *Don't Look Now* in 1973 as an ill-fated art historian married to Julie Christie who gets into creepy things having to do with omens and the trauma of coping with the death of their young daughter. Then there was *Invasion of the Body Snatchers* (1978), one of the few remakes infinitely better than its original (1956), in no small part due to Sutherland's performance. A short summary may not make much sense, but basically aliens land and turn humans into mindless, placid pod people. He and co-star Elizabeth Driscoll barely escape the dreaded fate for almost the whole movie.

Secondly, Sutherland is still as au courant as heartthrobs half his age, such as Brad Pitt. There is a very unforgiving but endlessly entertaining website called RottenTomatoes.com that rates movies and actors based on the percentage of good vs. bad reviews, both professional and amateur. Mr. Sutherland retains a "fresh" rating of 63%, tied with Mr. Pitt, not bad for an energetic veteran who is past 70. Both are way ahead of Ben Affleck and Nicole Kidman and just trail Sean Connery and Denzel Washington. Of course, all are far behind the heavyweight Tomato champion Marilyn Monroe at 91%.

Four of Sutherland's films achieved perfection, a 100% approval rating. *Don't Look Now* hit 96%, but that may have had more to do with the legendary sex scene between him and Julie Christie. The pictures of Tomato perfection are:

The Bedford Incident, a military classic featuring Sidney Poitier, in which Sutherland plays a minor role. *The Dirty Dozen*, perhaps the greatest "guy" flick of all time, in which twelve quite despicable prison inmates are made into an elite World War II unit to take out a decadent den of German generals. Sutherland described his role as "one of the bottom six," a psycho-farmboy killer. *The Day of the Locust* registered 100%, as did the minor 1971 classic *Klute*, in which Sutherland plays the low-key title character of a stolid, suburban detective on a missing-persons case, while Jane Fonda turns on the megawatts. The movie should have been called "Bree" after the high-rent call girl she plays, Bree Daniels, riveting enough to win the Oscar for Best Actress. It was the kind of performance that blows the rest of the cast away, but Sutherland's was praised as well, like a reliable rhythm section underscoring Fonda's dazzling dramatic riffs:

> With Fonda and Sutherland, you have actors who understand and sym-
> pathize with their characters, and you have a vehicle worthy of that
> sort of intelligence.

Sutherland's early interest in the arts was limited to a part-time radio job in his teens. While studying engineering at the University of Toronto, out of nowhere, he auditioned for a play, did it and soon after left the country, determined to become an actor in England. As the usual starving actor, he did repertory theatre and played some classics, even the BBC's *Hamlet*, with fellow Canadian Christopher Plummer, and Michael Redgrave (now Sir Michael). He was especially awestruck at the presence of Robert Shaw, perhaps best known for his role in the Redford/Newman blockbuster *The Sting* (also the convincing lead in the Canadian adaptation of the classic Brian Moore novel *The Luck of Ginger Coffey*). Sutherland also got gigs in the classic 1960s British TV series *The Saint* and *The Avengers*.

In 1964 the actor got his first big break, making his screen debut in the Italian

*As John Klute in **Klute** 1971. With Jane Fonda. Photofest*

horror film *The Castle of the Living Dead*. His dual role as a young soldier and an old hag was enough to convince various casting directors of a certain kind of versatility, and Sutherland was soon appearing in a number of remarkably schlocky films, including *Dr. Terror's House of Horrors* and *Die! Die! Darling* (both 1965). He recalled how his long, ungainly appearance led him to unusual roles:

I was always cast as an artistic homicidal maniac. But at least I was artistic!

This brings us back up to Dirty Dozen time, when he was about to break through in a big way. Major critics discovered his new work, revisited the old and found him intriguing. *The Split*, a heist movie from 1968 put him firmly on the radar screen, as yet another cold-blooded killer type, e.g., "The last man I killed for $5,000. For $85,000 I'd kill you 17 times."

The *Times* applauded:

> Although his role is not major, Donald Sutherland is remarkable. As the baby-faced soldier who impersonates a colonel in *The Dirty Dozen*, as the troubled friend of the family in *Interlude* and particularly as an aristocrat dying of leukemia in *Joanna*, Mr. Sutherland has shown a range of comic-sentimental talent that is absolutely star quality.

Suddenly *Time* magazine was doing very friendly features on him:

> Sutherland is very much the un-Hollywood man. Most of his clothes are hand-me-downs from his movies, and his only two luxuries are his sports cars, a Ferrari and a Lotus (on which he is still making payments). A big evening is dinner with his wife in an obscure restaurant, a movie, listening to records (anything from Mahler to the Cream) or playing with his three children.

Sutherland also became deeply involved in the anti-Vietnam war movement. In his breakout year, 1970, there were two films that reflected his emerging passion and anti-establishment persona. First (and definitely on the festival list) was *Kelly's Heroes*, a dark wartime comedy, a send-up of the usual homage-to-brave-soldiers genre like *The Longest Day* and *A Bridge Too Far*. A group of World War II GIs abandon their unit to hunt for a huge treasure of German gold bars. The key to success is the small tank unit, headed by a gum-chewing space cadet named Oddball. The character is brilliantly played by Sutherland as a hippy somehow magically transported from the Age of Aquarius in San Francisco to the European killing ground of the 1940s, complete with an aversion to anyone with "negative vibes." It may be more about American disillusionment with Vietnam and their military icons than World War II, but still it's a minor classic.

That same year also saw, for Sutherland, the cinematic version of a long, tape-measure home run. As the play-by-play man would say, "He got all of that one, folks." *M*A*S*H* (the acronym stands for Mobile Army Surgical Hospital), was directed by

As Captain Benjamin Franklin "Hawkeye" Pierce in **M*A*S*H** *1970. With Elliott Gould. Corbis*

Robert Altman and set in the Korean War. Sutherland and sidekick Elliott Gould play supremely talented army surgeons, wittily but bitterly cynical and resentful of authority of any kind. Almost sacrilegiously named Benjamin Franklin Pierce, a.k.a. "Hawkeye," Sutherland's character makes but one concession to the circumstances of that war, though officially it wasn't *called* a war at that time but a "military action." Waving his dry martini around the tent, lamenting the absence of olives, he declares, "We have to make some concessions. We are only three miles from the front."

There is one quality that sets this apart from other satirical war movies, as Roger Ebert perceptively observes that

> it is the flat-out, poker-faced hatred in M*A*S*H that makes it work. Most comedies want us to laugh at things that aren't really funny; in this one we laugh precisely because they're not funny. We laugh, that we may not cry.

Time magazine described the effect of M*A*S*H on Sutherland's career:

> Until recently Actor Donald Sutherland was the kind of person who got overlooked at cocktail parties. The face was familiar, but then hundreds of guys are tall and skinny with a resemblance to a tall pencil or a short television tower. Meanwhile, in one film after another for the past two years, Sutherland has been filling the screen with a low-key presence that has left critics grasping for adjectives and audiences grasping for his name. All that is changing, however, for he is becoming established as one of the finest talents in the cinematic youth movement.

Strange how Hollywood movies can reflect the profound, painful divisions in society. M*A*S*H just won one major Academy Award for Best Writing by Ring Lardner Jr. The runaway Oscar winner the year that Sutherland had literally acted out his heart and soul as Oddball and Hawkeye, was *Patton*, the red-white-and-blue biography of the much-revered, though controversial American warrior as played, brilliantly, by George C. Scott.

A complete look at Sutherland's films, to show their breadth and diversity, would merit a book. Great directors called on him: Fellini for *Casanova* (1976) and Bertolucci for *1900* (1976), in which he played a psychopathic, fascist rapist-murderer. The sexual predator became the clumsiest waiter ever in *Kentucky Fried Movie* (1977) and a dope-smoking underachieving prof in *Animal House* (1978). His best personal reviews came for meaty and quirky supporting roles: the father in *Ordinary People* (1980) an extraordinarily insightful and engaging film; Stockard Channing's husband in *Six Degrees of Separation* (1993); Mr. X in 1991's *JFK*; the title hero in *Bethune* (1990); the pyromaniac in Ron Howard's *Backdraft* (1991). They really liked him as Jerry O'Neil, one of the aging astronauts in *Space Cowboys* (2000):

> Mr. Sutherland, nearly sneaks off with the movie in his hip pocket . . . (his) reedy whisper delivers a stream of pickup lines that seem to come

from the October 1958 issue of Playboy his younger self is seen perusing early in the movie.

It's tough to "sneak off" with a movie with a cast that includes accomplished screenhogs Clint Eastwood, Tommy Lee Jones and James Garner. Sutherland became one of that extremely rare Hollywood breed, the "star-character actor."

The Guardian claimed his best work came in John Frankenheimer's TV movie *Path to War* set in the Lyndon Johnson White House in the worst of the Vietnam quagmire:

> But his finest role in recent years was as presidential adviser Clark
> Clifford, opposite Michael Gambon's explosive LBJ. Sutherland's slow,
> horrified head-turn as LBJ announces his decision not to run for re-
> election is a 10-second lesson in all the things that make Donald
> Sutherland a great actor.

And he by no means coasted into the 21st century, making some fifteen films between 2003 and 2006. There was yet more critical acclaim for his "pitch-perfect" portrayal of Colin Farrell's boozy, talkative neighbour in Robert Towne's *Ask the Dust*. And all this was on top of his deliciously repulsive character, Nathan Templeton on TV's weekly drama series *Commander-in-Chief*.

A *New York Times* critic wrote this nice little tribute to Sutherland, ostensibly for a 2001 film called *Panic*:

> Once a year or so, Donald Sutherland shakes the boredom out of his
> voice, runs a steady hand over the lapels of one of his immaculately
> hand-tailored jackets and gives a performance. That alone is reason
> enough to see *Panic*.

But it could also be the reason the Sutherland Film Festival would be a grand time. If you have somehow managed to miss his films, you may not even know how familiar his voice has become, narrating a remarkable number of radio and television commercials — or it could be his son Kiefer as they do sound very much alike. And as postscript, he named son Kiefer after Warren Kiefer, who gave him his first big break in *The Castle of the Living Dead*, and another son, Roeg, for Nicholas Roeg who directed him in the still riveting *Don't Look Now*.

Norman Jewison

B. TORONTO, ONTARIO, 21 JULY 1926

NORMAN JEWISON'S FILM CAREER BEGAN IN ADOLESCENCE at Kew Beach in Toronto's East End. He begged and borrowed dimes, the price of admission to the Beach Theatre to see not one, but two features each Saturday. That evening he would regale the gang by recreating every scene, especially the ones that involved dying. According to him, that melodramatic bent plus the salesmanship he discovered in his father's store laid the foundations of his future craft.

> Years later I would find myself in New York, pitching a story, playing
> all the parts, prancing, declaiming, hoping they would like the pitch
> enough to give me the green light. It's not much different from my
> performances I put on in the Beach, only the stakes are higher."

"Doin' the dance" is what he called it. Convincing studios and networks to spend millions on his projects. He even rated others directors on the same scale: "Coppola was a terrific dancer. So was Fellini. Hitchcock may have been the best." But it took a little while for the Dance to work.

After an uneventful stint in the military, he enrolled at the University of Toronto (with Johnny Wayne and Frank Shuster), constantly putting on shows and working menial jobs. One summer at the Banff Springs Hotel, he wrangled a role as an extra in the long-forgotten movie *Canadian Pacific* (1949) with big-time cowboy star Randolph Scott. Everyone, it seemed to him, said, "Come to Hollywood and give me a call." So he did. But they didn't call back. His first foray to Tinseltown was disastrous. He ran out of money, sleeping on the beach in Santa Monica until the cold forced him into some apartment lobby for the night. He hitchhiked all the way back to Toronto, drove a cab for a while and then inexplicably decided to seek fame and fortune in "this terrible business" in London, England.

He got by, even doing some writing for the legendary Bernard Braden. He wasn't sleeping on park benches. He had a flat in Notting Hill, but by Christmas 1951, he didn't have enough coins to heat it. When a friend offered to pay his way home to try out for the newly formed CBC-TV network, he jumped at the chance. He ended up directing hundreds of live shows at CBC, with their stomach-churning, nerve-rattling pressure.

CBS recruited him and he was noticed for stewarding Judy Garland, then a deeply troubled and erratic diva, through an entire series without mishap. It was his entree to the world of Hollywood and feature film. As he began his first feature, *Forty Pounds of Trouble* (1962), the star of the movie, Tony Curtis introduced him to the cast and crew. "This is Norman Jewison. He may look like your paper boy, but he's your director."

"The Dance" began to pay off. There were a few successful light comedies with Doris Day, Rock Hudson and Carl Reiner. Then came his first (but by no means last) "bomb," *The Art of Love* (1965). He sank into a depression that he could only alleviate by lying face down on the linoleum floor in his house. He hired a high-powered, table-banging American agent, and, in his memoirs, urged all Canadian performers to get one. Canadians are learning but still too polite, according to Jewison. If it weren't for American agents, he said, Jim Carrey would still be doing bar mitzvahs in Toronto.

So despite the sordid fate of *The Art of Love*, his new fire-breathing advocate, Abe Lastfogel, got him a hot property to direct with impressive Hollywood legends. *The Cincinnati Kid* (1965) is a story about the world of high-stakes poker. The new young hotshot who bets on anything, played by Steve McQueen, inexorably works his way to a showdown with the reigning champ, played by Edward G. Robinson. The ending is anything but conventional Hollywood, and the reviews were mixed, but Jewison called it his favourite movie of all. It was the one that finally made him feel like a "real" director.

With much-boosted confidence, he began displaying a distinctly liberal social conscience and a willingness to step fearlessly into the frying pan. In 1965, the world was still breathing a sigh of relief, just months after the Cuban Missile crisis brought the US and USSR to the brink of nuclear war. Jewison picked up a Robert Benchley novel about a hapless Soviet submarine crew accidentally grounded near a bucolic New

England hamlet. They desperately try to hijack a boat big enough to tow them off the sandbar before the US Air Force blows them out of the water and starts World War III.

The Russians Are Coming, the Russians Are Coming (1966) was a deft comic political satire with wonderful performances from a then-unknown Alan Arkin, Jonathan Winters and Jewison's old pal, Carl Reiner (though Jack Lemmon had been his first choice). Portraying Russian sailors as ordinary human beings with things in common with the American townsfolk was nothing if not audacious. It was nominated for Best Picture, and Arkin for Best Actor. Not long after, Jewison was introduced to the great (and notoriously conservative) John Wayne who asked, "So are you one of those goddamned pinkos?" The movie made him famous, even controversial. And so he stepped right back into the frying pan.

He followed the next year with *In the Heat of the Night* (1967), which boldly barged into America's hot-button domestic issues — race relations, segregation and civil rights. In the movie, a young, intelligent, well-dressed detective from Philadelphia named Virgil Tibbs is seconded to a case in the Deep South. The incendiary twist is that Mr. Tibbs, superbly played by Sidney Poitier, is an African-American in an area where people could be lynched just for the colour of their skin. The script had a scene in which a wealthy Southern "gentleman" objects to Tibbs' tone of voice and slaps him. Tibbs slap him right back.

The premise and the plot were so fraught with tension that some of the cast and crew, including co-star Rod Steiger, weren't sure they could do it. No movie had ever dared to allow a black man strike a white man before. But, it was shot, and it won five Oscars in 1968, including Best Picture and Best Actor for Steiger's endearing portrayal of the gum-chewing, pot-bellied, redneck local PO-lice Chief who ends up with a (small) soft spot for Virgil.

Heat was Jewison's master work, a true cinema classic. Injustice and racism were two themes he often returned to. His hopes for a Best Director Oscar were dashed when the Academy chose Mike Nichols for *The Graduate*, but in tragic testament to how reflective of American society Jewison's film really was, the Oscars were postponed that year to mourn the assassination of Dr. Martin Luther King.

By this time, he could effortlessly cross thematic boundaries, from searing, to syrupy, to satire, to stylish. *The Thomas Crown Affair* (1968) did touch on themes of the individual versus the establishment, power struggles and betrayal. But as Jewison said himself, this film was more about style. It's a skilled piece of storytelling, with plots within plots and wheels within wheels, as heard in the Oscar-winning song "Windmills of Your Mind." Jewison reunited with Steve McQueen, casting him as a thief who raises stealing to an art form, and Faye Dunaway as the investigator who pursues him

*Directing **Jesus Christ Superstar** 1973. Universal*

professionally and otherwise. No male Baby Boomer who saw this as a teenager will never forget the things Faye could do with a chess board in their big love scene.

Jewison followed in 1969 with *Gaily, Gaily*, a comedy about turn-of-the-century Chicago, featuring fellow Canadian Hume Cronyn's devilish rendition of a corrupt politician.

Jewison, his wife, Dixie, and Melina Mercouri were having Chinese food en route to a meeting with the leading contender for the Democratic Party's presidential nomination (and one of Jewison's heroes) when word came that Bobby Kennedy had been shot. Jewison was devastated. He wrote that, for him, his American dream ended that moment. He fled the States in revulsion, and moved to England.

He had long wanted to make a musical and would now make two. Neither *Fiddler on the Roof* (1971) nor *Jesus Christ Superstar* (1973), with a score from no less than Andrew Lloyd Webber, were very well received. Jewison came back to Canada in 1985 to make one film in his native country. *Agnes of God* is an eerie religious mystery that stars a radiant Jane Fonda, but was stolen by Ann Bancroft's Mother Superior.

He continued to be able to do his dance and over the next fifteen years went from the whimsical romance of *Moonstruck* (1987) with Cher and Nicholas Cage, and the charm of *Only You* (1994) with Marisa Tomei and Robert Downey Jr, , to the power of Denzel Washington's lead role as the wronged boxer in *The Hurricane* (1999).

The Academy finally bestowed an Oscar to him in 1998, the Irving Thalberg Award for a body of work of high quality. "I have intended," he has written, "to show humanity as fallible, sensitive, befuddled but redeemable, rather than mindlessly, relentlessly violent."

Beginning in the 1980s he was the driving force behind the establishment of the Canadian Film Centre to promote the production of more Canadian films. He blamed funding institutions for the lack of Canadian movies. "They will bankroll real estate and Cuban tomatoes, transit systems in Brazil and oil in the Sudan. But go see a Canadian banker about a movie and he'll throw up his hands."

Still long after a normal retirement age, there are projects on the go. As the great William Wyler once told him, "It's not over till your legs give out, kid."

Arthur Hiller

B. EDMONTON, ALBERTA, 22 NOVEMBER 1923

OVER THE YEARS, MOVIE REVIEWERS have officially changed his name to Arthur (*Love Story*) Hiller, as if the director can't be named without the insertion of the 1970 blockbuster hit that earned him an Oscar nomination.

Critics have loved him:

> Over a long and distinguished career, Arthur Hiller has consistently managed . . . riveting storytelling in a unique way that few film makers have done.

And loved him not:

> The translation from theatrical musical to movie musical doesn't get much more disastrous than in *Man of La Mancha*, a cheap, muddled, and badly put-together debacle that resoundingly establishes Arthur Hiller (who directed *Love Story* and *Silver Streak*) as one of cinemas' most hit-and-miss directors.

Until *Love Story*, Hiller had followed a conventional, linear career path from war service in the Royal Canadian Air Force, to a Masters in Psychology, to directing live television at the CBC. He went on to Los Angeles and throughout the 1950s and 1960s directed hundreds of episodes of some of the biggest series on television: *Gunsmoke*, *Perry Mason*, *Playhouse 90*, *Route 66*.

He directed his first feature in 1957, although the tagline for *The Careless Years* suggests something better left alone:

> Girls From the "Right" Kind of Home . . . Stumbling Into the "Wrong" Kind of Love!

Next came *The Wheeler Dealers* in 1963, with Lee Remick and James Garner as a Texas oilman wheelin', dealin' and romancin' in New York.

The following year, the Hiller/Garner collaboration continued, and produced a minor classic. Perhaps more important for Hiller and his career, it was his first collaboration with screenwriter Paddy Chayevsky, best known for his Oscar-winning script for *Network* (1976). Hiller later said that Chayevsky was the only real genius he ever worked with. *The Americanization of Emily* (1964) is the best movie you've never heard of. Hiller claimed he only got the job because more senior directors considered it too dark, too anti-American and too anti-war. In fact, you can find it on a website about classic anti-war films. But it's more a dark satire than anti-war, and as for anti-American, Garner as Commander Charlie Madison, the would-be "Ugly American" gives as good as he gets to Julie Andrews, his British assistant and love interest.

Madison has a charming thesis that cowardice will save the world, but there is seriously thoughtful stuff beneath: It's not war that's bad, it's the glorification of war that will be the end of us all. The razor-sharp script, the tremendous chemistry between Garner and fellow officer James Coburn, Hiller's controversial choice to shoot in black and white when colour had become the Next Big Thing, his almost dialogue-free montage that delivers the gut-wrenching terror of the last yards in the landing craft before hitting the beach, and the very satisfying and unexpected plot twist at the end all might make *Emily* the only war satire that may leave you trying not to sniffle at the end. Hiller called it the favourite of all his films, and so did Garner.

There were a series of competent, forgettable movies for the rest of the 1960s, though Hiller had no trouble attracting major talent. He directed Warren Beatty and Leslie Caron in *Promise Her Anything* (1965), Natalie Wood, Peter Falk and Jonathon Winters in *Penelope* (1966), and Alan Arkin in *Popi* (1969).

British and American film makers were fascinated by the dramatic battles in North Africa in World War II between the Allies' famed Desert Rats under Field Marshal Montgomery and the German Afrika Corps under General Rommel. In 1967, Hiller contributed one of the better versions in *Tobruk*, the real story of a suicide mission crossing the desert to destroy the German fuel depot in the town of Tobruk. The cast was led by Rock Hudson (as Canadian Major Donald Craig), and *TV Guide* called

On set of **The Lonely Guy** 1984. Universal

it a "well-paced and frequently exciting effort." *Tobruk* was nominated for the Oscar for Special Effects.

Hiller then directed a heroic performance by Jack Lemmon in *The Out of Towners* (1970), and followed that with *Love Story*, the top box-office hit of 1970 that received seven Oscar nominations. *Love Story* was a shameless tear-jerker that critics hated and audiences loved.

> What can you say about a twenty-five-year-old girl who died? That she was beautiful and brilliant? That she loved Mozart and Bach, the Beatles, and me?

Those opening lines are from Oliver Barrett IV (Ryan O'Neal) on the recent loss of his beautiful young wife, Jenny Cavalleri (Ali McGraw). Maybe parts of it jar now because it is all so antiseptically Hollywood, given that it was released the same year as the student shootings at Kent State, the US invasion of Cambodia, and the October Crisis in Canada. In *Love Story*, no one has a hair out of place, and violent confrontation tops out at snowball fights — all of which probably explains its runaway success. Roger Ebert said that he read the book by Erich Segal in fourteen minutes. His film review makes Hiller sound like an absolute genius for making something of such thin material:

> The fact is, however, that the film of *Love Story* is infinitely better than the book. I think it has something to do with the quiet taste of Arthur Hiller, its director, who has put in all the things that Segal thought he was being clever to leave out. Things like color, character, personality, detail, and background.

The biggest rave reviews of all likely came from Hiller's bank manager, but they are unrecorded.

1975 would bring a great Oscar-nominated performance from Maximilian Schell in *The Man in the Glass Booth*, adapted from the powerful play written by actor Robert Shaw (you'd recognize him from *The Sting*) and based on the life of Nazi Adolph Eichmann. Ebert lauded the film's director:

> Hiller's direction is effective at gradually uncovering the hell of Goldman-Dorf's torturous past. At first we're uncertain how to take this strange character, striding about his penthouse and changing the subject — obsessively and urgently — every 30 seconds. But without ever seeming to explain, Hiller quietly leads us into his world.

The Silver Streak (1976) was a comedy shot around Toronto's Union Station that involves murder on a train and stars Gene Wilder, Richard Pryor and Jill Clayburgh. The scene where Mr. Pryor tries to disguise the very pallid Mr. Wilder as an African American and teach him how to act like one is comedy gold. It got less than stellar reviews, but made a lot of money and is still well worth a look.

Critics never ever write about his efforts outside the film world. In awarding him their 2004 Humanitarian Award, the Israeli Film Festival cited the risky work he'd undertaken:

> In the 1970s, Mr. Hiller and his wife risked their freedom when they smuggled books and clothing into the Soviet Union for the "Refuseniks," who had been stripped of their jobs and rights after applying to leave. Mr. Hiller had secret meetings with them, and he and his wife were instrumental in getting some of the families out.

He also worked for the Friends of Israel Disabled Veterans. In 2002, Hiller received the Jean Hersholt Humanitarian Award from the Academy of Motion Picture Arts and Sciences, and in fact served four terms as the Academy's president.

Despite his humanitarian awards and though he rarely made box-office flops, he was never granted membership in the charmed circle of critics' favourites whose stinkers were excused for "striving too high" or for having a faulty screenplay. But then having an Oscar nomination and a greatly enhanced bank account from a movie like *Love Story* means never having to say you're sorry.

Zacharias Kunuk

B. KAPUIVIK, BAFFIN ISLAND, 1957

ATANARJUAT (*THE FAST RUNNER*), DIRECTED BY ZACHARIAS KUNUK, was the first feature film ever made in the Inuit language of Inuktikut. In 2001, the Inuit director won the coveted Caméra d'Or (Golden Camera) for Best First Feature.

The following is a sample of the reviews that celebrated the film's stunning success:

From A. O. Scott of the *New York Times*:

The Fast Runner, however, is not merely an interesting document from a far-off place; it is a masterpiece. Mr. Kunuk's film, which won the Caméra d'Or for best first feature at last year's Cannes International Film Festival, is much more than an ethnographic curiosity. It is, by any standard, an extraordinary film, a work of narrative sweep and visual beauty that honors the history of the art form even as it extends its perspective.

From *The Village Voice*:

Mysterious, bawdy, emotionally intense, and replete with virtuoso throat singing, this three-hour movie is engrossing from first image to last, so devoid of stereotype and cosmic in its vision it could suggest the rebirth of cinema. As the arctic light and landscape beggar description, so the performances go beyond acting, and the production itself seems little short of miraculous.

From *The (Manchester) Guardian:*

> A naked Inuit man, long dark hair flying behind him, runs for his life across a limitless, frozen Arctic plain, leaping across the icy waters, pursued by three fellow Inuit, hunting spears in hand, bent on internecine slaughter. It is hard to think of a more striking image in recent film – and it is just one of many reasons why *Atanarjuat (the Fast Runner)* will take cinemagoers' breath away like an unplanned plunge into Baffin Bay.

As might be expected, the intersection of an ancient culture with an oral tradition with the film industry of the 21st century makes for stories within stories within stories. *The Fast Runner* is a film adaptation of the ancient Inuit legend of Atanarjuat. It is an epic tale reminiscent of Homer and Shakespeare. Traditionally, it is a cautionary tale told to young people to keep them on what we would call "the straight and narrow."

Set in an unspecified time that could be any time in the last thousand years, the rivalry between two would-be suitors, Atanarjuat (actor Natar Unguulak) and Oki (Peter-Henry Arnatsiaq) escalates into a huge feud, replete with murder, rape and adultery wrought by evil spirits that have been unleashed by the breaking of taboos, and crude humour that the spirits have nothing to do with.

Atanarjuat escapes the murderous wrath of Oki the only way he can — by running, completely naked, as fast as he can, over the icy infinity of the eastern Arctic. Spirits guide him across the treacherous ice, his feet bleeding profusely as if from stigmata. He is found passed out on the ice, his determined killer not far behind, and rescued. The runner returns home and the resolution of the movie deals with the Inuit ways of dealing with evil, of putting the genie back in the bottle.

There are at least two scenes that the critics refer to above that are unforgettable. The first is the naked man, running and running into the unforgiving landscape, as if descending into deeper levels of Dante's hell. The other is the utterly brutal fighting ritual that involves the two combatants taking turns pounding on each other's temples, with no self-defense allowed, until only one remains standing.

Most of the cast are non-professionals, and though Kunuk conveys many things through his camera, above all he portrays his people with dignity and resolve. Even the extra highlights on the DVD are a must-watch, in some ways as fascinating as the film itself. You'll laugh at Unguulak (as he does himself), wrapped in a blanket in a blanket between takes, hopping up and down to warm his feet (couldn't someone have brought

*Cast of **The Journals of Knud Rasmussen** 2004. Isuma Productions*

an extra pair of boots?). In contrast is Arnatsiaq, who portrays Oki's homicidal rage in a way that brings to mind Jack Nicholson in *The Shining*, also between takes, wearing a leather jacket and listening to his MP3 player.

There is also a description of the way that the running scene was shot, with a team of men pulling the cameraman on a sled alongside the actor, and a description of shooting the scene in which Unguulak stumbles and falls into a shallow pool of frigid water, how his "belly was numb for a day and a half." Just another day at the office in Igloolik.

It is difficult to think of another film that is shot in such loving, definitive detail. In his interview on the DVD, Kunuk talks repeatedly about the need to "get things right," down to the minutiae, things that Southerners haven't taken the care to portray properly, clearly much to his annoyance. Things like the real way to handle a seal-oil lamp or fresh-killed meat; how to make and light an igloo. He explains that he grew tired of seeing his people misrepresented and therefore took up a camera and has been documenting "The Ways" for twenty-five years.

Strictly speaking, tradition should have dictated that Kunuk follow his father into being a nomadic hunter. But he was sent to school in Igloolik (population 1,200), where despite that fact that there was no television at the time, he became enthralled with "Cowboy and Indian" movies. He began making soapstone carvings and in 1981 traded some of them for a camera. He described his motivation to become a film maker in an interview with *Cineaste Magazine*:

> My old man would come back from hunting and sit around with his buddies, drinking tea and telling terrific stories, and you wished you would have been there to see it. One way of capturing it was through the camera.

Kunuk eventually became the senior producer and station manager for Inuit Broadcasting, where he was able to make TV series and documentaries.

Principal photography for his first feature began in 1996, but chronic money problems shut them down more than once because of bizarre regulations that capped funding for Aboriginal film projects at $100,000, a pittance compared to English and French productions, and a tiny fraction of the nearly $2 million dollars they ended up needing and eventually finding. As he told National Public Radio, the experience seemed more than unfair:

> How oppressed can a race of people be? Because you're in English, you get a bigger budget. Because you're French, you get a bigger budget. Because you're an Aboriginal, you get the lowest budget. In the land of freedom, that doesn't sound right at all. Everybody should be equal because we all pay taxes. As Canadians, I thought we had the right to make this film. And we did have the right to make this film but we had to go into battle and defeat the system.

He succeeded and his success fundamentally changed the funding system in Canada and has been a boon to young Aboriginal film makers who benefit both from Kunuk's inspiration and the wake-up call to people who finance films.

Home base for Kunuk is still Igloolik, thousands of kilometers north of Montreal, and a company called Igloolik Isuma Productions that is 75% Inuit-owned and the producer of *Atanarjuat*. The film proved to be Canada's highest-grossing film of 2002, earning receipts of over US$6 million. It is also an important employer in a town that is sadly plagued by the too-usual sad, indefensible statistics in Aboriginal towns. Isuma's website states its mission:

> Isuma's mission is to produce independent community-based media — video, audio, TV and now Internet — to preserve and enhance Inuit culture and language, and to create jobs and needed economic development in Igloolik and Nunavut. In 1991, with support from Canada Council of the Arts, Isuma created Tarriaksuk Video Centre, a non-profit TV training and equipment centre. Tarriaksuk sponsored Arnait Video Productions (Women's Video Workshop), Inuusiq Youth Drama Workshop and began local broadcasting through cable TV Channel 24. Since 1995 Channel 24 has produced over 300 news and current affairs programs called *Nunatinniit* (*At Our Place*).

Isuma's second feature, *The Journals Of Knud Rasmussen* is, in the company's own words, "an epic tragedy set in and around Igloolik in the 1920s." It tells the story of the last great Inuit Shaman, besieged by the modern onslaught of Christianity and capitalism. It's an important era and topic for Kunuk:

> My parents are very religious and Christian, but when you start to think about it, you start to think about this 4,000-year history, and in the last 50 years, 75 years maybe, people became Christian and become from top of the food chain to the bottom of the food chain. Doesn't really make sense. As I get older, I start to think how come we dumped our religion for this new religion. You start to ask about it and they say, "Oh, our old religion had hundreds of taboos. We traded them for Ten Commandments."

Atanarjuat was made with obvious pride. Making a statement for a neglected, misunderstood society, Kunuk's mission is to cure the Southerners of their bias and misconceptions about his people with tough, yet awesomely beautiful works of art. He has become a nomad like his father, but of a much different sort, travelling the world now, as if hunting, not for walrus and caribou, but for recognition and respect for his people.

Back home in Igloolik the tradition is honoured. Kunuk is a hunter, and a member of the Board of Igloolik Co-op and Hunters and Trappers.

*One of 6 Genies for **Atanajurat (The Fast Runner)** 2002. Toronto Star*

Sandra Oh

B. NEPEAN, ONTARIO, 20 JULY 1971

THERE ARE MANY LEVELS TO SANDRA OH, all of them interesting. She has a well-earned place in that elite category of youthful veteran, as a precociously talented actress who can lay claim to a list of commercial and critical successes while still young. Many people would agree that just her famous last scene in *Sideways* in 2004 should instantly qualify her as a Screen Legend. (You know, the one that makes you suddenly and profoundly understand that old quote about hell, fury and a woman scorned?)

But there are more important, substantive reasons for her inclusion here. And since her days as an Honours student at Sir Robert Borden High in Nepean (just a little west down the Queensway from Ottawa), Ms. Oh has been a substantive woman.

She is among, if not atop, the cadre of a new generation of Canadian stars in Hollywood. But she is also a woman with a mission. She has taken on the formidable task of forcing the movie-making establishment, still largely male and white, to consider issues of race and gender on her terms. And now, not later. Just consider that it took the film industry over seventy years to make a film allowing a white female to have an African-American boyfriend (Catherine Houghton and the devastatingly charismatic Sidney Poitier in *Guess Who's Coming to Dinner?* [1967]). So, Oh's is no small task. But then there has always been something about her style and career choices that suggest a fearless heart — not to mention that she can handle the business end of a motorcycle helmet.

Born to a family of Korean descent, Oh's first two hugely attention-grabbing roles were as young Chinese women in *The Diary of Evelyn Lau* (1993) and *Double Happiness* (1994). What enraged her was the misguided political correctness that suggested Koreans should play Koreans, Chinese should play Chinese, etc, etc, putting constraints on her career that white males don't even think about. She put it this way on her website:

> I completely understand saying that you want to be specific to the ethnicity, but that rule never applies to white people . . . Ralph Fiennes can play an English person, a German person, a Polish person, a Jewish person. He can play anything, and no one questions him. He is a handsome, Caucasian-looking-ish man. But what I have big problems with is when people put those limits on me . . . there always has to be a quantifier or qualifier when it comes to me.

So far, hers appears to be the loudest voice on the issue, and, it seems, forceful enough to be making some sort of progress. Of course Hollywood is the kind of place whose interest in your sense of social justice is directly related to the gross revenue of your last movie. For instance, Denzel Washington has the awards, track record and screen/box-office credentials to decide he'd like to play Brutus in *Julius Caesar* on Broadway, as he did in 2005.

When reading Oh's convictions on racially based career limitations, there is a strong echo of another Legend in this book, Jay Silverheels, whose agenda also went beyond fame and fortune to enhancing the opportunities for aspiring actors from a cinematically marginalized community.

Nepean, Ontario is a short commute from Ottawa and a perfectly fine piece of suburbia with clean, safe streets and a Junior B hockey team. But it is in so many ways a long way from the beach at Malibu. Oh's first passion was dance, starting with ballet lessons at the age of 4. A precocious talent, in her teens she was acting well enough professionally to be accepted into Canada's National Theatre School. She recalled in a 2005 interview with *Time* magazine that she had a dramatic flair on and off the stage:

> I was a typical drama freak who needed to express herself. My favorite outfit was bright orange palazzo pants that I'd wear with this beat-up tuxedo jacket. And I'd have my hair up with a giant bow."

She prevailed over a thousand others for the high-profile role of the title character in the 1993 CBC production of *The Diary of Evelyn Lau*, the TV adaptation of the real-life memoirs of Lau, a teenage poet who descended into and escaped a life of drugs and prostitution. Oh's performance won plaudits in Canada and abroad.

Then, completely across spectrum, she played legendary Canadian broadcaster and future Governor General, Adrienne Clarkson in a CBC biopic.

Oh's feature film breakthrough came in 1994's *Double Happiness*, playing Jade Li, a young Chinese-Canadian woman in a coming of age movie, as a young person trying to escape the lovingly oppressive web of family traditions. *MSN Movies* describes her impressive range in the movie:

> Here Oh proved a remarkable screen presence, brimming with an understated but nevertheless luminous vitality and charm. She capably handled both the lighter romantic moments of the film and the family-clashing dramatic fare. For her exceptional turn, she was awarded that year's Best Actress Genie."

Janet Maslin in the *New York Times* somehow picked up on a subplot that perfectly illustrates Oh's real life professional frustrations:

> She's an aspiring actress who wishes she could play Blanche DuBois, but the jobs for which she's considered are strictly typecast. "You don't stand a chance," she's told at one audition. "They're looking for a Filipino."

Maclean's magazine put her on their 1995 Honour Roll as a rising star to keep an eye on, and she was off to Los Angeles.

She got a part in the HBO comedy series *Arli$$*, as the long-suffering, hyper-efficient Rita Wu, assistant to a big-time sports agent, like Jerry Maguire but nowhere near as cute and with no redeeming qualities whatsoever.

Then she had a small but memorable turn in 1997's *Bean* with Rowan Atkinson. Teaming up with fellow Canadian Don McKellar, she won a second Genie for her work in *Last Night*, a 1998 film about the end of the world. She had a risky but terrific role opposite Darryl Hanna and Meg Tilly in *Dancing at the Blue Iguana* as a lonely, exotic dancer. The film critic for the prestigious British magazine *The New Statesman* found her entrancing:

> But there is one other actress who would be worth the price of admission alone, and she is Sandra Oh, who plays Jasmine, a Chinese-American stripper who writes poetry and attends writers' workshops . . . the scene where Jasmine reads some of her work to an equally sad and lonely porn starlet is very, very good, perhaps the best in the movie. Looking at Oh's tear-stained face, a picture of miserable beauty,

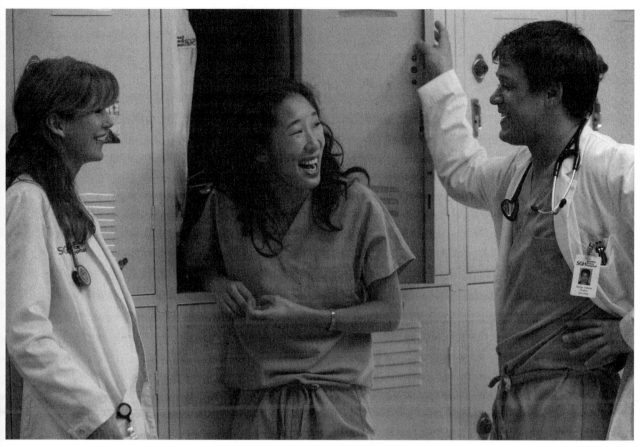

*As Dr. Cristina Yang in **Grey's Anatomy**. Photofest*

I felt I could have been looking at Edgar Degas' wonderful painting *L'Absinthe*, a portrait of the actress Ellen Andrée staring bleakly over the top of her opalescent glass.

She was on the roll that still shows every sign of accelerating. She showed up often on some of TV's hottest series, such as *Judging Amy* and *Six Feet Under*.

2003 brought another high-profile role as Diane Lane's friend Patti in *Under the Tuscan Sun*.

Ms. Oh's clear, sharp performance is the kind of work that solidifies careers. She is the voice of common sense, and she makes up for years of toiling on the third-rate sitcom *Arli$$* with the spiritual smarts she gives Patti.

If *Under the Tuscan Sun* was work that solidified careers, then the huge hit *Sideways* was work that makes them.

> Oh is just dazzling (or as *Variety* put it "a gas") as Stephanie, a motor-cycle-riding, sexy, very obliging single mother who pours the wine at tastings for a Californian vineyard.

In *Sideways*, aspiring author Miles Raymond (Paul Giamatti) takes his friend Jack (Thomas Haden Church) out for one last pre-nuptial, wine-sodden toot. The posters say, "In search of wine. In search of women. In search of themselves."

Her edgy, award-winning role as Cristina Yang, the bitchy Stanford-graduated intern on the weekly hospital TV series *Grey's Anatomy* has made her a full-fledged star. *The MSN Movies* website describes Oh as "one of Canada's most respected actresses."

And in the summer of 2006, she, just like Denzel Washington, fulfilled a lifelong dream, starring on Broadway. For her, it was in a play called *Satellites*. Should her current trajectory continue, she could play Brutus some day, if she wanted. Just watch out for that Colm Feore fellow.

It's amazing where talent, determination and box-office grosses can take you.

Deepa Mehta

B. AMRITSAR, INDIA, 1950

WATCHING DIRECTOR DEEPA MEHTA'S FILMS CAN BE HARD on your self-esteem. They are intelligent and exquisitely lovely. Every frame is a gem, the ensemble of actors near perfection. Even the sound tracks are beautiful in an almost ungodly way.

For those of us who consider ourselves reasonably well-informed, who listen to CBC and PBS and have the *New York Times* online edition bookmarked on our computers, it is completely mortifying to suddenly feel abjectly ignorant of the realities of modern-day India. Considering India is the largest film producer in the world; that there is ongoing controversy about North American jobs heading there; and that it's the world's largest democracy in a constant nuclear showdown with neighbouring Pakistan, any level of ignorance is just not a good thing.

Mehta's relentless feminist magnifying glass produces revelations. Do divorced and widowed Indian women really become outcasts? Is a wife in the 21st century who is accused of disrespecting her husband really expected to kiss his feet and ask for forgiveness? Could a film with a very discreet and loving depiction of a same-sex relationship, tame by Western standards, actually cause riots and destruction in India? Does the director really need to go to the Indian Supreme Court to ensure that her film is shown and not censured? And to venture out in Indian cities, does she need to travel with armed guards?

The answer to all of the above is: apparently so. And it's thanks to Deepa Mehta that we're all paying more attention to these things.

Deepa Mehta was born in Amritsar, home to the Golden Temple, near the Pakistan border. She graduated in philosophy at university and came to Canada in 1973. She worked in children's films until she made her first feature in 1991. *Sam and Me* tells the story of a cross-cultural friendship that grows between a cranky old Jewish man and the young Muslim man hired as his caregiver. Neither family approves and bad things happen. The movie won an Honorable Mention at the Cannes Film Festival.

In 1994, Mehta made *Camilla*, Jessica Tandy's second-to-last film and a real tour de force from the classic actress as a free spirit befriending an unhappy Bridget Fonda.

It was the first film of Mehta's self-styled *Elemental Trilogy*, called *Fire*, in 1996 that sparked the controversy. In it two sisters-in-law trapped in miserable marriages by the crushing weight of the "tradition" that Mehta makes so palpable, you can feel its stifling presence on the screen. Sita, the younger free spirit, has a louse for a husband who half-lives with his Chinese girlfriend, while his wife observes "traditions" like fasting for the long life of your good husband. Radha's husband has a vow of celibacy running thirteen years and counting. Sita laments, "Someone just has to press my button called tradition and I start acting like a trained monkey."

The two women find each other in a tender and moving way, but their relationship is discovered and has the effect a cluster bomb would on the family. The ubiquitous, ancient grandmother, silenced by a stroke, rings her bell in disapproval whenever the two are left alone. Near the end, the incarnation of Old India rings for Radha, who has looked after her for years, raises her head with great effort, and spits in her face. Sita's husband slaps her when he finds out. She defiantly, shockingly, slaps him right back. She pleads with Radha to run away with her (shades of *Thelma & Louise*), saying, "They don't even have a word for how we feel about each other."

The film is many things, but subtle is not one of them. Men can have mistresses, watch porn, demand to be waited on hand and foot by wives, but the message is that women pay the price of either a soulless existence or exile for daring to be equal. Mehta said that *Fire* transcends the Indian experience:

> The struggle between tradition and individual expression is one that takes place in every culture. *Fire* deals with this specifically in the context of Indian society. What appealed to me was that the story had a resonance that transcended geographic and cultural boundaries.

Earth (1998) depicts the sorrowful decline into bloodcurdling mass homicide in the once-civil city of Lahore. For Roger Ebert, it was a revelation about the horrible violence that ensued from the British pullout from India and the subsequent partition with Pakistan:

On *set of* **Camilla** *1994.*

It is hard for us to imagine the upheaval and suffering unleashed when the British washed their hands of the jewel in their crown. Imagine a United States in which those with a last name beginning with a vowel had to leave their homes and belongings and trek north, while those with a consonant had to leave everything behind and trek south. Now add bloodthirsty mobs of zealots on all sides.

It is all seen and told through the eyes of an eight-year-old girl.

Mehta began the third film of the trilogy, *Water*, in 2000. But Hindu fundamentalists destroyed her set and shut down the production. An author who heard about the film thought it sounded a lot like the plot of one of his books. She eventually settled out of court, but at the time, Mehta shut *Water* down and for fun made *Hollywood, Bollywood* in 2002, an homage to the campy Bollywood genre of India.

Mehta recalls that she then "fell in love" with Carol Shield's book *The Republic of Love*. "I realized I had to walk into this world Carol Shields had created and embrace it." The reviews more or less agreed that it was a touching movie with special chemistry between leads Bruce Greenwood and Emilia Fox. For Mehta, it was seen as a marked improvement on *Hollywood, Bollywood*, but below the level of *Fire*. A perceptive review in *Variety* noted it meant something more:

> It also marks the Indian-born, Canadian-based helmer's most complete immersion in Canada's Anglo world, with the only indication of her roots in the oddly applied tabla-meets-techno score by Talvin Singh."

She returned to filming *Water*, switching locations to Sri Lanka to complete it, undisturbed by Hindu fundamentalists. Near the beginning is a scene that is low key and unremarkable …that gobsmacks the unfamiliar Western ear. It is 1938 in India, during the rise of Gandhi. A grownup walks into a room and curtly informs an 8-year-old girl that she is now a widow, and that she must go off to spend the rest of her life in an isolated Hindu ashram for widows, who are regarded as bad karma and a senseless expense for their families.

It's an amazing performance by the young actor, Sarala, and it also features the stunning Lisa Ray as a widow forced into prostitution. *Water* is another in the new wave of Indian movies that seek to bring Indian culture and cinema to audiences beyond the Indian diaspora . . .

> Mehta and cinematographer Giles Nuttgens light and create images of startling beauty. Indeed the calm magnificence and spirituality of the landscape make a violent contrast to the oppression these widows in white saris suffer and the complacency of a society soon to be torn apart first by Gandhi and then by Partition.

Mike Myers

B. SCARBOROUGH, ONTARIO, 25 MAY 1963

IT'S NOT THAT SCARBOROUGH, ONTARIO IS A HORRIBLE PLACE. Parts of it are quite pretty, really. If you stand atop the bluffs overlooking Lake Ontario, you might think this is so nice it can't possibly be part of Toronto.

But it has been a public tradition in Hogtown to treat Scarborough with disdain. Like Rodney Dangerfield it gets no respect whatsoever. It is commonly referred to as "Scarberia." During the last Referendum, (the one we almost lost), when concerned Anglo Canadians put bumper stickers on their cars declaiming "My Canada Includes Quebec," some car drivers in Toronto sported ones saying, "My Canada includes Scarborough," as a gesture of the ultimate in inclusiveness.

So how did Mike Myers come to transcend his working-class roots in the urban equivalent of Wonder Bread to become one of a precious few who commands salaries in excess of US$20 million a film in Hollywood?

His mother, Alice was a trained actor and decided that, of her three sons, Michael could be one too. Dancing lessons began at the age of 8. All through school appearing in commercials was his part-time job.

He got his first trip to Hollywood to make one, and on another he was deeply impressed with "co-star" Gilda Radner, the gifted comic who would become one of the early stars of *Saturday Night Live* and who would sadly die far too early.

Father, Eric, was a Britisher through and through, proud of his Liverpool roots. He was one of the top salesmen for the *Encyclopedia Britannica*, earning enough for a comfy house in the suburbs, with a rec room that would be immortalized in *Wayne's World*. Myers said much later that he made *Austin Powers* in honour of his father.

After writing his last high school exam, Myers went to audition for the rising Toronto-based comedy troupe Second City and was hired.

Moving on at 21, when most aspiring comics head to New York or Los Angeles, Myers went to London to pay homage to the English comedy traditions of *The Goon Show*, Monty Python and Benny Hill. He worked, got paid little, starved in a flat in Notting Hill and got a lot of the "ice time" young comics need to develop.

He returned to Canada and bounced around in a short-lived show at the CBC and a stint with the Chicago Second City troupe that had graduated illustrious funny men like Bill Murray and John Candy.

A guest appearance at the Toronto Second City's fifteenth anniversary, where he stole the show in front of an audience of the elite of the entertainment industry, led to a phone call from Lorne Michaels, the head of *Saturday Night Live*, hereafter called *SNL*. Myers entered the 1990s in the Big Time.

He was a prolific writer as well as performer. A month into the season, he introduced Wayne Campbell, your "excellent" host, as if live from the rec room in Scarborough. Looking back there seemed to have been many memorable or classic *SNL* shticks: Dan Aykroyd and Jane Curtin as the Coneheads ("We are from France"); Garrett Morris's "Base-a-balla bin berry, berry gude to me"; Billy Crystal's "You look mahvelous."

But none approached the extensive use in the public vernacular as the signature lines of Wayne and Garth, the heavy-metal dweebs with bad hair. "That is such a nice outfit . . . NOT!!!"; "Way"(as the opposite of "No way"); "Party on"; "Excellent"; "She's a Major Babe" and "We are not worthy" can still be heard, even if the people saying these classic phrases never saw *SNL*. By the early 1990s Wayne and Garth had become stars in their own right.

Myers invented other well-known characters. There isn't actually much of an intellectual deconstruction of his humour in terms of comic traditions. (He'd probably say that intellectual deconstructions of comics should be banned or at least classified as oxymoronic, in any case). He was just a guy with a funny imagination, who wrote exceptionally funny things and performed them in very funny ways.

Another of the most memorable of his creations was the emotional Linda Richman, the aging Jewish Princess host of her show, "Coffee Talk" (pronounced "koe-fee towk"), who would always be reduced to tears and unable to speak (*verklempt*), waving her bracelet-covered wrist, croaking "Discuss amongst yourselves." Dieter, the freaky German host of an arts show called "Shprockets," with his pet monkey, was another.

Then one night the *Wayne's World* sketch involved Wayne (Myers) kind of making out with (the real) Madonna. That was probably the night, for all practical purposes, that the late-night TV sketch went into development as a feature movie, *Wayne's World*.

The setting of *Wayne's World* had long been changed for US audiences to what had been suggested as the American equivalent of Scarberia: Aurora, Illinois, enraging the natives there. Tim Horton's donut shop became Stan Mikita's, but the rec room stayed the same.

There was a plot, but that's beside the point. Everyone just wanted to see the two guys do their gags, and see Tia Carrere wear very little except a big electric guitar. There are many more signs of functioning brain cells in this than in later examples of the genre like *Dumb and Dumber* (1994). (And isn't it great to have a "Stupidity Genre" . . . Not.)

In a clever-but-not-laugh-out-loud scene, the two guys wangle backstage passes to meet their idol, the demented, sick, twisted Alice Cooper, in Milwaukee, Wisconsin. They can't wait to witness the outrageous antics that were no doubt in store. But Myers has Cooper play a quiet intellectual who prefers discussing the First Nation derivation of the town's name. "Wow!" says Wayne. "You sure know how to party."

The reviews were mixed. Roger Ebert found it "dumb and vulgar but with a genuinely amusing, sometime intelligent undercurrent." Janet Maslin over at the *New York Times* was appalled. In a review titled "A Dim Duo Revel in Stupidity" she wrote,

> H. L. Mencken may have noted that no one ever went broke underestimating the intelligence of the American people, but not even he could have anticipated this. Wayne and Garth do their best to elevate stupidity to an art form.

Legend has it that Mike's mother called and floored him with the remark, "That Dana Carvey sure is funny."

All of that was beside the point, too.

Wayne's World was huge at the box office and suddenly a sequel was assumed and Myers could just about name his price. The movie people who had had doubts about the project and Myers' temperament ran to jump back on the bandwagon because that's what media people do. It was easily the best film adaptation of an *SNL* sketch.

The sequel, *Wayne's World 2* (1993), however, was neither a good idea nor a good product. In the same year, Myers released *So I Married an Axe Murderer*, which had been through so many incarnations and rewrites (Woody Allen, Gary Shandling,

Albert Brooks and others had all looked it over) that it was a dog's breakfast. Myers played two parts and he was funny as the Scottish grandfather, a sort of reprise of his grumpy old Scot on *SNL* ("If it's no' Sco'ish, it's crrraaap!).

Even a bevy of wonderful cameos couldn't save it: Steven Wright, Alan Arkin, Charles Grodin and, best of all, Phil Hartman as a tour guide in the infamous prison of Alcatraz who says, "My name is John Johnson, but everyone here just calls me Vicky." Myers had always been known for having a thin skin. He only half-joked that he was afraid that the Talent Police would arrive one day and take him away. The quick closing of *Axe-Murderer* and the flopping of *Wayne 2* must have made him feel that that day had arrived.

As Martin Knelman writes in *Mike's World*, the combination of professional adversity and the death of his father and his brother-in-law sent Myers into a "psychic meltdown." He went to war with the original writer of *Axe-Murderer*, insisting on a writer's credit. Why, only Myers knows. But it didn't do his reputation much good.

Four years would pass before Myers made it back to the big screen. According to Knelman's biography, the inspiration for *Austin Powers* (1997) came while hearing a Burt Bacharach song on the radio. It launched "a tremendous act of catharsis . . . a huge posthumous tribute to the obsessions of his departed father." Psychoanalysis aside and being mindful that, though unlikely, there may be readers who have not seen one of the Austin Powers "franchise" movies, here's the overview: Austin is a legendary secret agent from the London of the 1960s, Yuppie Ground Zero, the British Invasion of rock and roll, Carnaby Street, and Mods and Rockers. He is also a legendary playboy despite crooked teeth and terrible taste in clothes. He's a bumbling 98-pound-weakling version of James Bond, in the tradition of Inspector Gadget and Maxwell Smart with a touch of *Laugh-In* from TV.

Powers and his arch-enemy, Dr. Evil, who is bent on world domination (both played brilliantly by Myers) are cryogenically frozen in 1967 and unfrozen again to do battle in 1997. The fish-out-of-water humour is well played as a central part of the charmingly improbable theme. Austin's 1960s promiscuity runs headlong into the much different sensibilities of the 1990s. Dr. Evil is laughed at for his ransom demand of $1 million, a king's ransom in 1967, chump change for bad guys in 1997. He implores his bad guy entourage, "I've been frozen for thirty years. Throw me a frickin' bone here." There is also a surfeit of variations of the verb "to shag."

It would be fun to recount a few highlights from the truly inspired insanity Myers created with unknown director Jay Roach, but more interesting is the growing distaste that creeps into critics' reviews as the series progresses to *The Spy Who Shagged Me* (1999) and *Goldmember* (2002). The best laughs are:

Induction into Canada's Walk of Fame June 2003. Toronto Star

1. Dr. Evil and his son Scott go to group therapy (led by a wonderfully deadpan earnest Carrie Fisher). Scott: "I want to open maybe a petting zoo." Dr. Evil: "An *evil* petting zoo?"

2. Heather Graham, in form-fitting 1960s fashion, on being asked how you get into hot pants that tight: "Well, you can start by buying me a drink."

3. Dr. Evil's second-in-command, played by Robert Wagner, explaining to his out-of-touch boss that Austin and his colleague, Elizabeth Hurley, can't be thrown in a shark tank because sharks are an endangered species, so they have sea bass. "But very angry sea bass."

The single thing that critics consistently point out as the films' primary virtue is Myers' own wide-eyed enjoyment in playing his characters, especially Austin. His enthusiasm fills the screen, projecting a very comfortable, likable presence. But somewhere near the end of the original, reviewers got bored, and maybe a little insulted. What began as wacky display of a comic tour de force seemed to veer away from witty riffs on Culture Then and Now and dumbed way down.

They could forgive it once. Janet Maslin wrote in the *New York Times*:

> This comedy can be sophomoric, but at some moments it's also unexpectedly sharp. And the film's single-mindedness is so dauntless and just plain nutty that it's hard to resist . . . The film narrows its range and aims for a teen-age audience — a group that may be entirely oblivious to its jokey references — with bathroom jokes and frat house humor.

Patience wore thinner with the sequel, *The Spy Who Shagged Me*, and the introduction of the truly revolting character Fat Bastard:

> Despite an oversupply of bathroom jokes and scattered scenes that play like outtakes, this is still a crafty, intermittently hilarious comedy that deserves its place in the Smart-Stupid Hall of Fame. Mike Myers's neo-Sellers multiple-personality act guarantees that . . . In the third persona of a drooling, loutish Scotsman named Fat Bastard, this scatological slob plays as just a gross-out gambit to win the hearts of teen-age boys. Though Mr. Myers shows his versatility from behind the blubber, the film's wit is not heightened by the joke about the Scotsman's stool sample.

Roger Ebert gave it maybe a half-thumb up, but found something disturbing:

> This film obtained a PG-13 rating — depressing evidence of how comfortable with vulgarity American teenagers are presumed to be.

As for *Goldmember*, the praise for Myers' performance and talent remained lavish. But the reservations about the "groin-centred" humour turned to disgust, in some quarters. Like *Time* magazine. Ouch, baby. Very ouch. And a very perceptive question in a very scary kind of way:

> Myers' humor isn't even adolescent, really. It's infantile. It's babies blissfully playing with themselves and their poop. The only thing dirtier

than the gags in *Goldmember* is the money that's made from them. And what will the preteens raised on Austin Powers have to watch — or want to watch — when they grow up?

So, Mr. Myers' balance sheet is a complex one, and there is a postscript that muddies it even more.

In an incident the Hollywood press dubbed "Dietergate," Myers backed out of a film adaptation of the *SNL* character, Dieter in the summer of 2000, despite the promise of a hefty payday for its creator and putative star. This, claimed the American entertainment media, was the smoking gun, the proof that Myers was 'difficult' to work with.

On the other hand, we're talking about one of the first celebrities who took to the American airwaves to defend and promote his hometown, economically devastated by the outbreak of SARS.

And a fitting final note: What would you think the chances are that an *Encyclopedia Britannica* salesman's Scarberian-born son, who became a purveyor of potty humour, would have his own mention in the *Encyclopedia Britannica*? No way, right? Well, way.

> Among the actors and directors who have achieved international renown over the years are Mack Sennett, Norman Jewison, Ted Kotcheff, Jim Carrey, Mike Myers, Atom Egoyan, David Cronenberg, and Denys Arcand.

I wonder if he knows? How shagadelic is that, baby?

Florence La Badie

B. MONTREAL, QUEBEC, 14 APRIL 1893
D. OSSINING, NEW YORK, 13 OCTOBER 1917

THE SADLY SHORT BUT PROLIFIC LIFE OF FLORENCE LA BADIE is as full of mystery, conjecture and conspiracy theories as *The Da Vinci Code*. She was one of the biggest stars of the early Silent Movie era, and was, for a brief time, at the top of the cadre of Canadian actors and directors who helped break new ground in establishing the oh-so-tenuous credentials of the new entertainment medium of film.

Most sources record her entry into the world in 1893, ostensibly in Montreal, to a successful lawyer and his European wife. She certainly grew up there, attending school at a Catholic convent, and her first performing experience was reliably recorded there at age 8. But many (usually American) online biographies record her birthplace as New York, in 1888, to be later adopted by the Montreal La Badies for no stated reason. In 1917, however, a New York woman named Marie Russ filed a suspiciously timed court order claiming to be Florence's birth mother. This just a few days before Florence's untimely and suspicious death. The fact that Americans were willing to fight to take credit for her has traditionally been, for Canadians, the ultimate proof that she must have been good.

Florence La Badie was born (or adopted) into a life of wealth and privilege, with mansions and butlers. In his highly readable collection of profiles of prominent Canadians in Hollywood's early days, *Stardust and Shadows*, author Charles Foster paints a portrait of a precocious young woman, a musical prodigy proficient in English,

French and German. Other biographies, mostly online, describe a tiny superwoman who learned the arts of painting, sculpting, classical piano and singing. And as if that weren't enough, she was an excellent athlete who would do her own, sometimes extremely risky, stunts.

Who knows what combination of happenstance, connections and youthful ambition brought her to audition for a Montreal production of a play featuring the huge American stage star Chauncey Olcott? Surely any association with the lowly regarded world of theatre should have risked excommunication by the pious Sisters of the Convent at Notre Dame. Olcott, according to Foster, recalled his deep and lasting impressions of the future star:

> I cannot recall in my lengthy career, directing an actress so knowledge-able and yet so eager as Florence La Badie. She was, at eight, a polished professional. At eighteen she was astounding directors and fellow performers . . .

Florence's parents seemed remarkably unconventional for their time. When asked for their permission for their daughter to act in Olcott's play, they replied it was up to her. And as they wouldn't consider taking money for her performance, they suggested Olcott discuss a contribution to the convent to obtain their blessing. The good Sisters at Notre Dame apparently had a voracious business sense, recognizing they had to cash in on a valuable, expiring asset. Olcott recalled that

> I wish I had a manager as capable of bargaining on my behalf as did the Sisters at the Convent.

And so began the remarkable career of little Flo as an angel in a play called *Ragged Robin*. Foster quotes Olcott graciously paying tribute to his young discovery:

> She upstaged me at every turn, and so totally stole the show that I took her hand in mine and walked out with her in front of the final curtain after each performance. I am sure that ninety percent of the applause was for her.

Her musical talents were renowned by the time she was ten. She both sang and played piano, appearing with the newly-formed Philadelphia Orchestra, later to be one of the great orchestras of the world. She wowed the conductor who proclaimed her a great piano prodigy who must study with him.

When her father died in 1908, she and her mother moved to New York. First and foremost there was Flo's acting career to pursue. They also had relatives in New

Jersey, as well as a very good friend of her father's, the president of Princeton who was about to become Governor of New Jersey. Woodrow Wilson would go on to become the 28th President of the United States.

Their first meeting may have been a fateful one. Rumours, neither proven nor disproved, persisted through the decades, that from the moment Wilson set eyes on her, the clock began ticking toward her early demise. In the meantime, it was as if New York had just been waiting for her to show up. She was quickly hired to act in a major play where she was seen by David Belasco, the undisputed heavyweight champ of New York impresarios, producers and agents. Aspiring actors would try for months to get a brief audience just to grovel for him. But *he* asked *Flo* if he could be her agent.

She had also been modelling for Penrhyn Stanislaws, the renowned photographer. It's likely that neither Florence nor her mother needed to work a day in their life, such was the estate left by her father. Considering the astounding adversity that other Canadians at the time had to overcome — Mack Sennett and Norma Shearer, to name just two — it's intriguing that good fortune continued to smile on someone like Florence, who really didn't need it.

Another of Belasco's stable of stars was the up and coming Canadian Mary Pickford who took young La Badie under her wing and soon had her making films at the legendary Biograph studios in downtown Manhattan. Biograph depended heavily on two other Canadians, Mack Sennett and Florence Lawrence. But the King of the Company was the great failed actor turned genius director D. W. Griffith.

La Badie made a number of films for him between 1909 and 1911, including *Serious Sixteen*, *Paradise Lost*, *Diamond Star*, and *Her Great Sacrifice*. Foster has found a number of obscure original sources, such as a 1916 interview with La Badie in *Picture Play* magazine.

> It didn't take me long to realize that Pickford and Lawrence were going to get all the best parts with the crumbs being thrown my way. I knew I had to go somewhere else if I was to achieve success.

Somewhere else would be Thanhauser Studios in New Rochelle, New York. The *All Movie Guide* described her tenure there:

> Florence La Badie's sweetly feminine presence enhanced many dozens of films made by the Thanhouser Studios, where she was one of the main stars. She was best known for the two serials she made for the company, the excellent *Million Dollar Mystery* (1914–1915) and the not-as-successful *Zudora*.

*Star billing as Eleanor Grayson in **When Love Was Blind**, 1917.*
Courtesy Ned Thanhauser

The *Thanhauser Official History* has this to say:

> Several hundred actors and actresses achieved recognition under the
> Thanhauser banner. Best known was Florence La Badie, who was the
> heroine in the 1914 serial, *The Million Dollar Mystery*, which lived up
> to its name and earned over a million dollars for its producer, thus

making it the most financially successful serial to that point. Florence, a veritable daredevil, leaped from cliffs, jumped from ship railings, and narrowly escaped death dozens of times.

The Million Dollar Mystery was a twenty-three-episode serial about a secret society called The Black Hundred and its attempts to gain control of a lost million dollars. Audience members were offered $10,000 to solve the mystery first. Each episode was just ten minutes, a "one-reeler" in the terminology of the early years. La Badie was always the hero.

Sadly, her most famous work is listed on a website called PresumedLost.com. She exists now only in little snippets of magazine articles, her picture as incomplete as an old jigsaw puzzle missing who knows how many pieces.

> In the meantime she received hundreds of proposals of marriage through the mail from her admirers. She counted these as they came in and considered it good luck to send the writer of each hundredth letter a little trinket and note.

An article in the March 1914 issue of *Photoplay* describes her as follows:

> Miss La Badie lived on Riverside Drive in New York City, and played the piano and sang. An accomplished pianist, Florence could play many classical selections from memory. She liked to dance but never had lessons. Art, sculpture and painting were among her spare-time interests.

She published two books of poetry. She was a tireless anti-war campaigner after receiving photos from a soldier and fan of hers in France. She turned them into a slide show and travelled around the US advocating for peace. At *Silentmovies.com*, William Drew claims she had another favourite hobby: reckless driving.

> A luminous, gifted actress, Florence was sensitive and poetic but was also known as a girl who feared nothing. Before switching to autos, she had at one time raced motorcycles. Characteristically, she exulted in speed when driving a car and was often ticketed.

Woodrow Wilson was a ranking member of the wealthy American East Coast aristocracy. He made Princeton the powerhouse institution and breeding ground for presidents it is today. Many found him insufferably overbearing. At the Versailles Peace Conference in 1919, France's Prime Minister Clemenceau said that being near Wilson was like "sitting next to Jesus Christ." Wilson brought his Fourteen Point plan to rebuild the world. Clemenceau sniffed that even God used only ten. Teddy Roosevelt, no shrinking violet himself, called Wilson "as insincere and cold-blooded an opportunist as we've ever had in the Presidency."

The La Badie family's old friend apparently began frequenting the Thanhauser studios. He told reporters that film making fascinated him. But even after becoming president, he continued to visit and you would think the American Head of State and Commander-in-Chief would have more pressing matters during the "War to End All Wars." They had to close the set during the filming of *Million Dollar Mystery* to keep plot lines from leaking out (there was after all the $10,000 reward). But Charles Foster quotes a source who claims Florence told her it was to keep the President from "slobbering over and pawing her."

Wilson's wife, Ellen, died in 1914 and that December the La Badies received an invitation to spend Christmas at the White House. La Badie returned a wreck in January, and soon requested a six-month leave of absence. The studio said that she needed to recover from a sudden nervous breakdown. The real reason was probably to have Wilson's illegitimate child. She recovered and went on to make twenty films in 1915, just nine in 1916 and likely wasn't aware that *The Man Without a Country*, a full-length sixty-minute feature in 1917 would be her last.

While out for a drive with her new fiancé near Ossining, New York, some stories say in August, most say in April, the brakes failed and the car plunged down the hill. The fiancé was able to leap to safety, unhurt, but Florence was seriously injured. Foster quotes a *New York World* report that she was recuperating and expected to leave the hospital within weeks. Six months later she died of septicemia. Suggestions that the brakes had been tampered with were never followed up, and the car allegedly disappeared.

Sadly, at the end of the day, this is not a titillating tale of scandal. It's the story of a brilliant young life cut short in its prime.

Catherine O'Hara

B. TORONTO, ONTARIO, 4 MARCH 1954

THERE IS THIS KIND OF FOOD CHAIN IN COMEDY where your status isn't registered somewhere in an inverted pyramid, but in terms of how far out on, and how high is, the branch you've chosen to park yourself on. Why anyone would choose to be there is another matter. But we're extremely grateful for all of them up and out there.

Simple standup can be the safest, or in the hands of a few (Robin Williams comes to mind), it can be right out there clinging with fingernails to the last leaf of autumn. In clubs, emcee is a step up. You get to introduce each act. Just the amount of face time requires one to hone sarcastic, demeaning insult skills for disgruntled patrons, as in, "The lab just called. Your brain is ready." Or the famous Billy Crystal line from *Mr. Saturday Night*: "THIS is what happens when cousins mate."

Sketch is another big step up and out, like *Saturday Night Live*.

And then there is improvisation, or "improv," the bungee-jumping of the comedy world. This is where casualties are high and medals for valour are quietly handed out.

And here begins our tribute to Catherine O'Hara, mistress of just about all of them, renowned for her gift at the most difficult and dangerous art of improv.

She'd already had a nice career, thank you very much, when she hooked up with improv guru Christopher Guest (a.k.a. Mr. Jamie Lee Curtis). If he didn't invent the "mock-documentary" genre, he certainly made it famous with *This is Spinal Tap* in 1984, a fictitious account of a non-existent rock band made essentially by putting funny people in front of a camera, preferably without a real script, letting it roll and stringing the best stuff together in the edit suite. The *New York Times* raved about it, with praise lavish and dubious at the same time:

> Guest, in particular, does a wonderful job of capturing his character's
> sincere idiocy.

O'Hara joined the Guest "mockumentary" troupe in 1996 for the first of several cult classic collaborations with Guest and fellow Torontonian and SCTV grad Eugene Levy. In *Waiting for Guffman*, she plays Sheila Albertson, a travel agent in the hamlet of Blaine, Missouri who is convinced that she and her equally untalented husband are the next Fred Astaire and Ginger Rogers. All are preparing a Red, White and Blue Revue for a mysterious big-time agent named Guffman, who, not to give away the ending, is the Godot of the piece.

O'Hara compared making *Guffman* to jumping off a cliff. She ad-libbed a scene in which she gets drunk and reveals the story about her husband's penis reduction surgery. It's very funny, but in a different way because you know its coming spontaneously from the warped recesses of otherwise stable minds. The same thing done in dramas by twenty-somethings sounds irritatingly pompous, but from a veteran comic actor it's an art form. The successful improv is the product of absolute trust between actor and director, O'Hara says.

> It makes you feel like you have so much to offer and if what you offer
> doesn't work, Chris will edit it out.

O'Hara also starred in *Best in Show* (2000), based on the bizarre world of competitive dog shows.

> [T]he actors improvising from a bare-bones screenplay (by Mr. Guest
> and Eugene Levy) riff off one another like jazz musicians to create
> what may be the cleverest on-the-spot caricatures since the heyday of
> Mike Nichols and Elaine May.

O'Hara plays Cookie Fleck, wife of the memorably geeky Gerry (Levy), who has two left feet, and owner of their terrier, Winky.

Of the third of the collaborations, *A Mighty Wind* (2003), allegedly depicting the reuniting of a once-legendary musical couple, *Times* critic A. O. Scott wrote:

> Of all of them, Mr. Levy and Ms. O'Hara are the two who have, histor-
> ically, been the funniest. If I had a dollar for every kernel of popcorn
> they have made me aspirate, separately and together, since their SCTV

*Bottom left with **SCTV** cast.* CBC

days in the 1970s, I'd be rich. This time, though, Mr. Levy, while sufficiently ridiculous with his vacant stare, hesitant diction and swept-back
gray hair, is also a lovable, vulnerable lost soul. And Ms. O'Hara has the
sublime wit to play Mickey completely straight.

*As Cookie Fleck in **Best in Show** 2000 with Eugene Levy. Photofest*

O'Hara's stature in the film industry rests solidly on her longevity, versatility and that legendary high-wire improv ability. To the larger public, she is indelibly etched in the annals of popular culture as Kate McAllister, the loving but hopeless mother in *Home Alone* and its sequel, who travels and manages to lose poor little Macaulay Culkin . . . twice. *Home Alone* was the top-grossing movie of 1990 and replays on small screens everywhere each Christmas right up there with the more traditional classics.

Her film career began inauspiciously in 1980 with *Nothing Personal* and *Double Negative*. She must have been doing something right because Martin Scorcese cast her in a small role in his dark 1985 comedy *After Hours*, where O'Hara got to work with not only one of the best-known directors of his generation, but with future stars Teri Garr and Rosanna Arquette. It was perhaps her first orbit near the edge, playing the flaky driver of a Mr. Softee ice cream truck. She followed as Meryl Streep's gossipy friend in *Heartburn* (1986) and Winona Ryder's mother in *Beetlejuice* (1988).

Oddly, few have seen two of her best performances. Ebert described O'Hara's portrayal as Beatrice Leaver in *Home Fries* in 1986, with Drew Barrymore and Luke Wilson:

> . . . one of O'Hara's best screen performances. The former Second City star is sweetness and reason as she manipulates her two luggy sons and brazenly acts her way through meetings with the cops and her late husband's young lover. She is so calm, so cool, she implies scary depths that she never has to reveal.

She also had a terrific role as Gabriel Byrne's chain-smoking, Guinness-swilling Irish Nationalist wife in 1996's *The Last of the High Kings*:

> The Irish charm does filter through somewhat, together with subtly amusing lines, and all in all, this is a film that has promise, but never delivers. Catherine O'Hara is engaging and gives a most entertaining performance as the extremist mother.

But aside from O'Hara the quality was such that it went direct to video.

She began doing voices for animated films like Tim Burton's *The Nightmare Before Christmas* (1993) and, in the ultimate confirmation of star status, *The Simpsons*.

As one of her fan sites recounts, the commercial and critical acclaim of the mature, risk-taking actor started in a very satisfying way: as a waitress:

> In 1973, Catherine took a job as a waitress at the Toronto Second City Theatre Company. When Gilda Radner left the cast in 1974, Catherine took her place as a cast regular. From Second City Theatre she went on to star on the legendary show SCTV. In 1983 she was part of the writing team that won an Emmy for their work on SCTV.

O'Hara is one of those endearing souls apparently content to be out of the mainstream, resigned, happily, to forgoing "major" awards.

"We're too specialized," she's said. "We're the *idiot savants* of comedy."

Christopher Plummer

B. MONTREAL, QUEBEC, 13 DECEMBER 1929

IT'S A DAUNTING TASK TO WRITE A FEW HUNDRED WORDS about Christopher Plummer. A two-volume biography maybe, but a short survey of nearly sixty years of success and acclaim is tough. He has been called the greatest actor to have never won an Academy Award, a handle he is probably very tired of hearing. But then he is nothing if not a most gracious man. His essay for his fellow Canadian Raymond Massey's autobiography is as eloquent, affectionate and respectful a tribute as you'll ever read.

The *Internet Movie Database* lists 158 screen appearances, and that's not even mentioning one of the most distinguished stage careers of all time, in England, at Stratford in Canada and on Broadway with six Tony nominations and two Best Actor wins for the musical *Cyrano* (1974) and *Barrymore* (1994).

He has given definitive interpretations of Iago in *Othello* and in 2004 of the lead in *King Lear*, begun at Stratford and taken on, to much critical acclaim and box-office success, to Broadway.

Plummer has another distinction, and one he's quite proud of. Being born on the infamous "Black Friday," the day the stock market crashed and began the Great Depression. The investment world lost fortunes that day, but the acting world had gained a future blue-chip asset.

Raised and educated in Montreal, Plummer apprenticed with the Montreal Repertory Theatre and made his professional debut in 1948 with Ottawa's Stage Society, performing over 100 roles with its successor, the Canadian Repertory Theatre.

*With Julie Andrews in **The Sound of Music**, 1965. Photofest*

Performances in Bermuda led to a US tour of *Nina* (1953) and Broadway recognition in *The Starcross* Story (1954), *The Lark* (1955) and as Marc Antony in the American Shakespeare Festival's 1955 inaugural season.

In 1961 he appeared at Stratford-upon-Avon in England as Richard III, while alternating in London as Henry II in *Becket* (winning the *Evening Standard* Award). He continued his British career at the National Theatre in revivals of *Amphitryon 38* and *Danton's Death* in 1971 and *The Scarlet Pimpernel* at Chichester in 1985. His first *King Lear* was directed by Sir Peter Hall in 2001.

Between 1956 and 1967 he starred at Canada's Stratford Festival, playing Henry V,

*As **King Lear** at the Stratford Festival 2002. Tony Hauser*

Hamlet, Andrew Aguecheek, Mercutio, Leontes, Macbeth, Cyrano de Bergerac and Marc Antony, as well as other roles. He returned twenty-six years later on 13 July 1993 to help the festival celebrate its exact 40th anniversary day with a gala one-man show entitled *A Word or Two, Before You Go. Barrymore* made its 1996 Canadian debut at Stratford before going on to Broadway.

His film career began with two releases in 1958. First, director Sidney Lumet (*Dog Day Afternoon, Serpico*) cast him as Joe Sheridan in *Stage Struck*, playing star Susan Strasberg's love interest, which made the *New York Times* sit up and take notice:

> Christopher Plummer, who is making his film debut as the playwright whose love she finally spurns, is restrained but effective.

In *Wind Across the Everglades*, by Nicholas Ray (*Rebel Without a Cause, In a Lonely Place*) Plummer had a larger role opposite Burl Ives and Gypsy Rose Lee. It was critically less well-received but he had begun his film career under two of Hollywood's best directors and he was definitely on the ascent.

This brings us to 1965 and *The Sound of Music*, one of the biggest hits of all time. It made Plummer famous worldwide and for a time the most bankable star in Tinseltown. It also launched Julie Andrews' distinguished career. The story of the singing Von Trapp family and how the governess (Andrews) tames a gaggle of rowdy children with love and song and falls in love with the dashing retired naval Captain Von Trapp (Plummer) leaves people weeping to this day. The Rogers and Hammerstein score was either enchanting or cloyingly sweet depending on taste, though some songs have been made into jazz classics (especially "My Favourite Things"). The film was nominated for ten Academy Awards and won Best Picture, Best Director, Best Musical Score, Best Film Editing and Best Sound.

The range of roles he sought and mastered is truly astonishing. From the heavy-duty title character in *Oedipus the King* (1967) to a delightful Sherlock Holmes opposite James Mason's splendid Watson in *Murder by Decree* (1979).

> With Christopher Plummer as a charming, cultivated Holmes, a fellow who reveals himself to be a man of unexpected social and political conscience, and with James Mason as an especially fond and steadfast Watson, Murder by Decree is a good deal of uncomplicated fun . . .

From Rudyard Kipling in *The Man Who Would Be King* (1975) to the deliciously evil, Shakespeare-quoting Klingon General Khan in *Star Trek VI: The Undiscovered Country*, Plummer could do it all.

From 2000, when he turned 71, to 2006 he made 29 film appearances, including a strong supporting turn in George Clooney's *Syriana* (2005). In 2006 he received an honorary Doctor of Letters from McGill University, and no doubt, Oscar will surely recognize a brilliant career before Mr. Plummer's days are through.

Jim Carrey

B. NEWMARKET, ONTARIO, 17 JANUARY 1962

FROM THAT TIMELESS MOMENT EARLY ON IN 1994's *Ace Ventura: Pet Detective* when Ace (Carrey) bends over and conducts a conversation by manipulating his rear end, he instantly became an idol to 12-year-old boys and their parents. Everywhere there were kids, his signature line could be heard: "Allllrighty-then!"

1994 was a magical year for Carrey, with an unexpected and most unholy trinity of smash hits that transformed the troubled, struggling young comic to superstar.

He has been accused of dumbing down the medium of film, if not the entire Western World with his lowbrow humour that seemed to straddle the line of sanity. His salary, per film, reads like the area code for Saturn. But he has endured a lot to get there.

His is a true rags-to-riches story, but unlike any other you've heard. It poses difficult questions. How can childlike funniness with mass appeal come from a young life of poverty, shame and adversity? How can traumas and demons contribute to the making of a comic legend?

Carrey's father Percy was a frustrated musician who had trouble finding and keeping enough work to raise a family. Always broke or close to it, they once had to live for a spell in a Volkswagen bus. ("I'm Canadian. I thought we were camping," he later joked.)

Young Jimmy was a goofy, skinny kid who just knew how to get laughs. When a class at school got boring, his pals would plead with teachers to let him get up and perform. By the time he became a teenager, he was saddled with the almost unthinkable pressure of being the family's salvation. Not only did he have to keep them laughing, he was going to be a star, make them respectable and more.

He dropped out of school after Grade 9 and started hanging out at comedy clubs. Everyone saw the natural talent, but his material, including Jimmy Stewart impersonations, seemed tame and lacking any edge. Once he was so bad they actually gave him the hook. It was humiliating and suddenly scary to contemplate life with a Grade 9 education and no skills. But he regrouped and at just 19 hit the comeback trail with a well-received performance before a tony Yorkville audience. One critic gushed that the world "saw a genuine star coming to life."

In comedy as in life, timing is everything. He ventured to New York, going from club to club just looking for his ten minutes of stage time. It was a break in more ways than one when he got a paying gig at Dangerfield's, the comedy dinner club of the legendary Rodney "I-get-no-respect" Dangerfield (as in "I know I'm ugly. When I was born, the doctor took one look at me and slapped my mother."). He liked the young Carrey's stuff.

In his biography of Carrey, *The Joker is Wild*, Martin Knelman writes that this was more than a professional break. Though the great veteran would give the young beginner a huge leg up by taking him on tour, he also became a mentor, almost a father figure. His income bumped up as well. He could afford to move his parents into the lavish luxury of a basement apartment in Toronto.

By the fall of 1981, he was in Los Angeles, full of promise and with the tremendous good fortune to have Linda Ronstadt as a girlfriend. He did some small stuff on TV and in film and got the lead in a new, much-heralded NBC-TV series *The Duck Factory*. If you've never heard of it, no worries. Millions haven't. It crashed and burned and with it, it seemed, Carrey's career and self-esteem.

His parents had moved to LA and in with him. They drove him crazy and he actually ordered them to go home. He was at loose ends, trying to reinvent himself away from the impersonations he'd relied on.

He tried new material that could only be described as "experimental," stuff that mystified his friends and appeared to be the product of an unstable creative mind. His "from-another-planet" reputation took hold.

In the mid 1980s he lucked into two good movies and, as Knelman notes, made two more important friends. In *Peggy Sue Got Married* (1986) he had just a small role as Walter Getz, the future geeky, substance-abusing dentist. The legendary Francis Ford Coppola directed, and Carrey befriended the legend's nephew who starred in the movie, Nicolas Cage.

Clint Eastwood also took a liking to Carrey and cast him in *The Dead Pool*

*The Grinch in **How the Grinch Stole Christmas** 2004. Universal*

(1988). Both Cage and Eastwood would be there years later when Carrey got his star on Hollywood's Walk of Fame.

Given his otherworldly reputation, it made perfect sense to audition as an actual alien for *Earth Girls are Easy* (1988). A slight but amusing sci-fi comedy, it stars Geena Davis as a manicurist with a swimming pool in her back yard, into which plunges the out-of-control spacecraft from the planet Jhazzala with its zany trio of astronauts Jeff Goldblum, Damon Wayans and Jim Carrey as Wiploc. Regarded by many as a spaceman in real life, Carrey spoke fluent Jhazzalian throughout almost the entire movie. More important, Wayans found him crazy, in a good way. Wayans and his brother Keenen, still huge on the African-American film and comedy scene, were developing the groundbreaking TV series *In Living Color*. Its mission was to be a Black *Saturday Night Live*, but it did have room for a "token" white guy and the virtuoso of craziness, Jim Carrey, won the part.

His second comeback was complete. It was the breakthrough he'd hung in for.

He grew in stature, range and celebrity as his watershed year of 1994 arrived. *Ace Ventura: Pet Detective* was the surprise hit of that year. More by luck than design the wacky yet charming movie was perfectly positioned against acclaimed and much heavier fare such as *Schindler's List* and *Philadelphia*. The plot, such as it was, featured a pet-friendly private eye called in to solve the disappearance of the National Football League's Miami Dolphin's mascot, Snowflake. It was also Carrey's good fortune to work with a gorgeous, then-little-known future 1990s icon, *Friends'* star Courtney Cox.

Critics seemed to try hard not to like it. The famous critic pair Siskel and Ebert gave it two thumbs down. Others were blown away by Carrey's irrepressible performance:

> As *Ace Ventura: Pet Detective*, the comic actor Jim Carrey gives one the most hyperactive performances ever brought to the screen. With his hair swept into a precarious leaning tower, his eyes wide as saucers, moving in spasms, he suggests Desi Arnaz as Don Knotts on speed.

> Only a child could love Mr. Carrey's character, but that may be the point. The movie has the metabolism, logic and attention span of a peevish 6-year-old. It's not the story that matters, but the silly asides, like the way Ace starts doing impersonations of *Star Trek* characters at odd moments or singing the theme from *Mission Impossible*.

The money it made on opening was stupendous.

He got $7 million to sign on for *Dumb and Dumber*, and the bouts of poverty were behind him for good. It was the kind of movie you hoped your kids wouldn't like.

But resistance was futile. They loved it. His co-star, Lauren Holly, wouldn't become an icon, but she would become his second wife. Carrey endured a messy, public divorce from his first wife, Melissa Womer. But he'd acquired the quality that Hollywood loves above all: he was money in the bank.

In *The Mask* (1994), he redeemed himself in the eyes of Thinking People everywhere. In it, he plays the mild-mannered likable loser of a bank clerk, Stanley Ipkiss. Fate intrudes as a magical mask that when put on, transforms poor old Stanley into a manic, frog-green being with superhero powers and great comic timing. Carrey's energy and the special effects are a memorable combo. Martin Knelman wrote that Carrey's father was fond of saying things like his son wasn't just a ham he was the whole pig. And *The Mask* was a showboater's dream.

Moviegoers who were still skeptical about this Next Big Thing saw the light. Even if they didn't realize it, they were won over by the gifted, broad physical comedy to which Carrey had become heir, passed on from Chaplin to Keaton to Skelton to Lewis. The law of averages dictates that even money in the bank can be fallible. The critics savaged his 1996 effort in *The Cable Guy*, with Matthew Broderick, but kids still loved it and him.

At this point his career Carrey settled into the usual pattern of an established star. Some movies were good (*The Truman Show*; *Man on the Moon*); some were OK (*Liar, Liar*; *How the Grinch Stole Christmas*) and some not so great (*The Majestic*; *Me, Myself and Irene*). True, he could and did command salaries in excess of US $20 million per film, plus a percentage of the merchandise sales. But had he really endured all that he did to grow old making 12-year-old boys squeal with laughter?

In 2004, he starred with Kate Winslet in *The Eternal Sunshine of the Spotless Mind*, a substantive drama so quirky it would take less time to watch the film than explain the plot. It impressed enough that the *New York Times* put it on their "Critic's List." Maybe there was more to life than huge paydays.

Legend has it that when Carrey was at one of his lowest ebbs, he followed the advice of a motivational expert and made himself out a cheque for $10 million to cash when he was rich and famous. When his father died in 1994, Carrey *was* rich and famous. He quietly slipped the uncashed cheque into Percy's pocket in the casket. A King's Ransom to ensure his hard-luck Dad a better break wherever he was bound.

Mordecai Richler

B. MONTREAL, QUEBEC, 27 JANUARY 1931
D. MONTRAL, QUEBEC, 3 JULY 2001

MORDECAI RICHLER'S BOOKS AND MAGAZINE PIECES are quite rightly acclaimed world-wide as masterpieces, big and small. (One of his best pieces, sadly forgotten, is his 1976 *Esquire* magazine essay called "The Spiritual Necessity of the Montreal Canadiens," a thing of beauty about his beloved Bleu, Blanc et Rouge. But that's for another book.) It is somewhat less well-known that he also excelled at writing for the screen. So much so that he was nominated for an Oscar.

This faculty of his had two great benefits. First, it made for some wonderful movies, often, but not always, adapted from his own superb novels. Secondly, his experience in the silliness of the movie industry, filtered through his grumpy, pitch perfect eyes and ears, provided memorable material recounted (with names changed to protect the guilty) in his later fiction, *Barney's Version* in particular.

Perhaps a short primer on the joys and frustrations of screen writing. If you want a visual portrayal of the utter vacuousness of the process, go and rent Robert Altman's *The Player* (1992) with Tim Robbins.

William Goldman, a two-time Oscar winner, for writing *All the President's Men* (1977) and *Butch Cassidy and the Sundance Kid* (1970), has also written a couple of "How-To" books, sort of "Screenwriting for Dummies" that are intentionally hilarious. He applies one time-honoured but unforgettable metaphor, to aspects of the film industry, likening it to a self-centred bird that flies in ever-decreasing concentric circles until eventually, it flies up its own ass.

The Apprenticeship of Mordecai Richler, 1986. *National Film Board of Canada*

Those who had the good fortune to know or at least meet Richler would be aware of his legendary eloquent but short fuse. Example: At a reception, the widow of a very wealthy purveyor of fine spirits complimented him on coming such a long way for a St. Urbain Street boy. He replied, "And you've come a long way for a bootlegger's wife."

It's really fun, though a tad daunting, to parse his films, trying to figure what parts are his, how your favourite passages from his own books play out and why some of the funniest, laugh-out-loud parts didn't make it. For instance, in the 1977 original *Fun With Dick and Jane*, splendidly played by George Segal and Jane Fonda, there are two Richlerian touches early on. Segal's drunken boss, Ed McMahon, waves his glass of scotch, leans over and says, *sotto voce*, "Can I be honest with you, Dick?" as if to impart some deeply personal insight. Dick, of course, says sure and McMahon continues, "You're fired." And it just seems absolutely certain that Richler had seen something very close if not exactly like that happen in his real life and filed it away for the right moment. Then, when Dick and Jane, who are renovating their already lavish house, let it slip he's been fired, the contractor blows a whistle and things come to a screeching halt.

Likewise, the brilliantly funny Biblical analysis of Joshua's father Reuben (an ex-boxer who breaks fingers and votes illegally for a living and who on occasion, has to quickly climb into trunks of cars that speed off) in the book *Joshua Then and Now* is a grand piece of writing. Joshua and a friend are going to lunch and spot another friend across the street. Joshua begins to raise his hand to wave, only to have his friend who is with him grab his hand and shush him. "Not him. He eats."

Of course Richler's filmic masterpiece is *The Apprenticeship of Duddy Kravitz* (1974), the coming of age story of his most famous character. At the time, Richler took a lot of heat for writing what many considered an anti-Semitic tract. That view has faded somewhat over time and from this distance, the film looks like a wonderfully captured piece of much-loved nostalgia, as written by Richler, directed by Ted Kotcheff and perfectly played by Richard Dreyfuss.

In George Woodcock's *Duddy Kravitz* reader guide, Richler says, "the state of a writer to reach was one where the reader could look at a page and know that nobody else could have written it." That is the book and film in a nutshell, the rendering of a place and time, like John Steinbeck's Monterey and Thomas Hardy's Wessex, Montreal's St. Urbain Street is forever Richler's.

Sources

MARIE DRESSLER

Hall, Mordaunt. "Anna Christie [review]" *New York Times*, March 15, 1930.

Hall, "Miss Dressler at Her Best [*Emma* review]" *New York Times*, February 6, 1932.

Hall, "Mr. Lubitsch's 'Design For Living' [*Christopher Bean* review]" *New York Times*, December 3, 1933.

RAYMOND BURR

Canby, Vincent. "The Screen: 'Godzilla 1985'" *New York Times*, August 30, 1985.

Hill, Ona, L. *Raymond Burr: A Film, Radio and Television Biography* (Jefferson, NC: McFarland, 1994).

Kelleher, Brian, and Diana Merrill. *The Perry Mason TV Show Book: The Complete Story of America's Favorite Television Lawyer, by Two of the Greatest Fans.* (New York: St Martin's Press, 1987); online at www.perrymasontvshowbook.com/.
www.raymondburrvineyards.com.

YVONNE DE CARLO

Crowther, Bosley. "The Screen: 'Rose's Diamond Horseshoe'" *New York Times*, May 3, 1945.

De Carlo, Yvonne, with Doug Warner. *Yvonne* (New York: St. Martin's Press, 1987).

"The New Pictures [*Salome* review]" *Time*, May 7, 1945.

"The New Pictures [*The Captain's Paradise* review" *Time*, October 12, 1953.

Yvonne de Carlo (http://movies.yahoo.com/).

CLAUDE JUTRA

Canby, Vincent. "The Screen: Coming of Age in Quebec" *New York Times*, April 18, 1972.

Canby. "The Screen: Claude Jutra's 'Kamouraska'" *New York Times*, July 14, 1975.

Crowther, Bosley. "The Screen: 'Take It All' Opens at Plaza" *New York Times*, April 26, 1966.

NORMA SHEARER

"Her Cardboard Lover." *All Movie Guide* (www.allmovie.com).

Foster, Charles. *Stardust and Shadows: Canadians in Early Hollywood* (Toronto: Dundurn, 2000).

Kael, Pauline. *5001 at the Movies* (New York: Holt, Rinehart and Winston, 1982).

Lambert, Gavin. *Norma Shearer: A Biography* (New York: Knopf, 1990).

Morris, Gary. "Queen Norma — Shearer" *Bright Lights Film Journal*, Issue 16 (April 1996) (www.brightlightsfilm.com).

Nugent, Frank S. *"The Women"* *New York Times*, September 22, 1939.

Sennwald, Andre. "The Capitol Presents a Brilliant Screen Version of 'The Barretts of Wimpole Street'" *New York Times*, September 29, 1934.

RAYMOND MASSEY

Crowther, Bosley. "The Screen: Gary Cooper Plays an Idealistic Architect in Film Version of 'The Fountainhead'" *New York Times*, July 9, 1949.

Donald, David Herbert. Personal e-mail.

Hall, Mordaunt. "The Screen: The Brave and the Fair, and a Thriller From the Sherlock Holmes Detective Series" *New York Times*, November 7, 1931.

Kael, Pauline. *5001 at the Movies* (New York: Holt, Rinehart and Winston, 1982).

Massey, Raymond. *When I Was Young* (Toronto: McClelland & Stewart, 1976).

Massey. *A Hundred Different Lives: An Autobiography* (Toronto: McClelland & Stewart, 1979).

Nugent, Frank S. "The Screen: The Music Hall Celebrates Washington's Birthday With a Brilliant Edition of Sherwood's 'Abe Lincoln in Illinois,'" *New York Times*, February 23, 1940.

P.P.K. "'Arsenic and Old Lace' With Cary Grant, in Premiere at Strand." *New York Times*, September 2, 1944.

MACK SENNETT

Foster, Charles. *Stardust and Shadows: Canadians in Early Hollywood* (Toronto: Dundurn, 2000).

Louvish, Simon. *Keystone: The Life and Clowns of Mack Sennett* (London: Faber & Faber, 2004).

Sennett, Mack with Cameron Shipp. *King of Comedy* (New York: Pinnacle Books, 1975).

COLLEEN DEWHURST

Barnes, Clive. "*A Moon for the Misbegotten* [review]" *New York Times*, December 31, 1973.

Dewhurst, Colleen and Tom Viola. *Colleen Dewhurst: Her Autobiography* (New York: Scribner, 1997).

Maslin, Janet. "Messed-Up Lives in 'Dying Young'" *New York Times*, June 21, 1991.

RUBY KEELER

Barnes, Clive. "No, No, Nanette" *New York Times*, January 20, 1971.

Hall, Mordaunt. "Patting On a Show" *New York Times*, March 10, 1933.

Nugent, Frank S. "At the Capitol" *New York Times*, May 4, 1935.

Thompson, David. *A Biographical Dictionary of Film* (New York: Knopf, 1994).

DEANNA DURBIN

The Deanna Durbin Database (www.geocities.com/bungalow743).

ALEXIS SMITH

Butler, Craig. "*Night and Day* [review]" *The All Movie Guide* (www.answers.com/topic/night-and-day-film).

Craig. "*Here Comes the Groom* [review]" in *The All Movie Guide* (www.answers.com/topic/here-comes-the-groom-film).

Lucas, Ralph. "Alexis Smith" *NorthernStars.ca* 2003 (www.northernstars.ca/actorsstu/smith_alexisbio.html).

"That Old Magic Relights Broadway" *Time*, May 3, 1971.

BEATRICE LILLIE

An Evening with Beatrice Lillie. Cover jacket, LP recording.

Laffey, Bruce. *Beatrice Lillie: The Funniest Woman in the World* (New York: Wynwood Press, 1989).

Lillie, Beatrice. *Every Other Inch a Lady* (New York: Doubleday, 1972).

"The Screen: Not Enough Lillie [*On Approval* review]" *New York Times*, January 29, 1945.

Sources

FAY WRAY

Fontana, Tony. "Biography for Fay Wray" *Internet Movie Database* (imdb.com/name/nm0942039/bio).

Hall, Mordaunt. "*King Kong* [review]" *New York Times*, March 3, 1933.

Wray, Fay. *On the Other Hand: A Life Story* (New York: St. Martin's Press, 1989).

FLORENCE LAWRENCE

Foster, Charles. *Stardust and Shadows: Canadians in Early Hollywood* (Toronto: Dundurn, 2000).

GLENN FORD

Kulzer, Dina-Marie. "Glenn Ford: An Interview (1990)" (www.classichollywoodbios.com/glennford.htm).

Thuresson, Mattias. "Biography on Glenn Ford" *Internet Movie Database* (www.imdb.com).

"Glenn Ford: A Silver Screen Legend" (glennfordsite.com).

HUME CRONYN

Cronyn, Hume. *A Terrible Liar: A Memoir* (New York: William Morrow, 1993).

Crowther, Bosley. "Shadow of a Doubt' a Thriller, With Teresa Wright, Joseph Cotten, at Rivoli — 'Tennessee Johnson' Is at the Astor" *New York Times*, January 13, 1943.

Crowther. "The Screen: '*The Postman Always Rings Twice*'" *New York Times*, May 3, 1946.

Crowther. "Seventh Cross," Anti-Nazi Drama, With Spencer Tracy, at Capitol" *New York Times*, September 29, 1944.

KATE REID

Crowther, Bosley. "The Screen: '*This Property Is Condemned*'" *New York Times*, August 4, 1966.

Ebert, Roger. "*A Delicate Balance* [review]" *RogerEbert.com*, November 12, 1973 (rogerebert.suntimes.com).

Ebert. "*Atlantic City* (1980)" *RogerEbert.com*, December 4, 2005 (rogerebert.suntimes.com).

Gardner, David. "Reid, Daphne Kate" in *The Canadian Encyclopedia* (www.thecanadianencyclopedia.com).

Scheib, Richard. "*The Andromeda Strain*" in *The Science Fiction, Horror and Fantasy Review*, 1999 (www.moria.co.nz/sf/andromeda.htm).

LORNE GREENE

H. H. T. "The Screen: 'Tight Spot'" *New York Times*, March 19, 1955.

LOUIS B MAYER

Schulberg, Budd. "Lion Of Hollywood" *Time*, December 7, 1998.

MARY PICKFORD

Eyman, Scott. *Mary Pickford: America's Sweetheart* (New York: Dutton, 1990).

Hall, Mordaunt. "New Pickford Film" *New York Times*, January 8, 1917.

"Hollywood Stars" (collections.ic.gc.ca/heirloom_series/volume4/312-317.html).

"The Screen: Rough Matrimonial Weather" *New York Times*, November 13, 1922.

"They Would Elope" *Internet Movie Database* (www.imdb.com).

Whitfield, Eileen. *The Woman Who Made Hollywood* (Toronto: Macfarlane Walter & Ross, 1999).

WALTER HUSTON

Crowther, Bosley. "'*Treasure of Sierra Madre*,'" *New York Times*, January 24, 1948.

Crowther. "Yankee Doodle Dandy" *New York Times*, May 30, 1942.

Sources

Grobel, Lawrence. *The Hustons* (New York: Charles Scribner's Sons, 1989).

"'The Bad Man" *New York Times*, September 27, 1930.

Hall, Mordaunt. "The Screen: Mr. Griffith's First Talker" *New York Times*, August 26, 1930.

Nugent, Frank S. "Samuel Goldwyn's Film of 'Dodsworth' Opens At the Rivoli" *New York Times*, September 24, 1936.

Stein, Elliott. "Old Hollywood's Sure Thing: William Wyler at Film Forum" *Village Voice*, September 11–17, 2002.

WALTER PIDGEON

Berger, Joseph. "Walter Pidgeon, Actor, Dies at 87" *New York Times*, September 26, 1984.

Crowther, Bosley. "Excellent Picture of England at War [*Mrs. Miniver* review]" *New York Times*, June 5, 1942.

Foster, Charles. *Stardust and Shadows: Canadians in Early Hollywood* (Toronto: Dundurn, 2000).

Troyan, Michael. *A Rose for Mrs. Miniver: The Life of Greer Garson* (Lexington: University Press of Kentucky, 1998).

JACK WARNER

Thomas, Bob. *Clown Prince of Hollywood: The Antic Life and Times of Jack L. Warner* (New York: McGraw-Hill, 1990).

Warner, Jack. *My First Hundred Years in Hollywood* (New York: Random House, 1965).

GENEVIÈVE BUJOLD

Canby, Vincent. "The Screen: On the Farm With 'Isabel'" *New York Times*, July 24, 1968.

Ebert, Roger. "*The Trojan Women* [review]" *RogerEbert.com*, June 4, 1972 (rogerebert.suntimes.com).

Kael, Pauline. *5001 at the Movies* (New York: Holt, Rinehart and Winston, 1982).

Maslin, Janet. "Review/Film: Another Marriage of Convenience" *New York Times*, June 21, 1991.

TES-WAH-NO (CHIEF DAN GEORGE)

Canby, Vincent. "*Little Big Man* [review]" *New York Times*, December 15, 1970.

Ebert, Roger. "*Little Big Man* [review]" *RogerEbert.com*, January 1, 1970 (rogerebert.suntimes.com).

Ebert. "*Harry and Tonto* [review]" *RogerEbert.com*, January 1, 1974 (rogerebert.suntimes.com).

Ebert. "*The Outlaw Josey Wales* [review]" *RogerEbert.com*, January 1, 1976 (rogerebert.suntimes.com).

Eder, Richard. "*The Outlaw Josey Wales* [review]" *New York Times*, August 5, 1976.

George, Chief Dan (Teswahno). "Lament for Confederation" Delivered at Empire Stadium, Vancouver, BC, July 1, 1967 (www.canadahistory.com/sections/documents/1967_dan_george.htm).

Kael, Pauline. *5001 at the Movies* (New York: Holt, Rinehart and Winston, 1982).

KATE NELLIGAN

"Best of '88: Theater" *Time*, January 2, 1989.

Maslin, Janet. "'*Eye Of Needle*,' Espionage and Passion" *New York Times*, July 24, 1981.

Maslin. "Short-Order Cookery and Dreams of Love [*Frankie & Johnny* review]" *New York Times*, October 11, 1991.

Schickel, Richard. "Anguished Aria [*A Moon For The Misbegotten* By Eugene O'Neill]" *Time*, May 14, 1984.

Schickel. "Stuffy Nonsense [*Dracula* review]" *Time*, July 23, 1979.

Webster, Brian. "*Eye of the Needle* [review]" *The Apollo Movie Guide* (apolloguide.com).

Sources

LESLIE NIELSEN

Canby, Vincent. "Review/Film: Lieutenant Drebin Whiffs the Smell of Fear (and Lobster) [*The Naked Gun 2 1/2: The Smell of Fear*]" *New York Times*, June 28, 1991.

Crowther, Bosley. "The Screen: Unrewarding 'Ransom'" *New York Times*, January 25, 1956.

Lumenick, Lou. "4GEDDABOUTIT [review *Scary Movie 4*]" *New York Post*, April 14, 2006.

Maslin, Janet. "The Screen: '*Airplane!*,' Disaster-Film Spoof" *New York Times*, July 2, 1980.

Nielsen, Leslie, David Fisher and David Kaestle. *The Naked Truth* (New York: Pocket Books, 1993).

DENYS ARCAND

Bennetts, Leslie. "Film View; A Film About Sex That's All Talk [*Decline of the American Empire* review]" *New York Times*, November 9, 1986.

Canby, Vincent. "The Screen: 'Decline.'" *New York Times*, November 14, 1986.

La Rochelle, Réal. *Denys Arcand: A Life in Film* (Toronto: McArthur & Company, 2005).

Wilmington, Michael. "Movie review: 'The Barbarian Invasions'" *Chicago Tribune*, December 17, 2003.

JOHN CANDY

Ebert, Roger. "*Planes, Trains and Automobiles* [review]" *RogerEbert.com*, November 12, 2000 (rogerebert.suntimes.com).

Knelman, Martin. *Laughing on the Outside* (New York: St. Martin's Press, 1996).

Maslin, Janet. "'*Stripes*' and the Biggest Wise Guy in the Army" *New York Times*, June 26, 1981.

Maslin. "Screen: '*Splash*,' A Mermaid's Love" *New York Times*, March 9, 1984.

Maslin. "Film: '*Summer Rental*'" *New York Times*, August 9, 1985.

Maslin. "Review/Film; When Mom Is a Monster and her Boy Meets a Girl" *New York Times*, May 24, 1991.

DOUGLAS SHEARER

Academy of Motion Picture Arts and Sciences Awards Database (awardsdatabase.oscars.org).

"Douglas Shearer" (collections.ic.ca/heirloom_series).

Foster, Charles. *Stardust and Shadows: Canadians in Early Hollywood* (Toronto: Dundurn, 2000).

Gilbert, Morris. "Pictorial Entertainment in Paris" *New York Times*, December 1, 1929.

Hall, Mordaunt. "The Screen; A Jail-Break [*The House* review]" *New York Times*, June 25, 1930.

Kael, Pauline. *5001 at the Movies* (New York: Holt, Rinehart and Winston, 1982).

"The Broadway Melody (1929)" *Classic Film Guide* (www.classicfilmguide.com).

MICHAEL SARRAZIN

Canby, Vincent. "Pollack's 'They Shoot Horses' Opens at the Fine Arts" *New York Times*, December 11, 1969.

Canby. "'Sometimes a Great Notion'" *New York Times*, March 2, 1972.

JAMES DOOHAN

Doohan, James, and Peter David. *Beam Me Up, Scotty* (New York: Pocket Books, 1996).

WILLIAM SHATNER

Gallagher, William. "*Star Trek: The Motion Picture* [review]" Updated September 4, 2001 (bbc.co.uk/films).

James, Caryn. "Review/Film; The Fifth 'Star Trek,' With Old, New and Evil" *New York Times*, June 9, 1989.

Maslin, Janet. "Review/Film; Aging Trekkers to the Rescue One Last Time. Really." *New York Times*, December 6, 1991.

Shatner, William. *Get a Life!* (New York: Pocket Books, 1999).

Star Trek TV series [[review] *Variety*, September 14, 1966.

Sources

MARGOT KIDDER

Canby, Vincent. "Screen: It's a Bird, It's a Plane, It's a Movie" *New York Times*, December 15, 1978.

Canby. "'*Willie and Phil*' 3 Lives, Sort of Shared" *New York Times*, August 15, 1980.

Canby. "Pryor in '*Some Kind Of Hero*'" *New York Times*, April 2, 1982.

DONALD SUTHERLAND

Adler, Renata. "Screen: Holdup at a Pro Football Game [*The Split* review]" *New York Times*, November 5, 1968.

Ebert, Roger. "*Klute* [review]" *RogerEbert.com*, January 1, 1971 (rogerebert.suntimes.com).

Ebert. "*M*A*S*H* [review]" *RogerEbert.com*, January 1, 1970.

Mitchell, Elvis. "Film Review: *Panic*" *New York Times*, January 19, 2001.

Patterson, John. "Total Recall" *The Guardian*, September 3, 2005.

Scott, A. O. "Film Review: Voices of Experience, Rocketing to the Rescue [*Space Cowboys* review]" *New York Times*, August 4, 2000.

"Who Was That Guy?" *Time*, February 2, 1970.

NORMAN JEWISON

Jewison. *This Terrible Business Has Been Good to Me* (Toronto: Key Porter, 2004).

ARTHUR HILLER

Ebert, Roger. "*Love Story* [review]" *RogerEbert.com*, January 1, 1970 (rogerebert.suntimes.com).

Ebert. "*The Man in the Glass Booth* [review]" *RogerEbert.com*, January 27, 1975.

Null, Christopher. "*Man of La Mancha* [review]" *FilmCritic.com*, 2004 (www.filmcritic.com).

ZACHARIAS KUNUK

Campbell, Duncan. "On top of the World" *The Guardian*, August 17, 2001.

Chun, Kimberly. "Storytelling in the Arctic Circle: An Interview with Zacharias Kunuk" *Cineaste*, December 22, 2002.

Hoberman, Jim. "Let There Be Light. *The Fast Runner* (*Atanarjuat*)" *The Village Voice*, June 5, 2002.

Isuma Distribution International website (www.isuma.ca).

Scott, A. O. "Film Festival Review: A Far-Off Inuit World, in a Dozen Shades of White" *New York Times*, March 30, 2002.

SANDRA OH

[*Dancing at the Blue Iguana* review] *The New Statesman*, July 1, 2002.

Maslin, Janet. "Film Review [*Double Happiness*]; A Delicate Asian Flower in a Motorcycle Jacket" *New York Times*, July 28, 1995.

Mitchell, Elvis. "Film Review [*Under the Tuscan Sun*]; Restoring a Villa While Repairing the Heart" *New York Times*, September 26, 2003.

"Sandra Oh: Biography" Hollywood.com (/www.hollywood.com).

SandraOh.com (www.sandraoh.com).

DEEPA MEHTA

"Canadian Women in Film: Deepa Mehta" (www.collectionscanada.ca/women/002026-708-e.html).

Ebert, Roger. "*Earth* [review]" *RogerEbert.com*, October 15, 1999 (rogerebert.suntimes.com).

Honeycutt, Kirk. "*Water* [review]" *The Hollywood Reporter*, September 9, 2005 (www.hollywoodreporter.com).

Koehler, Robert. "*The Republic of Love* [review]" *Variety* (www.variety.com).

MIKE MYERS

Corliss, Richard. "This Essay Is Rated PG-13" *Time*, July 22, 2002.

Ebert, Roger. "*Dumb And Dumber* [review]" *RogerEbert.com*, December 16, 1994 (rogerebert.suntimes.com).

Ebert. "*Austin Powers: The Spy Who Shagged Me* [review]" *RogerEbert.com*, June 11, 1999.

Knelman, Martin. *Mike's World: The Life of Mike Myers* (Toronto: Penguin Books, 2002).

Maslin, Janet. "Review/Film [*Dumb and Dumber*]: A Dim Duo In a Revel Of Stupidity" *New York Times*, February 14, 1992.

Maslin. "It's a Mod, Mod, Mod, Mod World [review *Austin Powers: International Man of Mystery*]" *New York Times*, May 2, 1997.

Maslin. "Film Review [*Austin Powers: The Spy Who Shagged Me*]; The Girls All Go For His Euphemism" *New York Times*, June 11, 1999.

FLORENCE LA BADIE

"Florence La Badie" *All Movie Guide* (allmovie.com).

"Florence La Badie" Thanhouser Company Film Preservation Inc. (www.thanhouser.org).

Foster, Charles. *Stardust and Shadows: Canadians in Early Hollywood* (Toronto: Dundurn, 2000).

Macmillan, Margaret. *Paris 1919: Six Months That Changed the World* (Toronto: Random House, 2001).

"Thanhouser Company History." Thanhouser Company Film Preservation Inc.

CATHERINE O'HARA

Ebert, Roger. "*Home Fries* [review]" *RogerEbert.com*, November 25, 1998 (rogerebert.suntimes.com).

Holden, Stephen. "Film Review [*Best in Show*]; Dog Owner Eat Dog Owner Kind Of World" *New York Times*, September 27, 2000.

Maslin, Janet. "Film: '*This Is Spinal Tap*,' A Mock Documentary" *New York Times*, March 2, 1984.

Scott, A. O. "Film Review [*A Mighty Wind*]; Nostalgic Sounds of Old Folkies Who Never Were" *New York Times*, April 16, 2003.

Sragow, Michael. "The Once and Future Queen of Comedy Catherine O'Hara roars back to the top of the heap in '*Best in Show*'" *Salon.com*, September 28, 2000 (archive.salon.com).

CHRISTOPHER PLUMMER

Canby, Vincent. "Film: '*Murder by Decree*' in Foggy Old London: Ripper Redux" *New York Times*, February 9, 1979.

Weiler, A. H. "A Tale of the Theatre Retold; 'Stage Struck' Bows at the Normandie" *New York Times*, April 23, 1958.

JIM CARREY

Holden, Stephen. "Reviews/Film [*Ace Ventura: Pet Detective*]; On the Trail Of a Lost Fish" *New York Times*, February 4, 1994.

Knelman, Martin. *The Joker is Wild: The Jim Carrey Story* (Toronto: Penguin Canada, 2000).

Photo Acknowledgments

Page 4:   Marie Dressler – Keystone Film Company
Page 6:   Raymond Burr – Corbis
Page 13:   Yvonne DeCarlo – Universal
Page 19:   Claude Jutra – Brune Massenet
Page 24:   Norma Shearer – Corbis
Page 32:   Raymond Massey – Photofest
Page 39:   Mack Sennett – Corbis
Page 46:   Colleen Dewhurst – Sullivan Films
Page 51:   Ruby Keeler – Warner Brothers
Page 57:   Deanna Durbin – Universal
Page 61:   Alexis Smith – Associated Press
Page 66:   Beatrice Lillie – Photofest
Page 73:   Fay Wray – Copyright unknown
Page 79:   Florence Lawrence – Copyright unknown
Page 83:   Glenn Ford – Copyright unknown
Page 89:   Hume Cronyn – Copyright unknown
Page 94:   Jay Silverheels – Photofest
Page 100: Kate Reid – Copyright unknown
Page 105: Lorne Greene – Andrew J. Klyde Collection
Page 110: Louis B. Mayer – Corbis
Page 115: Mary Pickford – Copyright unknown
Page 122: Walter Huston – Copyright unknown
Page 128: Walter Pidgeon – Universal
Page 133: Jack Warner – Corbis
Page 140: Geneviève Bujold – Photofest
Page 145: Chief Dan George – Toronto Star
Page 152: Kate Nelligan – Copyright unknown
Page 158: Leslie Nielsen – Universal
Page 164: Denys Arcand – Toronto Star
Page 170: John Candy – Toronto Star
Page 178: Douglas Shearer – Photofest

Page 185: Michael Sarrazin – Universal

Page 189: Arthur Hill – Universal

Page 194: James Doohan – Canadian Broadcast Corporation

Page 198: William Shatner – Copyright unknown

Page 203: Margot Kidder – Universal

Page 206: Jack Carson – Photofest

Page 208: Monique Mercure – Copyright unknown

Page 213: Donald Sutherland – Corbis

Page 220: Norman Jewison – Universal

Page 225: Arthur Hiller – Universal

Page 232: Zacharias Kunuk – Isuma Productions

Page 236: Sandra Oh – Photofest

Page 241: Deepa Mehta – Toronto Star

Page 245: Mike Myers – Toronto Star

Page 252: Florence Labadie – Ned Thanhouser

Page 258: Catherine O'Hara – Canadian Broadcast Corporation

Page 263: Christopher Plummer – Corbis

Page 267: Jim Carrey – Universal

Page 272: Mordecai Richler – Copyright unknown

Cover photos courtesy:

      Photofest (Mike Myers),

      Toronto Star (Sandra Oh),

      Andrew J. Klyde Collection (Lorne Greene),

      Corbis (Jack Warner and Louis B. Mayer)

Index